Adolescent Assertiveness and Social Skills Training

A Clinical Handbook

Iris G. Fodor received her Ph.D. in clinical psychology from Boston University. She has been a staff psychologist at Boston Children's Hospital, Massachusetts General Hospital and Harvard Medical School, and a postdoctoral trainee at the Palo Alto V.A. Hospital in California. For the past twenty-one years she has been a Professor in the School Psychology Program program and is currently its director in the Department of Applied Psychology at New York University, where she trains students in cognitive therapy. She has numerous publications on assertiveness training, mother–daughter issues, cognitive therapy and women and mental health. Her most recent work is in the area of psychotherapy integration, with an emphasis on the integration of cognitive and gestalt therapy.

Adolescent Assertiveness and Social Skills Training

A Clinical Handbook

Iris G. Fodor
Editor

SPRINGER PUBLISHING COMPANY
New York

Springer Publishing Company, Inc.
536 Broadway
New York, NY 10012

92 93 94 95 96 / 5 4 3 2 1

Library of Congress Cataloging-in-Publication Data

Adolescent assertiveness and social skills training : a clinical
  handbook / Iris G. Fodor, editor.
      p.   cm.
   Includes bibliographical references and index.
   ISBN 0–8261–7490–6
   1. Assertiveness training for teenagers.   2. Social skills—Study
and teaching (Secondary)   I. Fodor, Iris G.
   [DNLM: 1. Assertiveness—in adolescence.   2. Behavior Therapy—in
adolescence.   3. Interpersonal Relations—in adolescence.   WS 462
A23852]
RJ505.A75A36   1992
158'.2—dc20
DNLM / DLC
for Library of Congress   92–20357
                                                                        CIP

Printed in the United States of America

This book is dedicated to Professor Gil Trachtman, former Chair of the School Psychology Program at New York University.
For more than 25 years he has provided caring, creative leadership and direction to generations of students.
He continues to be a role model for us all in his ethical and moral concerns for children, schools, and the community.

Contents

Preface

For the past 20 years, I have been training psychologists for the schools at New York University. Since the early 1970s, with the advent of assertiveness training, my doctoral students and I have been engaged in collaborative research and practice in applying assertiveness and social skills assessments and training in a variety of clinical and school settings.

For adolescents, social skills and the ability to assert themselves are essential. On a daily basis they are confronted with situations that call for social interaction. Adolescents still live with their families, spend most of their day in schools, and are expected to participate in peer culture. When adolescents do not function competently in these interactive situations, they are noticed, singled out, or suffer social ostracism and humiliation. Many adolescents, when faced with problematic social interactive situations, withdraw; act immaturely, inappropriately, or aggressively; and then have to face the consequences of social disapproval, punishment, and lower self-esteem for these actions.

During this past decade, mental health professions working with adolescents, both in the community and in schools, have become interested in addressing these social interactive problems. Social and developmental psychologists have studied "social competence" in children and adolescence, whereas behavioral psychologists have highlighted the skills aspects of such interacting. Whether the focus is on social skills or social competency, the research draws heavily on the assertiveness training literature of the previous 20 years for its theory, assessments, and training programs. In many respects, these three terms have been used interchangeably.

This book represents the collective efforts and cumulative knowledge of a group of working school psychologists and clinicians covering a wide range of issues pertinent to assertiveness and social skills assessment and training with adolescents. All of the authors are doctoral students or graduates of the New York University School Psychology Program whose chapters were completed as part of their scholarly paper requirement. They have applied these assertiveness and social skills assessments and interventions with adolescents in a variety of settings representative of the multicultural nature of the New York metropolitan area. Some of the authors work in the inner city with minority populations. Others work in the suburbs with more affluent populations.

Given the lack of research and attention to adolescent assertiveness and social skills training in the past, most of the programs described in this book are pilot projects. The psychologists adapted standardized assessments, or developed their own assessment as needed, for their special populations. The book is more of a hands-on clinical handbook than a research manual. From our experience at New York University, we have discovered that most teachers and personnel working in schools and clinics need to tailor the standardized assessments and treatment programs to suit their particular population. This book provides practitioners and school psychologists with details of such customized programming. In many respects, there is a gap between the research literature, which focuses on standardized assessments and treatment manuals, and the clinician, who with the client develops individualized assessment and treatments. This book is in the latter tradition.

IRIS G. FODOR

Contributors

Carol Lampert Barrish has been working with learning disabled adolescents for the past 20 years as a learning disabilities specialist, lecturer, curriculum consultant and teacher trainer. Ms. Barrish is completing her Ph.D. in school psychology at New York University. She completed a clinical internship at the Rusk Institute for Rehabilitative Medicine in New York City. Her current research interests are in areas related to the neuropsychology of learning disabilities and irrational beliefs and their influence on assertive behavior in learning disabled adolescents.

Diana Planells-Bloom, M.A., is currently completing work on her Ph.D. in school psychology at New York University. She received her master's degree in educational psychology in 1982 from New York University. She served her psychology internship in the Department of Psychiatry at Elizabeth General Medical Center. Her research interests include bilingual and bicultural issues as they influence child and adolescent behavior.

Ernest A. Collabolletta received his Psy.D. in child/school psychology at New York University. He received his master's degree in Spanish education from Iona College and his master's in counseling from Fordham University. Since 1980 he has been teaching Spanish at Scarsdale High School and directs a psycho-educational program for disaffected students there. He is a psychotherapist at Scarsdale Family Counseling Services, where many of his clients are individuals, couples, and families whose difficulties revolve around substance abuse.

Diane Duggan-Ali is a doctoral candidate in school psychology at New York University. She is a certified sex educator and has worked extensively with adolescents in regular and special education. She is the author of a book about sexuality for learning disabled adolescents and has trained teachers in developing sexuality education programs for learning disabled and developmentally delayed adolescents. She received her M.A. in school psychology from New York University in 1990 and is currently employed by the New York City Board of Education as a psychologist.

Catherine J. Hsu is presently working towards her Psy.D. degree in school/child psychology at New York University. For the past two years she has actively worked with substance abusers and the chronically mentally ill in providing counseling and social work services at Bellevue Hospital. Her interests include psychological issues for the Asian–American family.

Lesley Koegel is currently working on her Psy.D. degree in school psychology at New York University. She received her master's degree in educational psychology from N.Y.U. in 1984. She has taught in the New York City public schools for over ten years, as a primary-level classroom teacher, a reading specialist, and a teacher in a drop-out prevention program at the high-school level.

Tulsa Knox received her master's degree and advanced certificate in school psychology from CUNY Brooklyn College in 1985. She is a doctoral student in school psychology at New York University. Her research interests include the battered woman syndrome and maladaptive behaviors among minority groups.

Dianne Ollech is currently completing work on her Psy.D. in professional child/school psychology at New York University. She graduated from New York University with a B.S. in dance therapy, and has been an extern at Manhattan Children's Psychiatric Center.

Marilyn Bernstein Shendell, Psy.D., received her doctorate from New York University in 1989. She is the School Psychologist in a high school in Westchester County, in addition to having a private practice in White Plains, New York.

Laura Parsons received her master's degree in early childhood special education from Teachers College, Columbia University, New York City, in 1982. She will soon be receiving her doctoral degree in school/child psychology from New York University. Her research interests include adolescent depression, developmental disabilities and consultation.

Rena C. Schwartzbaum, Psy.D., obtained her doctoral degree in 1989 from New York University and completed her clinical child psychology internship at Roosevelt Hospital in New York City. She served as a school psychologist for the Mamaroneck, New York, school district and is currently in private practice in White Plains, New York.

Danya Vardi completed her master's degree in school psychology at New York University. She has been working with adolescent mothers for the past few years at several high schools and clinics in New York City. She is currently finishing her doctorate at New York University in school psychology. Her research interests are in the areas of parent education and training, women's studies, sexual abuse and other psychic trauma.

Steve Yarris, Psy.D., received his doctoral degree in professional child/school psychology from New York University in 1988. During his training, he completed a clinical internship at St. Luke's Hospital, in the Department of Child Psychiatry, in New York City. He has worked as a school psychologist with the New York City Board of Education and has served as a panel psychologist for the New York State Department of Vocational and Educational Services for Individuals with Disabilities (VESID). He continues to serve as an adjunct professor in the Department of Rehabilitation Counseling at New York University. He also has a private practice in which the interpersonal effectiveness of children is a special area of concentration.

Part I

Introduction to Assertiveness and Social Skills Training for Adolescents

Introduction

Iris G. Fodor

In the 1970s, assertiveness training techniques were adopted by the general public and publicized in the media. Assertiveness training became one of the cornerstones of behavior therapy. Alberti and Emmons (1970) further popularized the concept of assertiveness as a human right and provided a commonly accepted definition of assertive behavior. With the publication of their best seller, *Your Perfect Right,* followed by many other popular books on assertiveness training, Alberti and Emmons promoted a movement that mainstreamed assertiveness training into educational and counseling programs, and generated hundreds of research studies. Most of the original work in assertiveness training was focused on adults. In the 1980s, however, attention was directed toward extending this training to children and adolescents. For child and adolescent work there was a shift to viewing assertiveness as a component of social skills training. Researchers such as Michelson, Sugai, Wood, and Kazdan (1983) provided training modules adapted from adult programs for children and adolescents. Goldstein, Sprafkin, Gershaw, and Klein (1980) developed extensions of their structured learning programs for adolescents. Their "skillstreaming" approach for adolescents was widely adapted by clinicians, school and community personnel, as well as by parents and paraprofessionals.

In the 1980s development psychologists began to study social competency in children and stress peer interactions as crucial. Although most of the research has focused on young children, a few researchers have highlighted issues of social competency for adolescents (Ford, 1982; Dodge & Murphy, 1984). Adolescents who are judged to be socially competent were reported to be skilled in helping others, show emphathetic concerns, to be self-disclosing, and to communicate effectively and share interests with others (Ford, 1982; Smoller & Youniss, 1982). In addition, recent work has emphasized the importance of prosocial behaviors for optimal adolescent functioning, highlighting not only peer relationships, but relations with siblings and parents as crucial (Seltzer, 1989).

The chapters in Part I of this book will highlight key variables for understanding assertiveness and social skills training in general and the specific issues relevant for adolescents in particular. We begin with an overview by Iris Fodor, who presents a model for assertiveness and social skills training, drawing on her experience in training clinicians and school psychologists. After reviewing the basic principles of assertiveness and social skills training, she presents guidelines for conducting such workshops. Next, Marilyn Bernstein Shendell reviews major theories of adolescence, highlighting adolescent social emotional development and social competency. Leslie Koegel completes the section with a comprehensive review of the assessment literature. She begins by considering the lack of consensus in deciding just who is an adolescent. Next, she discusses assessment issues as well as scale development. Finally, she presents a comprehensive review of the major assertiveness and social skills scales used in adolescent assessment.

REFERENCES

Alberti, R. E., & Emmons, M. A. (1970). *Your perfect right*. San Luis Obispo: Impact.

Dodge, K. A., and Murphy, R. R. (1984). The assessment of social competence in adolescents. In P. Karoly & J. Steffen (Eds.), *Adolescent behavior disorder: Foundations and contemporary concerns*. Lexington, MA: D. C. Heath.

Ford, M. E. (1982). Social cognition and social competence in adolescence. *Developmental Psychology, 18*, 322–341.

Goldstein, A. P., Sprafkin, R. P., Gershaw, N. J., & Klein, P. (1980). *Skillstreaming the adolescent*. Champaign, IL: Research Press.

Michelson, L., Sugai, D. P., Wood, R., & Kazdin, A. E. (1983). *Social skills assessment and training with children: An empirically based handbook*. New York: Plenum.

Seltzer, V. C. (1989). *The psychosocial worlds of the adolescent: Public and private*. New York: Wiley.

Smoller, J., & Youniss, J. (1982). Social development through friendships. In K. H. Rubin & H. S. Ross (Eds.), *Peer relationships and social skills in childhood* (pp. 279–298). New York: Springer-Verlag.

1

Assertiveness and Social Skills Training: Clinical Overview

Iris G. Fodor

INTRODUCTION: A HISTORICAL OVERVIEW

Assertiveness and social skills concepts have an overlapping history. Although assertiveness is still considered a useful concept and tool by the public, psychologists and researchers for the most part now place assertiveness under the umbrella of social skills training. Furthermore, as the training in social interactive skills has been applied to children and adolescents, the term *social skills* is typically used to describe such work. The shift occurred as researchers in the United States and England highlighted the situationally specific nature of assertiveness (Eisler, Hersen, Miller, & Blanchard, 1975; Galassi, Galassi, & Vedder, 1981). The theoretical framing in the United States borrowed heavily from social learning theory (Bandura, 1971), whereas in England the theoretical formulations were drawn from information-processing models and social and organizational psychology (Argyle, 1969). Yet, as one examines in detail the social skills programs developed for children and adolescents, we see that assertiveness concepts and framing are still very central to this work (Hops, Lewinsohn, Andrews, & Roberts, 1990; Michelson, Sugai, Woods, & Kazdin, 1983).

In this chapter, I present an overview of both assertiveness and social skills training. I begin with assertiveness training, drawing heavily from my work in training mental health professionals. I highlight the issues raised by clinicians as they grapple with these concepts for their own personal and professional growth. I also illustrate the multifaceted nature of assertiveness highlighting its clinical underpinnings (Fodor,

1980). Next, I discuss social skills training and its integration with assertiveness concepts. I specifically focus on such training as it applies to work with adolescents in groups.

ASSERTIVENESS: ITS BEGINNING

Salter (1949) and later Wolpe (1958) are both credited with the clinical development of assertiveness techniques within the context of learning theory. Salter spoke of "inhibited" people with a pattern of shyness for whom he recommended "excitatory" training in expressiveness. Wolpe first used the term *assertive* to refer to "not only more or less aggressive behaviors, but also the outward expression of friendly, affectionate and non-anxious feelings" (Wolpe, 1958, p. 1124).

Assertive behavior is usually defined by leading trainers, such as Alberti and Emmons (1970), Lang and Jakubowski (1976), among others as involving an open, honest communication. It is essentially risk taking, being up front, and stating the facts. This philosophy reflects the underlying assumption that unassertive people lead a self-denying life that causes them to suffer in interpersonal relationships and sometimes leads to emotional and physical consequences (Fodor, 1980). Furthermore, Eisler and Miller (1973) who studied the "socially skilled" found them to be more assertive.

From its beginning, lack of assertiveness was seen as a clinical problem akin to phobia and other anxiety disorders. Treatment was conceptualized within a learning theory framework as training the non-assertive to become assertive. Furthermore, as the clinical work expanded, aggressiveness was also viewed as a lack of appropriate assertive behavior and training in shifting aggressive responses to assertive ones. With the movement toward cognitive therapy, the cognitive underpinnings of assertive and unassertive behavior were highlighted, and cognitive interventions were integrated into the behavioral treatment (Fodor, 1980). Today, work on assertiveness as a form of self-expressiveness is a feature of most standard cognitive behavioral treatments for a variety of disorders.

More so than almost any other behavior technique, assertiveness training in the 1970s moved from its clinical focus to adaptation by the public. Assertiveness training programs were developed to address a host of common problems (fear of public speaking, job interviewing, dating anxiety, etc.) In particular, assertive techniques were adapted by the women's movement to help women stand up for their rights, overcome socialization in passivity and compliance, and fight for equity. Assertiveness training programs were developed at Ys, schools, and community centers; although the popularity has waned somewhat since the 1970s, this work has continued (Fodor, 1988).

ASSERTIVENESS AND SOCIAL SKILLS AND THE PRACTITIONER'S ROLE

More and more, school psychologists and clinicians are called on to assess assertiveness and social skills, deficits in children and adolescents, and design individual and group interventions formally. Special populations are often singled out for such work, for example, the learning disabled, impulsive–aggressive, or depressed adolescents (Dodge & Murphy, 1984; Hops & Greenwood, 1980; Michelson et al., 1983). In addition, social skills or assertiveness training is often called for as part of wider programs for sexuality training, pregnancy prevention, AIDS prevention, practice in saying no to drugs, job interviewing, and so on (Bernard & Joyce, 1984; Feindler & Ecton, 1986; Hazel, 1990; Hops et al., 1990; Stern & Fodor, 1990). Most school psychologists and clinicians working with adolescents will do such work in schools, and inpatient–outpatient mental health facilities. Increasingly, they will be called on to provide social skills assistance in consultation with parents and teachers as well as develop programs for individual and group work with the adolescents themselves. Each social skills–assertiveness training context raises specific issues for the practitioner. This section will discuss assertiveness concerns raised by clinicians.

Training

Often the school psychologist or clinician is called on to train other staff in assertiveness and social skills. Such training might involve setting up staff training workshops, conducting a course, or working with teachers in setting up social skills curriculum in the classroom. Further didactic training might involve staff participation in parent–child and adolescent social skills groups.

Social Skills–Assertiveness Training in Clinical and School Settings

Most school psychologists and clinicians working with adolescents function in schools, community agencies, mental health clinics, and hospitals that operate within a bureaucratic structure. Therefore, these work settings particularly lend themselves to issues that involve power hierarchies. School psychologists in particular operate at different levels of authority and have multiple roles in such a setting.

This author has conducted training workshops for educators, school psychologists, and clinicians in social skills and assertiveness training in such settings. The model for trainers typically involves the psychologists bringing to the workshop their own assertiveness issues (Fodor, 1980,1988). The most frequently reported problem raised in these workshops is dealing with people in authority, for example, supervising psychiatrists and psychologists, principals, and head teachers, among others. In confronting authority, the workshop participants report feeling submissive, subservient, out of control, or helpless and angry at their superiors.

These same clinicians and school personnel are often in positions in which they exert power over others. They supervise teachers, trainees, younger staff, students, and others. In these cases, they report feeling frustrated and thwarted when they cannot get others to follow their directions. Often they are unprepared by their training programs to function comfortably with exercising authority and supervising others.

Other issues brought up in these workshops for professionals include getting along with colleagues, handling disagreements, speaking up at committee meetings, and disagreeing with other's recommendations. The problem of power issues within and among staff seems most absorbing regardless of work setting.

Assertiveness and Role of Psychologists–Mental Health Professionals

To be effective as a clinician or school psychologist calls for assertive skills. In a mental health clinic, after doing an evaluation, a psychologist is often asked to make recommendations to principals, teachers, psychotherapists, parents, and courts. Often, the presentation of the results of psychological testing calls for a particular type of assertive skill, for example, the psychologist needs to convince a parent that an adolescent needs a special class. Often the parent will disagree with test findings or recommendations or be unwilling to cooperate with the psychologist's recommendations. In abusive situations, mental health professionals need to be assertive in their reports and interactions with adolescents, parents, principals, and courts.

PRINCIPLES OF ASSERTIVENESS

Because psychologists, like their clients, are often dealing with their own issues of assertiveness, they may not have a clear understanding of relevant conceptual, behavioral, and interactive skills. In our workshops we begin by achieving some group consensus in defining and illustrating appropriate assertive behavior.

A central issue in the definition of assertiveness has been the distinction between assertive and aggressive behavior. These concepts are often confused. Most trainers distinguish between assertive, nonassertive, passive, and aggressive behavior following the proposals of Alberti and Emmons (1970) in their popular book *Your Perfect Right* (Gambrill & Richey, 1976; Lang & Jakubowski, 1976; Michelson et al., 1983; Wolfe & Fodor, 1975). Assertive behavior is usually considered by leading trainers, such as Alberti and Emmons (1970), Lang and Jakubowski (1976), as involving a direct, open, honest communication that is self-expressive but respectful of the other.

Distinction Between Types of Behavior

To recognize assertive behavior, consider the following example. A teenager and her best friend are experiencing unexpressed tension over anger and rivalry for the affections of a male classmate. An assertive response would involve one teenager stating directly to her friend, "I think we better talk; I feel a lot of tension between us because of Jim." Or, "I am angry that you are dating Jim; you knew I wanted to date him." Essentially assertiveness involves ownership of one's experience and a willingness to express it to the other.

Conversely, unassertive behavior can be defined as inhibited or passive behavior. It is avoidant behavior. For example, in the disagreement with the friend mentioned previously, an unassertive teenager would hold back the feelings, avoid eye contact, avoid groups where they might run into each other, or drop out of a shared activity group without ever discussing the matter. Unassertive behavior is indirect, a withholding of feelings and an avoidance of dealing with the issues. Usually, because unexpressed feelings are difficult to keep under control, these feelings do indeed surface, often in the form of sadness, weepiness, depression, or anger. For the most part, unassertive people do not feel good about their lack of assertiveness and will down themselves, which creates additional bad feelings.

One variant of unassertiveness is passive–aggressive behavior. For example, the teenager discussed earlier may not express her anger at her friend, but the anger may be expressed indirectly and often out of awareness by passive–aggressive acts. She may forget to bring back notes she borrowed before an examination. Or, she may bad-mouth her friend to other people and complain about her flirtatious behavior.

Another form of unassertive behavior is aggressive behavior. Aggressiveness and assertiveness have been confused in the literature. It is considered assertive to express anger directly. "I'm angry at you." Typically, however, aggressive behavior is attacking, escalating the confrontation.

In the example discussed previously, the friend may now express her anger. Instead of just assertively saying, "I'm angry," however, she blames and accuses her friend. "You've been awful to me; you've betrayed our friendship. What kind of friend are you?" Furthermore, this angry expression is often said in a hostile accusatory voice tone. It is self-enhancing at the expense of the other person. One person lets the other know in a loud, hostile tone that it is the other's fault. One friend in the previous example might say, "You should have known I was waiting for him to ask me out. You should have known how hurt I'd feel if you started dating him."

Most people who behave aggressively often get responded to in kind. With adolescents, arguments and fights can escalate from aggressive responding. Too often, unassertive people retreat further when confronted with an aggressive onslaught, which infuriates the aggressive person, so they shout and scream even louder. Regardless of whether aggressive people achieve what they want, however, they too often end up like the unassertive person, feeling bad about themselves after aggressive encounters. Also, aggressive adolescents are ranked lowest in popularity by their peers (Seltzer, 1989).

Often an unassertive person will become aggressive. The person is initially unassertive and there is a buildup until there is a last-straw kind of provocation and then a blowup. For example, the teenager might try to overlook her friend's dating someone she had wanted to see. Later, however, after not expressing her resentment, when she sees them together the teenager blows up out of control. She then berates her friend, shouting out all the resentments she has been repressing. Such outbursts often come out in a hysterical, angry way: "You never care about my feelings; you are selfish." At these times, everything that has been contained spills out. Sometimes, the other person begins to tie this slight onto a list of other injustices, presenting her friend with a list of grievances, often in an angry accusatory tone. Too often, the person who is the target of the tirade wonders what is the matter with the person venting, because she may never have mentioned being upset before, or the response is excessive to the provocation. Furthermore, aggressive behavior often has unpredictable consequences. It can create in the person under attack withdrawal, avoidance, or an aggressive response in return. Too often, the person under attack discounts what the venter is saying, brushing them off with, "She's gone mad!" or "He's acting like a child."

Assertiveness and Styles of Communication

Another way of looking at assertiveness is as an interpersonal communication style (Fodor, 1980; Lang & Jakubowski, 1976; McKay, Davis, & Fanning, 1983). The following are communication styles tied to assertive, nonassertive, and aggressive responding.

Assertiveness involves the willingness to make what is called "I" statements. That it, to be direct and honest about one's emotional states, by owning what one is feeling, one says "I." For example, "I'm upset, I am angry, I feel smothered, I feel overworked, I would like to go to the movies tonight."

Unassertive people will often ask questions of others rather than state their own preferences or express their own feelings. Too often a question indirectly disguises an unexpressed "I" statement. Instead of stating that she wants to go out, a wife asks her husband, "Are you tired?" Alternatively, instead of expressing his own anger, a husband asks his wife if she is upset.

Blamers usually are not willing to own what they are feeling or take responsibility for their emotions and behavior. Instead, they say: "You are a good for nothing. You make me mad. It's your fault that I'm angry."

Male–Female Differences and Assertiveness

There are also male–female differences connected to assertive and aggressive responding. In our culture men and women have been socialized differently regarding assertive communication styles (Jakubowski-Spector, 1973; Osborn & Harris, 1975; Phelps & Austin, 1975; Wolfe & Fodor, 1975,1977). Men have been trained to see assertiveness as part of the masculine role from early childhood on. They often confuse assertive, aggressive and competitive. Thus, a man may consider that he is behaving in an assertive manner when he is engaging in bullying or loud dominating actions. Typically, he is not criticized because this behavior is considered role appropriate (Fodor, 1988).

Another reported male problem is the inability to let people see their soft, vulnerable, or helpless side. So, if a man needs help or is feeling upset, it is difficult for him to ask for help, particularly from another man, or show the pain.

Women have too often been socialized in the more traditional female role, which stresses niceness, gentleness, care of others, and avoidance of making waves and expressing anger. Angry women are particularly castigated in our culture, and many women still feel they are behaving aggressively when they are asserting themselves. Many people will la-

bel appropriately assertive behavior on the part of a woman as aggressive (Fodor, 1988; Rich & Schroeder, 1976; Solomon & Rothblum,
1985).

Today, many adolescents still adhere to the more traditionally defined male and female roles, and their struggles with assertive issues
are inherently tied up with their own sex role definitions. (See chapters
by Duggan-Ali, Bernstein Shendell, and Plannells-Bloom for a fuller
discussion of these issues.)

Stages in Learning to Be Assertive

Assertiveness is not a unitary trait. We can approach learning to be assertive as a development process with individuals showing assertiveness difficulties around a particular stage (Fodor, 1980). Let us assume
a recently hired psychologist and her supervisor are having a disagreement about clarity of assignments. For example, the supervisor is un-
clear about how many cases her supervisee is to test a week. She
frequently changes her mind about which cases have priorities and
deadlines.

The first stage of assertive awareness is to clarify the feelings being
elicited by the situation. Sometimes people do not know what they are
feeling or just have a vague notion of feeling upset. Often people are not
aware they are upset until some time later. Feeling training might focus on awareness of feelings related to triggering incidents as well as
learning to distinguish anger, excitement, anxiety, and general upset.

The next step is to delineate the rights in that situation. This has
been an important contribution to assertiveness training (Alberti &
Emmons, 1970). For example, does the new psychologist have a right to
express herself to her supervisor? Does she have a right to a clear definition of her workload? Does she have a right to be treated with equal
respect for her professional role? Should there be a list of rights for
teachers, mental health professionals, and psychometricians in every
department? What types of rights do adolescents have in schools, families, and with friends? (Adolescent rights might include freedom to
make choices, express themselves, not to be labeled, make mistakes,
and be included in the decision making process in school and family.)

The next step is to address goals. What does the person want to
achieve? For example, in the disagreement with the supervisor, does
the supervisee just want to be negativistic or to fight with her supervisor, or does she want a precise schedule of her testing assignments and
due dates?

The next stage involves the skills aspect of assertiveness. Is the psychologist willing to risk a clear, open communication with her supervisor? Does she have the social skills to be direct and honest, and make "I statements"? Can she state her position clearly while maintaining a steady voice flow, strong body language, and good eye contact? Can she clearly say to her supervisor, "I'm upset about how my testing assignments keep changing each day. I have trouble knowing what I'm supposed to do. We need to arrange a time to talk about this matter." When responding assertively, can she spell out what she wants: "Let's get together first thing each morning, and go over the testing assignments and discuss supervision."

As one works toward assertion, can one express oneself clearly and keep feelings of upset, anxiety, and anger under control? Sometimes people know what they want to say and as they start to talk they are overwhelmed with anxiety or anger. Naturally, most people feel some discomfort in charged encounters, but for some people the anxiety and anger interfere with effective responding. Here cognitive factors need to be identified and challenged that are interfering or inhibiting assertive responding.

After one's position has been articulated, can the person listen to the other view point? What does the supervisor have to say about this matter? How assertive is she in articulating her position? Can the new supervisee put herself in the other's shoes? Many people are so preoccupied with making their own points, they neglect to focus on what it may be like for someone to be on the other side of an issue.

When it is clear that you still have disagreement, is it possible to compromise? If that is not possible because of a real impasse, or the other person is unreasonable, irrational, or stubborn can the person state their disappointment? Can they accept the reality of an impasse? Can they be clear about realistic barriers or organizational systems that are operating to prevent their goal achievement?

At this point, another set of problems often emerges. When one gets assertive, that behavior may escalate into aggression. For example, the supervisee still insists that her supervisor sees the situation from her own viewpoint. She does not drop the matter and blames the supervisor for the disagreement ("It's all your fault that I'm not getting my work done, or the department is in such a mess"). The insistence that things be different from what they are, that the other person change, often leads to escalating anger. If this type of behavior persists, others now perceive the person who may have had a valid grievance in a negative way.

Having all the appropriately assertive responses in one's repertoire does not guarantee that one's goals are achieved. Sometimes by becoming assertive, one can get a clearer picture about how impossible or rigid the supervisor is, how this job is not meeting one's needs, or how impossible change is in a bureaucratic structure. By accepting the realities of the situation, one can then look elsewhere for satisfaction.

Such an impasse, however, also provides an opportunity to use other resources. Is there another way to solve the problem? For example, if the supervisor ignores your suggestions, are there alternatives to withdrawal? Can one discuss these issues with other members of the staff, or work with others together to foster change in the department?

Whether or not your assertive goals have been reached, is it possible to be pleased with how one dealt with the situation? For example, can you feel good about trying to address a problem, rather than just walking away from a difficult supervisory situation? Can you praise yourself for some of the new behaviors? Can you highlight what you did well and where you need to work for further improvement.

Categories of Assertiveness

Assertiveness is not a global trait. Some people have problems in only one category, and others have problems in many categories. The same person who seems to have it together and knows how to handle one situation may not be able to do as well in others (Eisler & Frederiksen, 1980; Galassi & Galassi, 1978; Gambrill & Richey, 1976; Lang & Jakubowski, 1976; Michelson et al., 1983). The following are some typical problematic categories for adolescents.

Initiating interactions is one area of difficulty for some teenagers. Can they enter a classroom, cafeteria, or be at a party and begin a conversation? Is it easier or more difficult to talk to another student, a stranger, a teacher, or a person in authority?

Dealing with dating situations and sexual concerns is another challenge for those struggling with assertiveness. Can they ask another adolescent for a date? Can they express positive feelings in intimate relationships? How comfortable are they in talking about sex?

Learning how to say no is an additional problem area for some. Can they refuse a request, reasonable or unreasonable? Can they say no to someone who requests a favor they do not wish to grant? Examples include taking on extra work assignments, baby sitting for their parents, helping a friend with homework, or lending their clothing, notes, or car. Can they say no to a reasonable request without being apologetic? Is it more of a problem with a close friend, parent, or teacher?

Disagreeing is another difficulty for unassertive adolescents. Can they ever express disagreement? An example might come up in class discussion or in a club where a teacher or student might suggest one plan of action when they prefer another. How comfortable are they in opposing this plan or presenting one of their own? Is this more of a problem with a fellow student, parent, or teacher?

Dealing with both positive and negative reactions presents an additional challenge for some teenagers. Can they give and receive feedback, praise, and complaints? Do they find it easier to focus on what they do not like, ignoring what is good and only commenting on the negative? Sometimes receiving negative feedback appears to be unjustified. How do they handle such feedback?

Asking for help is another problematic area for some. How comfortable are they in asking for help? Do they feel they have to do it all themselves? Sometimes adolescents expect others to be mind readers.

Coping with anger is an additional difficulty for unassertive adolescents. How comfortable are they in handling their own anger as well as others' aggressive responding?

Cutting across all these problematic categories, it is also important to ask oneself if the problem is responding to others' assertion or aggression. Some people have problems fielding responses that are being directed at them, whereas others are passive and cannot initiate a response. For example, a responder may only assert themselves when opposing another's view point, whereas an initiator will take the risk of discussing a tense matter directly. Most unassertive people have problems in both areas.

Self-Talk and Unassertive Scripts

Cognitive therapists link internal dialogues—what people think and say to themselves—with assertive, unassertive, and aggressive responding. These internal scripts serve either to inhibit an assertive response, or create anxiety and anger about the effect of such a response. These attitudes serve to limit assertive responding (Bernard & Joyce, 1984; Ellis, 1975; Feindler & Ecton, 1986; Wolfe & Fodor, 1975,1977).

For example, a school psychologist may be upset by a student's refusal to do her homework or attend counseling sessions. She calls the student in for a talk. She says to herself, however: "What's the use? She can't change, and nothing I do will make a difference. She has too many family problems." The psychologists talk to the student in a low voice, avoiding eye contact. The student, in experiencing such a passive interaction, feels relief at avoiding a challenge to her noncompliant behavior.

Cognitive Aspects of Assertiveness

The following are common unassertive scripts that are associated with inhibited assertive responding (Fodor & Wolfe, 1977; Wolfe and Fodor, 1975).

One unassertive script is that taking care of others is more important than tending to oneself. Women and people in the helping professions in general are quick to worry about hurting the other person's feelings, and these concerns are reflected in such self-talk as "I can't be direct; it isn't nice. I really worry about upsetting the other person. The other person's needs are more important than mine." Once one gets into this frame of mind, one moves away from a personal agenda. For example, Mae, a single parent, has asked Dee, her teenaged daughter, to mind her younger sister on Saturday evening. Dee would like her mother to find someone else but puts her mother's wishes above her own. Therefore, she says she will baby-sit, cancels her own plans for the evening, feels resentment, but says nothing.

Although I am not advocating selfishness, in the early stage of an assertive response, it is important to at least stay with oneself and not get pulled too quickly into taking care of the other person's needs.

Another common unassertive script is: "Don't make waves." It is easier in this scenario to avoid hassles than to face them. Why get upset about a particular problem? It is not worth it. In the preceding example, Dee, says to herself, "Why tell my mother I'm upset? It will make her upset. Maybe if I say nothing, she'll change her mind, and I can go out with my friends after all." Or, "I'll make myself too anxious or upset by talking to my mother about how I feel, so why bother?"

Unassertive people also think they are helpless and powerless to do much on their own. In the earlier example, Dee says to herself, "My mother is much stronger than me; she's the boss."

In addition, unassertive people believe they have no control over their feelings. For example, Dee says to herself, "My mother makes me angry by asking me to baby-sit at the last minute. There's nothing I can do about my feelings."

Another unassertive script is that it might be awful or catastrophic to be assertive. For example, Dee says to herself, "If, I told my mother how I felt, she might think I was an ungrateful daughter, and she might stop loving me. She might throw me out of the house or have a nervous breakdown."

The following are self-statements that are more likely to create angry or aggressive responses (Fodor & Wolfe, 1977; Wolfe & Fodor, 1973).

One self-statement is: "I can't control my anger." In the earlier example, Dee says to herself, "If I talk with my mother, I'll just let her have it." Low frustration tolerance often accompanies out-of-control, angry feelings. Again, Dee says, "How dare she do this to me, I'm going to get even. I'll show her she can't treat me this way!"

Another self-statement is: "The world should be fair and just." For example, Dee says, "Here am I a teenager. I should be the one to go out on Saturday night. My mother should take care of *my* needs."

A final example of this type of self-statement is: "People should do what I want them to do." For example, Dee says, "I can't stand it. My mother shouldn't do what she's doing. She has no right to ask me to baby-sit. How dare she make plans on a night I want to go out!"

In highlighting the cognitive factors, it is important to emphasize that the other person, in this case the mother, has her own self-statements that are driving her interactive behavior (e.g., the mother might be focusing on how she is the mother, and her daughter has to obey her rules, put her needs first, or has no right to defy her) (Fodor & Wolfe, 1977).

Typically, as assertiveness issues are discussed the underlying beliefs associated with the issues are identified. For example, if Dee is complaining about her avoidance of assertion with her mother, we might ask her to tell us what she is saying to herself. Next, following Ellis's (1975) system of rational emotive therapy, we dispute these beliefs. We also work on replacing the inhibiting beliefs with more facilitative and coping beliefs. What might you say to yourself differently? For example, "We both have rights. We need to cooperate better on planning our schedules." Finally, through behavioral rehearsal and homework assignments, the client is encouraged to integrate the newer beliefs with work on changing her assertive behaviors in the problematic situation. Ideally, in the situations described previously with parents and children, working with the dyads would facilitate the change process. For a fuller illustration of such cognitive behavioral work see Fodor and Wolfe's (1977) description of mother–daughter assertive groups.

Assertiveness and Social Skills Training for Adolescents

In assertiveness applications for children and adolescents, practitioners and researchers have incorporated assertiveness techniques under the umbrella of social skills training. Furthermore, recent work has highlighted enhancing social competency as a goal for such training.

Michelson et al. (1983) describe two general models for social skills training as follows: "The first model views social skills problems as instances of skills deficits . . . based on the assumption that children do not have their response repertoires the . . . skills to interact well with others. . . The goal of training would be to build the requisite skills to overcome problematic social behavior" (p. 35). "The second model is based on the view that children may have the requisite skills but experience competing emotional, affective or cognitive states or processes that interfere with the expression of the abilities" (p. 35).

In practice, however, both the skills training and cognitive components are incorporated into standard training programs. Most social skills assessments and treatments, however, have been developed first on adults and then adapted or reformatted for use with children. Adolescents have generally not been the focus for most of the research and training in this area.

Social skills research and training developed from two different thrusts in the United States and England. In this country, behavioral researchers focusing on the skills aspects of assertiveness stressed its situational specificity. In particular, they strove to assess and refine components of problematic situations and effective responding (Eisler et al., 1975; Galassi & Galassi, 1978). They also argued for the substitution of the term *social skill* for assertion, shifting from the emphasis on self-expression to delimitation of specific situations and target responses. From that time on, most psychologists preferred to use the term social skills in describing clinical and research work on social interactive behaviors. In England, Argyle (1969) and his associates at Oxford developed a research base for social interactive behaviors. They coined the phrase "social skills" to describe these behaviors. Their research brought to social skills assessment, information-processing models and social psychological theory. The focus of the English researchers was on specifying the behavioral components of effective social interactive skills. They used machine models and also stressed the importance of the social context. (For a fuller description of research on social skills, the reader is directed to L'Abate & Milan, 1985; Hollin & Trower, 1983.)

In adapting programs for addressing social interactive problems for children and adolescents, behavioral psychologists integrated features from the earlier assertiveness work and the later social skills research under the umbrella of social skills programs, focusing on specific assessments and interventions for problematic behaviors.

Michelson et al. (1983) present a comprehensive review of the many different ways of defining social skills that have relevance for children and adolescents. Central to most definitions is the view that social interactive skills are learned behaviors that are shaped by social interactions and the culture (Hops & Greenwood, 1980; Libert & Lewinsohn,

1973). Representative definitions discussed by Michelson et al. (1983) include the following.

One social skills definition is "the ability to interact with others in a given social context in specific ways that are socially accepted or valued and at the same time personally beneficial, mutually beneficial, or beneficial primarily to others" (Combs & Slaby, 1977, p. 162).

Another social skills definition is "a repertoire of verbal and nonverbal behaviors by which children affect the responses of other individuals (e.g., peers, parents, siblings and teachers) in the interpersonal context. This repertoire acts as a mechanism through which children influence their environment by obtaining, removing, or avoiding desirable and undesirable outcomes in the social sphere . . . the extent to which they are successful in obtaining desirable outcomes and avoiding or escaping undesirable ones without inflicting pain on others is the extent to which they are considered 'socially skilled'" (Rinn & Markle, 1979, p. 108).

Other social skills definitions highlight positive and negative behaviors associated with effective and deficient social skills. For example, Trower (1979) views goal attainment as "dependent or skilled behavior which involves a continuous cycle of monitoring and modifying performance in light of feedback. Failure in skill is defined as a breakdown or impairment at some point in the cycle . . . leading to negative outcomes" (p. 4). Argyle (1981) also highlights feedback, featuring "metaperception," a social cognitive focus on how the other person is evaluating or judging the interaction.

Social Competency and Its Relation to Social Skills

Consistent with the social context emphasis of skills researchers is the concept of social competency. Zigler and Phillips (1961) from research on institutionalized patients introduced the term *social competency* as a central predictor of the postadjustment process for these patients. Goldfried and D'Zurilla (1969) developed an assessment model that featured social competency as a component of social skills behavior.

Development psychologists have also featured social competence— the development of effective social interactive skills—as central for adolescents (Dodge & Murphy, 1984). Effective social skills for peer interactions are highlighted in this research. For example, researchers found lack of effective social interactive skills or social competency associated with psychopathology in adolescents. They report that adolescents who are rejected by peers, who are unpopular as children (Renshaw & Asher, 1982), have poor relationships with siblings and parents (Seltzer, 1989) are at high risk for psychopathology.

Hence, following the social competency model, we see that some social behaviors are claimed to be adaptive and appropriate, which leads to positive rewards, effective interaction, and satisfaction. Eisler, Miller, and Hersen (1973) link effective social skills and assertive behavior. They studied "socially skilled" individuals and claimed they were more assertive, made more requests, spoke in a louder voice, and were less compliant than less socially skilled individuals. Furthermore, adolescents who are socially competent are reported to have positive social interactive behavioral skills, and these in turn are associated with increased satisfaction, higher achievement, and effective peer and parental interactions (Ford, 1982; Seltzer, 1989).

Other adolescents are said to have "maladaptive," or "deficit or inappropriate" social skills. As we have noted previously, such negative social interactive behaviors are associated with poor school performance and adjustment, poor peer and parental interactions, and psychopathology (Seltzer, 1989). Emotional disorders said to be associated with lack of social competence include delinquency, inhibition, excessive shyness, depression and learning disability. (See chapters by Ollech, Parsons, and Barrish for a fuller discussion of these issues.)

It is also important to emphasize the value-laden sociocultural aspect of the previous framing of social interactive issues. The framework for assertiveness and most social skills concepts is derived from a mainstream American view of what are "appropriate and inappropriate behaviors" (Cheek, 1974). Too often minority adolescents, who are the majority in urban settings, are singled out as having "maladaptive" or deficit behaviors. (See chapters by Hsu, Knox, Planells-Bloom, and Scwartzbaum for a fuller discussion of ethics and ethnic issues associated with such framing.)

We must also ask what aspects of social skills are singled out by researchers for study and how sociocultural biases influence theory building. Furnham (1985) reports that in Britain assertiveness as an aspect of social skills research has been neglected. Instead, the British emphasize the importance of friendships and peer relations as central in their social skills research. We have little information about social skills research and practice in non-Western cultures.

Social Skills Training: Psychoeducational Perspective

In many respects social skills training serves as a bridge between therapy and education (L'Abate & Milan, 1985). It is therapy, in that the aim is usually some form of remediation for a target population with maladaptive or deficit behaviors. However, the treatment model is more educational than most therapies in that there it can be carried out by educators, as well as therapists, in groups or in courses that could be considered "social curriculum" (Phillips, 1985). The assumption is that adolescents who lack social skills may not have learned these skills, or they have the skills in their repertoire but do not know how to use them. Hence, skills instruction is central. Often there is an additional assumption that education in self-control or handling of emotional factors are also needed for effective skill development (Bernard & Joyce, 1984; Hazel, 1990). Social skills training fits the psychoeducational model in that the programs typically included modules developed to address specific deficiencies that are taught in a sequenced course (Michelson et al., 1983). Also, social curriculums could be developed by schools to address specific problems as needed.

Social Skills Training in Groups

In adapting the basic assertive and social skills format for adolescents, group training is ideal. The following points demonstrate the benefits of group training:

School environments and classrooms provide ideal opportunities for group interventions for assertiveness and social skills training. Following the psychoeducational model, assertiveness and social skills curriculum can be presented in a structured format.

A group situation encourages shared problem solving among adolescents with similar concerns (e.g., coping with anger, getting along with one's parents, dealing with the opposite sex, etc.).

A group provides a natural laboratory for the assessment of assertiveness problems. A shy or aggressive student's issues are immediately apparent to the group.

The situations that occur naturally in a group reflect a broader range of real-life situations with which adolescents cope. Also, schools can arrange theme-centered groups.

The group can devise creative assertive responses that might not occur to the trainer.

In a group adolescents have the opportunity to understand other viewpoints through role playing. For example, in a reverse role play, a student who is aggressive may experience the receiving end of bullying behavior.

Group members learn how to give support and reinforcement for change. The group provides experience in giving feedback and is a natural environment for new learning. (For illustrations of group process and assertiveness and social skills issues, see Fensterheim, 1974; Fodor, 1980; Lang & Jakubowski, 1976; and chapters by Bernstein Shendell, Dugan-Ali, and Collabolletta.)

Assertiveness and Social Skills:
Treatment Package

Most trainers use some variant of a flexible treatment package that includes performing assessment, learning to distinguish assertive and nonassertive behavior, skills training, and cognitive restructuring (Eisler & Frederiksen, 1980; Fodor, 1980; Gambrill & Richey, 1976; Goldstein, Sprafkin, Grenshaw, & Klein, 1980; Hazel, 1990; L'Abate & Milan, 1985; Michelson et al., 1983). Central to most treatment packages are the following:

1. *Assessment*: This initial assessment of assertiveness problems uses self-report questions. It involves setting up role-play situations, and training clients to self-monitor their own and others' behaviors.

2. *Instruction*: This introduction to assertive philosophy distinguishes between assertive, aggressive, and unassertive behavior. Guidelines and instruction in how to behave more assertively are provided. A discussion of rights and setting of assertive goals also occurs. The format may include lectures, group demonstrations, discussions, work books, or programmed materials.

3. *Skills training*: This includes direct teaching, practicing, and integrating of behavioral skills. The components of skills training are the following:

   a. Modeling—The participant observes the trainer, another participant, or a taped demonstration.
   b. Role play—The participant acts out an assertive response or appropriate behavior.
   c. Behavioral rehearsal—There is active practice of assertive responding with the trainer or other participants.
   d. Feedback—The trainer and other participants give explicit descriptions of how they viewed the response.
   e. Coaching—Suggestions for improvement are provided.
   f. Reinforcement—The trainer and group provide support for improved performance.

4. *Cognitive restructuring*: This element involves attending to self-statements and cognitions that may impede assertive responding and attainment of effective social skills. Standard procedures include discovering and challenging irrational beliefs or self-statements (Bernard & Joyce, 1984; Ellis, 1975); paying attention to societal sex role programming and other social

variables (Jakubowski, 1973; Wolfe & Fodor, 1975); and discussing expectations about the effects of new assertive behaviors (Bandura, 1977).

5. *Anxiety or anger management training*: This training focuses on self-control issues, impulse control training, relaxation techniques, desensitization, and "flooding" (Feindler & Ecton, 1986; Stern & Fodor, 1990; Wolpe, 1958). Central to anxiety and anger control are highlighting dysfunction cognitions that interfere with effective management (Bernard & Joyce, 1984).

6. *Practice and follow-up*: Clients practice new behaviors and integrate them into their repertoire and interactions in everyday life. Clients self-monitoring procedures and homework assignments, typically involving more practice and further refinements in skills acquisition.

Assessment and Social Skills Programs for Adolescents

As noted previously, there is a shortage of specific assessment and treatment packages developed for adolescents. Most of the chapter authors in this book adapted their specific assessments and training material for adolescents from the scales and modules developed by Michelson et al. (1983) for children. Their book is consistent with the assertiveness and social skills format presented in this chapter. Although the material of Michelson et al. is geared more to children than adolescents, many of the modules span the major assertiveness and social skills problematic categories, and a few do address teen issues or can be easily adapted for such use. In their program, 15 training modules are detailed, with specific instructions for trainers, sample lectures, practice scripts, questions, and homework assignments. Modules include standing up for rights, empathy, refusal, resolving conflicts, among others.

Most of the clinical chapters in this book will provide illustrations or adaptations of the assessment and treatment modules by Michelson et al. (1983) geared to the needs of their specific populations. (For a fuller discussion of details of these programs, their suitability for adolescents and special populations, and their limitations, see chapters by Barrish, Yarris, Duggan-Ali, Vardi, and Collabolletta.)

Structured Learning Approach

Goldstein et al. (1980) have developed an adolescent version of their popular structured learning (SL) approach. Basically, Goldstein et al.

incorporate the major features of assertiveness and social skills training described earlier into the programs that have been applied to various populations and age groups. The SL materials by Goldstein et al. are written for nonprofessionals who carry out this training in the community. They report that "the array of types of change agents who have functioned as SL trainers is quite broad . . . psychologists, social workers, teachers, nurses, occupational and recreational therapists, graduate, undergraduate and high school students, home, parent and teacher aides" (Goldstein, Gershaw, & Sprafkin, 1985, p. 298). Their approach has popular appeal and has provided a format for mainstreaming social skills curriculum into schools. (See the chapter by Bernstein Shendell for a fuller presentation of this approach in working with junior high students.)

CONCLUSION

In writing this introductory chapter, I have tried to highlight some of the differing approaches to assertiveness and social skills training. The beginning section draws heavily on my work in training psychologists and other professionals to use assertiveness techniques for their own professional growth and from therapy clients who seek treatment for assertiveness problems. The section on social skills training for adolescents is based on experience in training school psychologists and clinicians to work with children and adolescents in schools.

There are problems in adapting adult and child assessments for the adolescent population. Clearly, more research needs to be directed toward specifying what specific skills are needed for adolescents and developing appropriate materials. Although training can ideally be done within a psychoeducational model, assessments and treatments need to be tailored for specific populations. Different ethnic groups may also require redefinition of what is socially effective skilled behavior and what is not. Furthermore, there are emotional, cognitive, as well as social interactive features of social skills training that require a certain degree of clinical sensitivity and care in application. Although it would be desirable for social skills to be part of each adolescent's social curriculum in the school, we must remember that such training most likely will require continued involvement of school psychologists and mental health professionals in the assessment, development, and implementation of such programs.

REFERENCES

Alberti, R. E., & Emmons, M. L. (1970). *Your perfect right.* San Luis Obispo, CA: Impact.

Argyle, M. (1969). *Social interaction.* London: Methuen.

Bandura, A. (1971). *Social learning theory.* Morristown, NJ: Learning Press.

Bandura, A. (1977). Self-efficacy: Toward a unifying theory of behavioral change. *Psychological Review, 84,* 191–215.

Bernard, M., & Joyce, M. (1984). *Rational-emotive therapy with children and adolescents: Theory, treatment strategies, preventive methods.* New York: Wiley.

Cheek, D. (1974). *Assertive black/puzzled white.* San Luis Obispo, CA: Impact.

Combs, M. L., & Slaby, D. A. (1977). Social skills training with children. In B. B. Lahey & A. E. Kazdin (Eds.), *Advances in clinical child psychology* (Vol. 1). New York: Plenum.

Dodge, K. A., & Murphy, R. R. (1984). The assessment of social competence in adolescents. In P. Karoly & J. Steffen (Eds.), *Adolescent behavior disorders: Foundations and contemporary concerns.* Lexington, MA: D. C. Heath.

Eisler, R., & Frederiksen, L. (1980). *Perfecting social skills.* New York: Plenum.

Eisler, R., Hersen, M., Miller, P., & Blanchard, E. (1975). Situational determinants of assertive behavior. *Journal of Consulting and Clinical Psychology, 43,* 33–340.

Eisler, R., Miller, P., & Hersen, M. (1973). Components of assertive behavior. *Journal of Clinical Psychology, 29,* 295–299.

Ellis, A. (1975). *A new guide to rational living.* Englewood Cliffs, NJ: Prentice Hall.

Feindler, E. L., & Ecton, R. B. (1986). *Adolescent anger control: Cognitive behavioral techniques.* New York: Springer.

Fensterheim, H. (1974). Behavior therapy: Assertive training in groups. In C. J. Sager & H. S. Kaplan (Eds.), *Progress in group and family therapy.* New York: Brunner Mazel.

Fodor, I. (1980). The treatment of communication problems with assertiveness training. In A. Goldstein & E. Foa (Eds.), *Handbook of behavioral interventions.* New York: Wiley.

Fodor, I. (1988). Assertiveness training in the 80's: Moving beyond the personal. In L. Walker & L. Rosewater (Eds.), *Handbook of feminist therapy.* New York: Springer.

Fodor, I., & Epstein, R. (1983). Assertiveness training for women: Where are we failing? In P. Emmelkamp & E. Foa (Eds.), *Failures in behavior therapy.* New York: Wiley.

Fodor, I., & Wolfe, J. (1977). Assertiveness training for mothers and daughters. In R. Alberti (Ed.), *Assertiveness: Recent innovations.* San Luis Obispo, CA: Impact.

Ford, M. E. (1982). Social cognition and social competence in adolescence. *Developmental Psychology, 18,* 322–341.

Furnham, A. (1985). Social skills training: A European perspective. In L.L'Abate & M. Milan (Eds.), *Handbook of social skills training and research.* New York: Wiley.

Gallassi, J., Gallassi, M., & Vedder, M. (1981). Perspectives on assertion as a social skills model. In J. Wine & M. Smye (Eds.), *Social competence.* New York: Guilford Press.

Gambrill, E. D., & Richey, C. A. (1976). *Its up to you: Developing assertive and social skills.* Milbrae, CA: Les Femmes.

Goldfried, M. R., & D'Zurilla, T. J. (1969). A behavioral-analytic model for assessing competence. In C. D. Spielberger (Ed.), *Current topics in clinical and community psychology* (Vol. 1). New York: Academic Press.

Goldstein, A., Gershaw, N. J., & Sprafkin, R. (1985). Structured learning: Research and practice in psychological skill training. In L. L'Abate & M. Milan (Eds.), *Handbook of social skills training and research.* New York: Wiley.

Goldstein, A., Sprafkin, R., Gershaw, J., & Klein, P. (1980). *Skillstreaming the adolescent.* Champaign, IL: Research Press.

Hazel, J. S. (1990). Social skills training with adolescents. In E. Feindler & G. Kalfus (Eds.), *Adolescent behavior therapy handbook.* New York: Springer.

Hollin, C., & Trower, P. (1983). *Handbook of social skills training* (Vols. 1–2). New York: Pergamon Press.

Hops, H., & Greenwood, C. R. (1980). Assessment of children's social skills. In E. J. Marsh & L. G. Terdal (Eds.), *Behavioral assessment of childhood disorders.* New York: Guilford Press.

Hops, H., Lewinsohn, P., Andrews, J., & Roberts, R. (1990). Psychosocial correlates of depressive symptomatology among high school students. *Journal of Clinical Child Psychology, 19,* 211–220.

Jakubowski-Spector, P. (1973). Facilitating the growth of women through assertive training. *The Counseling Psychologist, 4,* 76–86.

L'Abate, L., & Milan, M. (Eds.). (1985). Preface. *Handbook of social skills training and research.* New York: Wiley.

Ladd, G., & Asher, S. (1985). Social skills training and children's peer relations. In L. L'Abate & M. Milan (Eds.), *Handbook of social skills training and research.* New York: Wiley.

Lang, A., & Jakubowski, P. (1976). *Responsible assertiveness training.* Champaign, IL: Research Press.

Libert, J. M., & Lewinsohn, P. M. (1973). Concept of social skill with special references to the behavior of depressed persons. *Journal of Consulting and Clinical Psychology, 40,* 304–312.

McKay, M., Davis, M., & Fanning, P. (1983). *Messages: The communication book.* Richmond, CA: New Harbinger Publications.

Michelson, L., Sugai, D., Wood, R., & Kazdin, A. (1983). *Social skills assessment and training with children: An empirically based handbook.* New York: Plenum.

Osborn, S. M., & Harris, G. G. (1975). *Assertive training for women.* Springfield, IL: Charles C. Thomas.

Phelps, S., & Austin, N. (1975). *The assertive woman*. San Luis Obispo, CA: Impact.

Phillips, E. L. (1985). Social skills: History and prospect. In L. L'Abate & M. Milan (Eds.), *Handbook of social skills training and research*. New York: Wiley.

Renshaw, P. D., & Asher, S. R. (1982). Social competence and peer status: The distinction between goals and strategies. In K. H. Rubin & H. D. Ross (Eds.), *Peer relationships and social skills in childhood*. New York: Springer-Verlag.

Rich, A., & Schroeder, H. (1976). Assertiveness training. *Psychological Bulletin, 83*, 1082–1096.

Rinn, R. C., & Markle, A. (1979). Modification of social skills deficits in children. In A. S. Bellack & M. Hersen (Eds.), *Research and practice in social skills training*. New York: Plenum Press.

Salter, A. (1949). *Conditioned reflex therapy*. New York: Creative Age Press.

Seltzer, V. S. (1989). *The psychosocial world of the adolescent: Public and private*. New York: Wiley.

Solomon, L., & Rothblum, E. (1985). Social skills problems experienced by women. In L. L'Abate & M. Milan (Eds.), *Handbook of social skills training and research*. New York: Wiley.

Stern, J., & Fodor, I. (1990). Anger control in children: A review of social skills and cognitive behavioral approaches to dealing with aggressive children. *Child & Family Behavior Therapy, 11*, 1–20.

Trower, P. M. (1979). Fundamentals of interpersonal behavior: A social-psychological perspective. In A. S. Bellack & M. Hersen (Eds.), *Research and practice in social skills training*. New York: Plenum Press.

Van Hasselt, V., Hersen, M., Whitehall, M., & Bellack, A. (1980). Social skills assessment and training for children: An evaluative review. *Behavioral Research & Therapy, 17*, 413–437.

Wolfe, J., & Fodor, I. (1975). A cognitive/behavioral approach to assertiveness training in women: Special issues on assertiveness. *The Counseling Psychologist, 5*, 45–59.

Wolfe, J., & Fodor, I. (1977). Modifying assertive behavior in women: A comparison of three approaches. *Behavior Therapy, 8*, 567–574.

Wolpe, J. (1958). *Psychotherapy by reciprocal inhibition*. Stanford, CA: Stanford University Press.

Zigler, E., & Phillips, L. (1961). Social competence and outcome in psychiatric disorder. *Journal of Abnormal and Social Psychology, 63*, 264–271.

2

Adolescent Development and Social Skills Training: a Multifaceted Perspective

Marilyn Bernstein Shendell

Jane needs more time to think through the answer to the teacher's question. Seeing raised hands dart quickly into the air, Jane withdraws and gives up. Jane thinks she is the dumbest person in the whole class.

Brian used to be the same height as his friends. This year, he is shorter than his friends. He would like to play basketball but does not know how to approach the coach. Besides, he hates his nickname "Short Stuff." Maybe it would be safer if he did not play!

Anna would like to die every time some jerk in her class makes a comment about her big breasts. She wishes she knew how to deal with their sexual remarks.

Tom would love to go into town with friends on Saturday, but he never seems to get asked. If he knew what to do, he would like to be included.

In this chapter, we will focus on early adolescence (12–15 years), a time of key changes in physiological, cognitive, socioemotional, and personality functioning as well as physical appearance (Lerner & Foch, 1987). This is also the time frame in which social skills are developed, and that has subsequent implications for later adolescence and adult development.

The developing adolescent is asked to meet, cope with, and master a complex set of social skills for personal and interpersonal life tasks. Goldstein, Sprafkin, Gershaw, and Klein (1980) point out that love, sex, and peer relationships are all likely to require social skills. In addition the young adolescent is asked to meet the challenges of the secondary school environment, necessitating a host of interactions between teachers and students alike. Skills are required to start a conversation, to ask a question, to make a date with a friend, to express one's feelings, to deal with stress, to assert one's position, plus a multitude of moment-to-moment interchanges that many of us take for granted. If an adolescent does not have the skills to negotiate his or her environment adequately, as school psychologists we are likely to see a teenager with low self-esteem who may handle a difficult or unresponsive environment by avoidance, aggressive responses, or use of alcohol or drugs to ease anxiety and stress from social pressures. Furthermore, there are also those youngsters who do not fit the mode in some way, such as the physically handicapped, minority group, learning disabled, or culturally different; these adolescents must master social skills as well as additional skills that surround their status. The chapters that follow highlight social skills training for select populations, whereas this chapter elucidates normal adolescent issues.

Adolescence is a time of change. Biological, psychological, and cognitive changes all contribute to the adolescent's problems with social interactions.

Adolescence can be described as a time of intense peer involvement along with a heightened pressure for conformity. The adolescent is often totally immersed in peer culture. Hair, clothing, language, tastes in movies, music, dance, and recreation all follow a prescribed pattern. Navigating this very circumscribed territory can be a precarious balancing act for many a youngster.

Adolescence is a shift from childhood to the period when individuals begin to take responsibility for developing significant relationships (Dowrick, 1986). Yet, adolescents have particular problems in forming those relationships (Meeks, 1980). The anxiety, uncertainty, and apprehension that accompanies much of this developmental phase may actively intrude on the adolescent's ability to form and use human relationships, as well as on their ability to communicate. Inability to communicate as well as self-defeating cognitions often result in the adolescent's feeling less well liked and accepted by their peers. Good social skills include many areas of social interaction, all of which enhance the adolescent's social functioning and contribute to their overall sense of competence as individuals. Adolescents lacking such social skills frequently have problems maintaining friendships (LeCroy, 1982) and mediating interactions between parents, friends, teachers, and other adults. These interactions are all significant in terms of identity and self-growth associated with this developmental period.

SEXUAL MATURITY

Biological changes herald the first signs of the adult body and may serve to contribute significantly to the adolescent's sense of awkwardness. The physical manifestations of this period, also known as pubescence, are characterized by the rapid growth of the skeletal and muscular systems, the maturing of the genitalia, and the appearance of the secondary sex characteristics such as pubic hair and breasts (Kaplan, 1984). The hormones estrogen and testosterone begin secreting, leading to sexual maturity.

The achievement of sexual maturity is of great importance to the adolescent. It can also be the source of embarrassment. The boy's sexual organs seem to react without his volition. Nocturnal emissions may embarrass him. Erections as a reaction to a wide variety of stimuli are commonplace. A girl's first menstruation may bring its own difficulties. The girl may worry that the pad she is wearing is showing, that boys can tell that she is menstruating, that her body odor has become offensive, or that her gym teacher will question her note saying that she cannot participate today.

As every system of the body is altered to some degree, these many changes have an influence on the behavior and intrapsychic processes of the adolescent. As secondary sexual characteristics occur such as the development of breasts, pubic hair, beard, and body contour, the maturing adolescent must now incorporate these new anatomical changes into his or her body concept. The youngster is often acutely aware that these changes are apparent for everyone to see and may bring forth unwelcomed notice. Biological maturation may manifest itself in problems with social interactions. The developing male teenager may cringe as his voice goes through uncontrollable changes. The big-breasted or flat-chested girl must learn how to deal with teasing or sexual remarks. The boy who does not develop as quickly as his friends must contend with often contentious nicknames such as "Shorty" or "Peewee."

Sexual maturity brings with it the need to assert one's position on sexuality. A recent poll conducted by Harris and Associates (1986) revealed that more than one half of American teenagers are sexually active by the time they are 17 years old. Therefore, the developing adolescent must learn to talk about sex, to be able to say no, to be comfortable with their own feelings, and not to feel coerced by their peers. In addition, today's teenagers are bombarded with material on sexuality and birth control methods. A new area of concern comes from the AIDS crisis—asking for a sexual history or negotiating the use of condoms can indeed be an uneasy and awkward situation. Saturated with sexual material, the developing adolescent is asked to deal with a subject that requires skills that they may not have.

PHYSICAL MATURATION

Physical growth is rapid just before and during early adolescence. There are differences in development between boys and girls, however. Among boys the curves for height and weight rise most sharply from ages 12 to 16 with additional smaller gains until age 18. During pubescence, while boys are acquiring adult sexual characteristics, they grow very rapidly. A boy may gain as much as 6 inches and 25 pounds in a single year. The boy's increased arm and leg growth is primarily responsible for his often ungainly appearance at this time as he begins to adapt to these sudden extended appendages.

Among girls, growth is rapid in preadolescence but slower during adolescence. Because girls develop in all respects faster than boys, however, their preadolescent growth begins sooner. The growth spurt in weight is considerably more marked than in height. On girls, the onset of puberty has the effect of slowing down the rate of growth. By the age of 14 most girls have begun to menstruate, and there is little further rise in weight (Cole & Hall, 1964). Considerable research has focused on the social implications of early versus later maturing youngsters (Weatherly, 1964). The results have suggested that the early maturing boy, because of his superior strength and size, is usually at a temporary social advantage, whereas the late maturing boy may suffer most of all as the butt of jokes and ridicule. In contrast, the early developing girl may feel out of place among her undeveloped age mates and may go to great lengths to hide her newly developing body. The self-consciousness that may be aroused by physical development is an important factor in the adolescent's sense of comfort in dealing with social situations.

COGNITIVE CHANGES

Adolescence also brings a change in cognitive processes. During the last stage in the development of intelligence (usually 12–15 years) there gradually emerges what Piaget calls formal operations, which, in effect, permits adolescents to think about their thoughts, to construct ideas, and to reason realistically about the future. The adolescent's thinking, according to Piaget, now enables him or her to achieve integration into the social relationships of adults.

Capacity for Thought Implications

With this new capacity for thought, particularly in social situations, the adolescent now sees a host of alternatives. It is now possible to deal with problems through trial action in the mind's eye, considering alternative plans for their solution before taking action in reality. The adolescent may now see alternatives in terms of parents' directives and may no longer be willing to comply with their decisions without question. In addition, Elkind (1970) describes changes in thinking about the self during early adolescence. He identifies changes in egocentrism in which young adolescents tend to play to an imaginary audience in which they anticipate reactions to themselves based on the premise that others are as admiring or critical of them as they are of themselves. One has only to watch a seventh grader prepare for speech class before a scheduled appearance to note the role this cognition plays in the often overwhelming sense of self-consciousness intrinsic to the adolescent.

Cognitive development may be very uneven across grade level, resulting in a wide range of ability from the most developed to those who lag behind. This spread in thinking and reasoning ability may take its toll on adolescents who pigeonhole themselves as less capable simply because their friends may catch on more quickly than they can.

Social Cognition

Social cognitions can be defined as how people think about other people and themselves. In addition, it deals with how the adolescent learns to understand others' thoughts, emotions, social behavior, and beliefs and values. These social cognitions operate within a particular framework. Adolescents, more than any other group, are concerned with what others think of them. Adolescence is a time in which everyone's status is known in every area: who is smart, dumb, popular, a loser, and which groups are "in" or "out", and so on. What people think about adolescents affects their daily life in school. Everyone knows how they did in a test or if they just got "dumped" in a relationship.

Rice (1984) points out that gaining social knowledge is more difficult because social rules are less uniform, less specific, and more situation dependent than physical phenomenon. The adolescent who has superior intellectual problem-solving skills does not necessarily have superior social-problem skills. Thus, although adolescents might be able to hold forth eloquently regarding their thoughts on the current upheavals in the marketplace along with well-delineated plans for economic recovery, they might still be in a quandary when preparing to ask for a first date.

DEVELOPMENTAL HURDLES:
THEORETICAL PERSPECTIVES

Many theoretical models have been proposed to explain adolescent development. We will explore three of these theoretical frameworks for the purpose of culling information that will be helpful to our understanding of adolescent development and its implications for social skills training. Although each model differs significantly in its conceptualization of the issues surrounding normal adolescent development, each nonetheless provides some understanding and contribution toward the development of a behavioral intervention to aid youngsters who are encountering barriers to establishing satisfying relationships with the significant people in their life.

PSYCHOANALYTICAL VIEWS OF ADOLESCENCE:
ANNA FREUD

Much of the seminal psychoanalytical work on adolescence was developed by Anna Freud (1958). Freud first stated the concept of developmental disturbance, describing the adolescent reaction as a prototypical example. A developmental disturbance is a normal reaction to internal conflict, leading to a sensible adaptation to the external world. Much of the conflicting behavior is produced by the internal psychic disequilibrium that is brought about by sexual maturation at puberty. This surge in instinctual drives at puberty increases the adolescent's sexual urges and intensifies aggressive impulses that may be seen as rebelliousness. These increased aggressive and sexual impulses present a direct challenge to the ego, which is the evaluating reasoning power of the individual. The superego is also brought to bear as the conscience and internalized social values of the parent. With the onset of adolescence, this equilibrium of psychic forces is disrupted by developmental tasks that directly affect the youngster's capacity to cope. According to Anna Freud, the risk at this state is that the child may allow the new genital urges to connect with old love objects, that is with his parents, brother or sister. Consequently, all of his defenses are mobilized in an effort to control his sexual and aggressive impulses. Thus, all of the ego's defenses are employed indiscriminately to win this battle. The adolescent uses a variety of defense mechanisms (e.g., repression, displacement, denial, and reversal of instincts) in an effort to cope with these unacceptable impulses. This produces a variety of fears, hysterical symptoms, and increased anxiety, which is brought about through obsessional thoughts and behaviors. Much of the erratic behavior observed in adolescence is the result of this internal struggle.

Defensive Solution

Anna Freud stated that ultimately nothing helps here except for a complete discarding of the people who were the important love objects of the child—the parents. Along with leaving the family, adolescents abandon their ideals, resulting in their need to replace both. Adolescents often fill this void with the peer group, which becomes the unquestioned authority in all matters.

PETER BLOS AND THE SECOND INDIVIDUATION PHASE OF DEVELOPMENT

Peter Blos expanded on the work of Anna Freud and Margaret Mahler. He coined this period of life "the second individuation process of adolescence." Blos defines adolescence as the period in which the child sheds family dependencies and loosens infantile object ties to become a member of the adult world. For Blos, it is essential that the adolescent disengage from what he calls primary internalized objects. To do so, however, the ego is necessarily weakened. Previous to adolescence the parental ego was available to the child and was indeed his legitimate ego extension. Blos thus regards the ego weakness of adolescence as not only due to the increasing strength of the drives as described by Anna Freud but also, in large measure, the disengagement from the parental ego support.

What Blos emphasizes is that adolescence is the only period in human life during which ego regression and drive regression constitute an obligatory component of normal development. It is these specific transient regressions that Blos believes account for much of the perplexing behavior and the unique emotional turbulence of this age. A poignant example of this was graphically depicted in the movie *Summer of '42* in which four young adolescents purchased prophylactics and then proceeded to use them as water balloons.

SOCIOPSYCHOANALYTICAL VIEWS OF ADOLESCENCE

Erik Erikson: Ego Identity

Erik Erikson modified Freud's theory by embracing social forces and the socialization process to explain development. The core concept of this eight-stage theory is the acquisition of an ego identity, and the identity crisis is the most essential characteristic of adolescence. Erikson emphasizes that adolescence is a normative crisis with increased conflict that is characterized by a fluctuation of ego strength. During this phase the adolescent must establish "a sense of personal identity" and avoid the dangers of "role diffusion" and "identity confusion." Muss (1962) notes that this implies that individuals must assess what their liabilities and assets are, and how they want to use them. This raises the age-old questions: Who am I? What will I become? The answers to these questions must be searched for and worked on by the adolescent; without an active striving and intent to resolve these questions, the adolescent faces the danger of role diffusion, which may result in alienation and a lasting sense of isolation and confusion.

Identity Resolution

Erikson states that adolescents who have established a positive identity have developed a sense of being all right, of accepting themselves. Identity has many components: It includes physical, sexual, social, vocational, moral, ideological, and psychological characteristics that make up the total self. If adolescents fail in their search for identity they will experience self-doubt, role diffusion, and role confusion, and they may then indulge in self-destructive preoccupations or activities. The adolescent may withdraw from the effort to shape an identity or may play with various options. Erikson quotes Bill in Arthur Miller's play *Death of a Salesman*: "I just can't take hold, Mom. I can't take hold of some kind of life."

Process of Falling in Love

Erikson believes that falling in love during adolescence is not as much of a sexual nature as it is an attempt to see oneself through the eyes of a love object to clarify and reflect one's own self-concept and ego identity. Through various love affairs adolescents are able to refine and revise their own definition of ego.

SULLIVAN: ROLE OF "CHUM"

It is Sullivan that is given credit (Youniss & Smollar, 1985) for the role that individual friendships serve in the course of the adolescent development. Sullivan states that it is friendship that can be a healing relationship that aids the adolescent in overcoming what had been the source of negative or uncomfortable self-attributions. His view casts the friend in the role of therapist. The friendship may also serve as a source of more neutral self-appraisal, devoid of the defensiveness that may be present in the parental relationship, which may arouse judgment and explicit standards. In contrast, he thinks that adolescents do not see friendship as a judgment relationship but one that has standards that allow friends to be critics of each other's behavior. In a friendship, adolescents may present a truer picture of themselves without exaggerating assets or denying weaknesses. Sullivan argues that having a close friendship during adolescence may be crucial in an individual's defensive structure.

IMPORTANCE OF GROUP

For the psychoanalytical school, the adolescent is therefore in the throes of newly emerging sexual drives of regressive pulls to an earlier, safer stage of development, and to an affective state characterized by internal object loss and concomitant ego impoverishment. Compensatory relief is therefore sought in the group, generally with contemporaries. "This social formation is a substitute, often literally, of the adolescent's family" (Blos, 1967). The group becomes of fundamental importance to adolescents. From it they extract stimulation, belongingness, loyalty, devotion, and empathy. It is the group that supplies contact without which individuation cannot be realized. The group additionally allows adolescents to try out various roles without commitment as they experiment with severing childhood dependencies. The group thus shares and alleviates individual guilt feelings that accompany the emancipation from childhood dependencies. It is the peer group for Blos that eases the way to membership in the new generation within which adolescents must establish their social, personal, and sexual identity.

ROLE OF FRIENDSHIP FOR PSYCHOANALYTICAL SCHOOL: ITS DERIVATION AND PURPOSE

For the most part, the psychoanalytical framework sees friendship as an escape from the uncomfortable attraction to parents. As Douvan and Adelson (1966) state, the adolescent does not choose friendship but is driven into it. Friendship becomes a means through which the ego capacities are nourished and enhanced. The adolescent escapes to friendship to deal with issues that cannot be confronted with parents. Thus, friendship serves numerous functions. It serves as a device for relieving guilt, obtaining reassurance, and establishing controls. Through identification with another peer the adolescent can be rid of distorting drives and yet experience them vicariously. If the adolescent runs too far afield in experimentations, the friend provides the external norms necessary to aid the weakened internal controls.

ATTEMPT TO FIND SOME ANSWERS

Erik Erikson: Adolescent Peer Group

Adolescents reject the older generation as an appropriate role model in their search for a personal identity and turn to the peer group. As Muss (1962) states "the importance of the peer group in the process of finding out 'Who am I?' cannot be overemphasized." The peer group provides social feedback as to how others feel and how they react to the individual. Interaction with other people is the key to finding an identity. The peer group therefore provides the means through which adolescents test roles to see whether and how they fit them. The group provides a role model as well as direct feedback about themselves. Group conformity is explained by Erikson as a defense against the dangers of role diffusion that exist as long as an identity has not yet been established. In the confusion brought about by physical maturation, emerging sexuality, and fantasies regarding the opposite sex, the group provides comfort for adolescents by stereotyping themselves, their ideals, and their adversaries.

SOCIAL LEARNING THEORY

Social learning theory explains social and developmental problems within the context of behavioristic constructs rather than biological or maturational factors. Learning and development are seen as derived from a combination of environmental, situational, and social interactions.

Different Perspective

Bandura (1977), the major exponent of social learning theory, does not see adolescence as a specific stage but rather as a continuous ongoing process that unfolds from infancy to adulthood. Bandura emphasizes that children learn through observing the behavior of others and by imitating this behavior. This process of learned socialization is accomplished in three ways: modeling, imitation, and identification.

Modeling

As children grow they imitate different models from their environment. Bandura and his associates have shown that children watching the behavior of a model are quick to imitate that behavior as well as to generalize response patterns of the model. The potency of observing and imitating a model has been studied in divergent areas. Bandura's (1977) studies investigating the influence of watching unusually aggressive behavior and then noting children's accurate imitations of the aggressive acts has led to much of the concern about the effects of watching television violence on children and adolescents.

Adolescent models.   With the onset of adolescence, Muss (1962) notes that parents and teachers frequently decline as important models, at least regarding issues and choices that are of immediate consequence. It is now the peer group and entertainment heros that become models for the adolescent in such areas as food, clothing, hair, verbal expressions, entertainment preferences, music, and decisions regarding changing social values.

Identification and Imitation

Bandura refers to identification as a more general way of modeling the behavior of a person even without his or her presence. This includes incorporating the model's values, beliefs, roles, and attitudes. Imitation, conversely, is more specific mimicking of behavior, such as mannerisms, sexual behavior, self-control, language, and more complex social behaviors.

Difference from Stage Theories

According to Bandura, when changes in behavior occur in adolescence, they are likely due to sudden changes in family structure, in peer group expectations, or the environmental factors, and not to hormonal or other biological changes. The same principles of learning that explain child development are applicable to adolescent development. Only the models and environmental influences change. External stimulus conditions, rather than hidden, subconscious, internal dynamics, control normal as well as deviant behavior. Likewise, aggressive behavior in adolescence is not due to biological or maturational changes but rather has its antecedent in behavior learned in the interaction between parent and child.

IMPLICATIONS FOR SOCIAL SKILLS PROGRAMS

There are different theoretical positions for defining this time of life, yet each finds the peer group of paramount importance in supporting the adolescent's successful transition to adulthood. Although theories stress the importance of the peer group, the literature also reminds us of a paradox. The adolescent is required to take a step forward toward independent social functioning, but can often be hampered by biological and psychological changes. These changes can make the formation of new relationships difficult, compounding the adolescent's heightened sense of disorganization and inadequacy.

Social skills would allow the adolescent the ability to mediate interactions between peers, parents, teachers, and other adults successfully. Social competence would be enhanced giving the adolescent the skills associated with peer acceptance and friendships. These skills would involve the construction of new strategies for dealing with changes in interpersonal relationships and for redefining the adolescent's sense of self in the light of his or her new social position and changing social realities (Selman & Demorest, 1984). Although many social skills programs have been designed to address the clinically pathological population (Sarason & Ganzer, 1973; Elder, Edelstin, & Narick, 1979; Matson, Esueldt-Dawson, & Andrasik, 1980), we propose that the need exists for the basically intact adolescent who struggles through this developmental phase. To date, most social skills programs have been based on the more pragmatic views of social learning theory leading to a limited or narrow focus on adolescent behavior that stresses skill deficits. By broadening these programs to include the many developmental tasks that confront the adolescent a social skills program can view the adolescent from a perspective that adds greater depth and complexity. These programs should be cognizant of biological, physiological, and cognitive changes, as well as the psychological issues of impulse control and identity formation that the psychoanalytical schools have contributed to our understanding of the adolescent years. A more multifaceted program needs to consider the adolescent's struggle, which is often reflected in behavior that does not serve the adolescent well. The youngster who avoids difficult situations, is overcontrolled or is too aggressive is no longer seen as simply lacking skills, but one whose behavior demonstrates a variety of age-appropriate issues and concerns.

To date, social skills programs have not addressed the psychodynamic issues that underlie behavior but have concerned themselves primarily with the mechanics of training. Programs geared for the adolescent need to consider the developmental issues raised by the psychodynamic schools such as issues surrounding defensiveness, rebellion, identity, self-esteem, separation, the best friend, and the peer group. In the following chapters we discuss specific adolescent groups and social skills training. A broader perspective incorporates a psychodynamic understanding behind the issues faced by various adolescent groups.

CONCLUSION

The theoretical literature converges on the importance of the peer group as essential to promoting the individuation process and to helping the adolescent establish a sense of identity. Social skills can provide the normally developing adolescent with the tools that are necessary to negotiate the peer group environment in interactions that are supportive of the developmental tasks the adolescent must achieve. A sense of social competence is therefore fundamental if the adolescent is to engage successfully in peer relationships that enhance growth and development.

REFERENCES

Adelson, J. (1980). *Handbook of adolescent psychology.* New York: Wiley.

Bandura, A. (1971). *Psychological modeling.* Hawthorne, NY: Aldine Altherton.

Bandura, A. (1977). *Social learning theory.* Englewood Cliffs, NJ: Prentice Hall.

Bandura, A. (1986). *Social foundations of thought and action.* Englewood Cliffs, NJ: Prentice Hall.

Berndt, T. (1982). The features and effects of friendships in early adolescence. *Child Development, 53,* 1447–1460.

Blos, P. (1967). Second individuation process of adolescence. *Psychoanalytic Study of the Child, 22,* 162–182.

Blos, P. (1979). *The adolescent passage.* New York: International Universities Press.

Blyth, D., & Serafica, F. (1985). Continuities and changes. *The Study of Friendships and Peer Groups During Early Adolescence, 5,* 267–283.

Caplan, G., & Lebovicki, S. (1960). *Adolescence: Psychosocial perspectives.* New York: Basic Books.

Cole, L., & Hall, I. (1964). *Psychology of adolescence.* New York: Holt, Rinehart and Winston.

Douvan, E., & Adelson, J. (1966). *The adolescent experience.* New York: Wiley.

Dowrick, P. W. (1986). *Social survival for children: A trainer's resource book.* New York: Brunner/Mazel.

Elder, J. P., Edelstin, B. A., & Narick, M. M. (1979). Adolescent psychiatric patients and modifying a juvenile behavior with social skills training. *Behavior Modification, 3,* 161–178.

Elkind, D. (1970). *Children and adolescents: Interpreting essays on Jean Piaget.* New York: Oxford University Press.

Erikson, E. H. (1963). *Childhood and society.* New York: Norton.

Erikson, E. (1968). *Identity: Youth and crisis.* New York: Norton.

Freud, A. (1958). *Psychoanalytic study of the child.* New York: International Universities Press.

Gallatin, J. E. (1975). *Adolescence and individuality.* New York: Harper & Row.

Goldstein, A., Sprafkin, R., Gershaw, N., & Klein, P. (1980). *Skill streaming the adolescent: A structured approach to teaching social skills.* Champaign, IL: Research Press.

Group for the Advancement of Psychiatry. (1968). *Normal adolescence: Its dynamics and impact.* New York: Charles Scribner's Sons.

Harris, L. & Associates. (1986). *American teen's speak: Sex, myths, T. V. & birth control.*

Jones, V. F. (1980). *Adolescents with behavior problems.* Newton, MA: Allyn & Bacon.

Kaplan, L. J. (1984). Adolescence. In *The farewell to childhood.* New York: Simon & Schuster.

LeCroy, C. W. (1982). Social skills training with adolescents: A review. *Child & Youth Services, 5,* 91–116.

Lerner, R. M., & Foch, T. T. (1987). *Biological–psychosocial interactions in early adolescence.* New York: Erlbaum.

Matson, J. L., Esueldt-Dawson, K., & Andrasik, F. (1980). Direct, observational and generalization effects of social skills training with emotionally disturbed children. *Behavior Therapy, 11,* 522–531.

McKenna, J. G. (1983). An evaluation of group theory for adolescents using social skills training. *Current Psychological Research, 2,* 151–159.

Meeks, J. E. (1980). *The fragile alliance.* Krieger.

Muss, R. E. (1962). *Theories of adolescence.* New York: Random House.

Offer, D. (1960). *The psychological world of the teen-ager.* New York: Basic Books.

Piaget, J. (1963). *The origins of intelligence in children.* New York: Norton.

Rice, F. P. (1984). *The adolescent.* Newton, MA: Allyn & Bacon.

Sarason, I., & Ganzer, V. (1973). Modeling and group discussion in the rehabilitation of juvenile delinquents. *The Journal of Counseling Psychology, 20,* 442–449.

Selman, R., & Demorest, A. (1984). Observing troubled children's interpersonal negotiation strategies: Implications of and for a developmental model. *Child Development, 55,* 288–304.

Spivack, G., & Shure, M. (1983). The cognition of social adjustment: Interpersonal cognitive problem-solving thinking. In B. Lahey & A. Kazdin (Eds.), *Advances in clinical child psychology* (Vol. 5, pp. 323–372). New York: Plenum Press.

Stone, L. J., & Church, J. (1984). *Childhood and adolescence.* New York: Random House.

Sullivan, H. S. (1953). *The interpersonal theory of psychiatry.* New York: Norton.

Weatherly, D. (1964). Self perceived rate of physical maturation and personality in late adolescence. *Child Development, 35,* 1197–1210.

Youniss, J., & Smollar, J. (1985). *Adolescent relations with mothers, fathers, and friends.* Chicago: University of Chicago Press.

3

Assessment of Assertiveness and Social Skills of Adolescents

Lesley Koegel

This chapter reviews the assessment of social skills as it has been applied to adolescents. First I look at the process of social skills assessment itself. In doing so, I delineate the adolescent age group, discover who defines its problems, and determine who rates its behavior. Next I review the various types of assessment measures, and discuss several commonly used and current standardized examples of these measures. Finally, I consider areas for future research.

OVERVIEW OF SOCIAL SKILLS AND ASSERTIVENESS ASSESSMENT ISSUES

In appraising social skills and assertiveness assessment issues, the following topics need to be addressed: (a) Who is an adolescent? (b) How are problems defined? (c) How is ongoing treatment appraised? (d) How is outcome of social skills and assertiveness training evaluated?

Who is an Adolescent?

In reviewing studies we see inconsistencies in the definition of adolescence. There is a large pool of people called "adolescent." Sometimes they are distinguished as "early" or "late." There is vagueness about what constitutes "early" and "late," and sometimes there is no distinction made. Furthermore, an age group that is called adolescent in one location may seem preadolescent or adult in others. For example, an inner-city 16-year-old male or female teenager may seem adult in many ways by the standards of another geographical area or culture. A

12-year-old may fall into the "school-aged" or "teenaged" group. The college population is usually specified as such, but it would seem to share many characteristics with late adolescents on one hand and with adults on the other.

Researchers and clinicians recognize that adolescents differ from children and adults psychologically. Adolescents deal with issues such as drug abuse, truancy, or delinquency in unique ways. Too often adolescents are assessed with child or adult instruments that have been reframed or modified. In the last decade, however, an increasing number of assessments have been tailor-made for teenagers.

How are Problems Defined?

For problem definition the generic measure developed by Goldfried and D'Zurilla (1969) is one of the most useful. These researchers developed a model for an assessment measure to identify deficient social skill behavior, target needy students, and implement treatment. Their five-step assessment procedure calls for compiling a detailed list of problematic situations, generating a list of possible successful responses, evaluating the effectiveness of each on a continuum, developing a measuring instrument format, and evaluating the measure. (For a fuller description of the use of this technique, see the chapters in this book by Yarris, Barrish, and Planells.)

Most researchers focusing on the social skills issues of adolescence have developed measures to identify problem areas using direct observation, role play, or dramatization. Interviews, sociometrics, self-ratings, and observer ratings are also used to identify problems. Most typically, the particular adolescent populations singled out for social skills training are those already in special education classes, in prison, or in hospitals.

How is Ongoing Treatment Appraised?

Once problems have been identified and treatment is underway, clinicians use assessment to determine if treatment is working, and to refine and evaluate it. Practitioners often use role plays or hypothetical situations that arise during treatment as a form of ongoing assessment.

In assessing social skills for any purpose, it is important to note that rating of an "appropriate" response depends on who is the judge (e.g., an adult or a peer). Researchers tend to have a priori ideas about what constitutes "skill," and those ideas influence their assessment. Skill is often determined by researchers' values and biases. Also, similar behaviors might have different meanings in different situations. They are not tied to actually operational indices. It is especially important to keep these situational factors in mind when studying adolescents because they are not a well-differentiated, discrete group.

How is Outcome of Treatment Evaluated?

To assess outcome of treatment, psychologists often rely on the same measure they used to identify the problem. Most of the techniques, such as self-reports and observer reports and behavioral measures that are used for evaluation of outcome, were devised for use in problem identification.

REVIEW OF STANDARDIZED ASSESSMENT MEASURES

We will now review standardized assessment measures of the past decade, including the older measures that have been updated or modified from a child or adult population, as well as the more recent work written for adolescents themselves. We must remember that different researchers define adolescence differently. Although the term *adolescent* is used, the measures have been standardized on different age groups. We will include an age range from 12 years (early) to 21 years (late). This review will highlight sociometric measures, observer ratings, self-report scales, behavioral measures, and assessment batteries.

Sociometric Measures

Researchers using sociometric measures ask subjects to rate one another. Both positive and negative ratings are culled. For example, an adolescent might be asked to name those who are popular or unpopular. Or, students may rank one another on a scale, for example, numbered from "1—very quiet" to "4—very talkative." Sociometric techniques are useful for screening purposes in classrooms because they help determine students' perceptions of other's behavior. They are used during and after social skills training to indicate if peers have changed their opinions and to measure progress. Sociometrics have good predictive validity with teenagers (Dodge & Murphy, 1984).

Because sociometric measures are often developed on-site for use in specific research, they are the least documented form of assessment. One popular standardized measure is the Social Competence Nomination Form (Ford, 1982). Students judge their peers' competence in handling six hypothetical situations pertaining to interactions at school, for example, the ability to present students' viewpoints to teachers. They rate each other on a 1- to 5-point scale.

Sociometrics have some drawbacks for adolescents. By junior high school, students have usually already been screened in the referral process (Gresham & Cavell, 1986). Sociometrics are normative measures and dependent on context. Thus, in an aggressive class, a quiet student might be disliked, or vice versa. So, sociometrics might be context or culture bound. Also, sociograms give little information about why a child is liked or disliked. As a way of appraising interventions, peer evaluations may suffer from a time lag between a child's acquisition of new skills and others' appreciation of the change (Michelson, Sugai, Wood, & Kazdin, 1983).

Observer Ratings

Ratings by teachers or other adults, like sociometric ratings, are most often used in classrooms for screening. They are socially valid for a high school student only in a particular classroom (Gresham & Cavell, 1986). This kind of assessment tends to focus on questions of a global nature and to render a global score. For example, does the student obey rules or ask for help appropriately? Examples of such rating scales that have been used in schools with adolescents are Social Behavior Assessment, the Walker Social Skills Curriculum, and the Teacher Rating Scale of Social Skills. Parent rating scales include the Child Behavior Checklist and the Behavior Problems Checklist. Not only teachers and parents, but also school psychologists or peers may serve as observers. In addition to assertion, these scales may survey other attributes such as sensitivity or anxiety.

Rating scales are inexpensive, quick, objective, and reliable (compared with projective techniques). It is difficult to choose the best instrument to use, however, because scales cover a wide range of domains and phenomena. The user should consider the following technical aspects of teacher rating scales: content (Do items refer to behavior or its consequences?); measurement of global versus specific behaviors; response categories (Are frequency, duration, or severity specified?); development (Was the scale developed empirically or theoretically?); length of time the informant was exposed to the subject; and standardization. Different informants have different qualifications, vocabularies, backgrounds, and experience (Edelbrock, 1983).

Adolescents are more difficult for teachers to rate on a scale than younger children because they are not usually seen in self-contained classrooms. Also, raters are subject to inadvertent and deliberate bias. On the positive side, however, there are more teachers involved, so more sources of data. It is often advantageous to enlist teachers' and parents' help because they usually have positive motivations. Rating scales can be used over extended periods. They may be underused by school psychologists (Knoff, 1986).

Some problems do exist with these scales. The factor structures of different behavior rating scales are discrepant. More work needs to be done on specifying age, race, and sex variables, and how they influence patterns of behavior disorders. The most frequent and reliable use of rating scales is for assessment of conduct problems, anxiety–withdrawal, and developmental level (Carlson & Lahey, 1983).

The Child Behavior Checklist (CBC) (Achenbach & Edelbrock, 1979) is a multiple-choice inventory that comes in two forms, one for teachers and one for parents. It assesses social competence and behavior problems in children up to age 16 and is useful in schools and clinics, although some people find it complicated to use. The CBC is scored by hand or computer on the Child Behavior Profile, which differentiates syndromes between sexes and among ages. The CBC was used as part of a study on the development of antisocial behavior (Snyder, Dishion, & Patterson, 1986). Mothers, teachers, and peers reported on behaviors such as arguing, bragging, cruelty, and disobedience among 4th-, 7th-, and 10th-grade boys. The CBC was used to identify factors related to association with deviant peers; to assess the importance of attitudinal versus behavioral variables in predicting association with deviant peers; and to explore the influences of parental practices, child skill levels, association with deviant peers, and antisocial attitudes.

The Revised Behavior Problem Checklist (BPC-R) (Quay, 1983) has been used for screening and assessment, and in epidemiological studies. Its 89 items are scored as "no problem," "mild problem," or "severe problem." Quay sought to line up subscale categories on his test with categories and dimensions in the *Diagnostic and Statistical Manual of Mental Disorders-III* (DSM III). Although the term *social skills* is not used in DSM III, disorders seem to overlap with social skills deficits, for example, "undersocialized aggressive" and "socialized nonaggressive." The four major categories on the (BPC-R) are conduct disorder, socialized aggression, attention problems–immaturity, and anxiety–withdrawal.

The correspondence between both parents' reports on the BPC has been questioned (Jacob, Grounds, & Haley, 1982). Parents of 10- to 18-year-old male adolescent were sampled to see how closely a couple's responses matched each other. In this way interrater reliability was also examined; responses of parents of disturbed versus normal children were compared; and sociodemographic variables were compared. Parent agreement was found to be generally only moderate and even lower between parents of disturbed children than parents of normal children. Demographics were relatively unimportant. One conclusion is that data should always be obtained from both parents.

The Waksman Social Skills Rating Scale (WSSRS) (Waksman, 1985) is a 21-item scale that assesses the social skills deficits of students from kindergarten to 12th grade. It has been used to help select children for social skills training or special counseling programs and for evaluating the effectiveness of those programs. Aggressive items on the WSSRS (e.g., "insults others") seem to be more reliable than passive items (e.g., "fails to initiate conversations"). Also, the scale seems to discriminate between students in regular classes and those in classes for the emotionally handicapped.

The Assessment for Integration into Mainstream Settings (AIMS) (Walker, 1986) is a very specific and long instrument consisting of five parts. It was designed to achieve one of the goals of Public Law 94-142: to mainstream as many handicapped students as possible so they may interact socially with their nonhandicapped peers. The test measures the behavioral demands that exist in mainstream settings and assesses the teacher's needs in working with handicapped students placed in his or her class. AIMS consists of two instruments for the receiving (i.e., less restrictive classroom) teacher and one for the sending teacher; the remaining two instruments are used to code direct observations.

Are peer and teacher ratings useful in making predictions of future social adjustment? The Pupil Evaluation Inventory, in which teachers and students assess aggression, social withdrawal, and likability, was administered to boys and girls in first grade (Tremblay, LeBlanc, & Schwartzman, 1988). Seven years later, when these students were in junior high school, they were retested with several other instrument. For boys, teachers and peers were found to be equally good predictors of aggression. For girls neither teachers nor peers by themselves were good predictors of future social adjustment, but taken together, they were better predictors than for boys.

Self-Report Scales

Self-report measures are one of the most common forms of assessment used with adolescents in measuring social skills and assertiveness. When these are well written, they require little inference on the part of the self-rater. They assume minimal reading skills, however. They have often been shown to have poor validity and are not well correlated to other kinds of measures (Gresham & Cavell, 1986; Gresham & Elliott, 1984). Examples of self-report measures created for children but used with adolescents are the Children's Assertive Behavior Scale (Michelson et al., 1983), the Perceived Competence Scale for Children (Harter, 1982), and the Matson Evaluation of Social Skills with Youngsters (Matson, Heinze, Helsel, & Kapperman, 1986). Children might be asked to respond "yes" or "no" to an item such as, "Most kids like me"; or to select their typical response to a situation such as, "What do you do if your friend doesn't pay attention to you?" The Adolescent Problems Inventory (Hunter & Kelley, 1986) and the Problem Inventory for Adolescent Girls (Gaffney, 1984), however, covers situations that are relevant and problematic for the adolescent age group, such as making and keeping friends, and dealing with teachers, siblings, and parents.

One problem with many existing self-report questionnaires is that their concept and definition of assertiveness is not always clear. Furnham and Henderson (1983) analyzed five popular assertiveness measures (none normed on adolescents, but all used with them) by content and correlation. Although each scale was designed to yield an overall assertiveness score, they found big differences among them. They concluded that many of these self-report assessments ignore the fact that assertive behaviors are situation specific, and that global scores omit important information.

Assertiveness Self-Report Scales

In the 1970s, assertiveness was broadly considered as positive, negative, or self-denying. Most scales developed from this three-part division. This was the approach used in defining assertiveness in the popular College Self-Expression Scale (Galassi, DeLo, & Bastien, 1974). The expression of personal feelings was considered an important developmental task for college-aged students. This instrument consists of 50 items, each rated on a 5-point scale. It covers such common social situations as refusing a date and asking a friend for a favor.

The Assertion Inventory (AI) (Gambrill & Richey, 1975) is a 40-item questionnaire that was normed on a college-aged population. One of the most popular self-report questionnaires, this inventory differs from others by asking the subject to think about three factors: (a) the degree of discomfort in each given situation, (b) the probability of a behavior occurring, and (c) the situations in which more assertiveness would be desirable. Each of the first two factors is rated on a 5-point scale. Gambrill and Richey categorized assertion in the following ways: refusing requests, expressing one's own limitations, initiating social contact, expressing positive feelings, handling criticism, differing with others, providing service, and giving negative feedback. They tried to account for varying degrees of relationship among people in wording their questions. For example, they ask about the ease of complimenting a friend or telling a coworker to stop being annoying.

Research has attempted to correlate the AI with a role-play format. Dickson, Hester, Alexander, Anderson, and Ritter (1984) asked college students to watch some live and videotaped vignettes in which people enacted scenes depicting the categories listed previously. The results from the videotaped scenes correlated with the AI, but the results from the live performances did not. The usefulness of role play as an outcome measure was therefore questioned, as well as the tendency of people to give socially desirable responses on the AI. McNamara and Delamater (1984) compared the AI with existing measures of social desirability and sensitivity to rejection. In their group of undergraduates, low assertion correlated with high sensitivity to rejection, and was related to a fear of being disliked, overconcern for others, perfectionism, and negative expectations and self-statements (particularly among female adolescents). They also found the AI to be substantially related to social-desirability response biases.

Recently Wills, Baker, and Bovin (1989) adapted the AI for use with suburban and inner-city early adolescents to see how specific aspects of assertion might be related to substance abuse in this population. They found assertion deficits to be related to adolescents' substance use, but they also found significant positive associations between substance abuse and assertiveness. Their results indicate that there are various aspects of assertion at play in determining if an adolescent will succumb to substance abuse. They emphasize the need to pay attention to the social context.

The Modified Rathus Assertiveness Schedule is a version of its popular parent scale consisting of 30 items rates on a 6-point scale (Rathus, 1973). Del Greco, Breitbach, Rumer, McCarthy, and Suissa (1986) found its reliability with white, suburban, middle-class seventh graders to be moderate but variable. For example, reliability might vary with the day of the week the test is administered. Giving the test on Monday could lead to different outcomes than giving it on Friday. Kimble, Marsh, and Kiska (1984) found that with older adolescents, the Rathus revealed differences in assertiveness associated with sex, age, culture, and birth order.

The Adolescent Assertive Expression Scale (Connor, Dann, & Twentyman, 1982) is a 60-item questionnaire using a 6-point response scale developed for adolescents. Noting the lack of attention to the adolescent population, its authors developed this assessment for research from the adolescent viewpoint, as well as that of teachers and parents. They conceptualize assertiveness as the ability to express one's thoughts and feelings without violating the rights of others, distinct from submissiveness and aggressiveness. Items ask, for example, if students allow others to take advantage of them, can easily make requests, or are disruptive in class.

The Personal Assertion Analysis (Hedlund & Lindquist, 1984) is a 30-item self-rating questionnaire that was normed on teens, college students, and adults to distinguish among passive, aggressive, and assertive behavior. Used for screening, it is based on current behaviors, not enduring personality traits. Responses emphasize actual behaviors, not knowledge of correct behaviors. This inventory is not used to assess general level of assertiveness, nor the appropriateness of responses, but to help subjects identify and classify their responses. In validating their scale, the authors included, along with assertive, passive, and aggressive, a passive–aggressive category. Their finding that this last response occurred frequently raises the interesting possibility of including passive–aggressive, a category often neglected by other researchers, as a fourth general category for assessment.

The Assertiveness Scale for Adolescents (Lee, Halberg, Slemon, & Haase, 1985), for grades 6 to 12, was designed for research and diagnosis as well as screening and treatment. Its purposes are to obtain information on the typical behavior of a group or individual; to identify problem areas for an individual; to screen for cases in which intervention is needed; and to obtain information for research on assertiveness. A 33-item questionnaire with three choices per item classified as "assertive," "unassertive," and "aggressive or passive–aggressive," it covers refusing others, making requests, initiating conversations, expressing positive and negative feelings, and standing up for one's rights.

Other Self-Report Measures of Social Skills

In the 1980s, moving beyond the focus on assertion, psychologists became interested in social competence and social skills assessments of special populations. (For other examples, see chapters in this book by Planells-Bloom, Barrish, Duggan-Ali, and Vardi.)

The Perceived Competence Scale for Children (Harter, 1982) measures competence in four domains: cognitive (school), social (friends, peers), physical (sports), and general self-worth (a superordinate construct, not the sum of the other three). Normed on third through ninth graders, and designed for use by clinicians, educators, and program evaluators, this scale measures different levels of competence in different domains. The scale proposes a new type of format that is not loaded toward socially desirable responses. Harter, recognizing that new domains probably emerge in adolescence (e.g., between same-gender and opposite-gender friendships), recommends that other scales be designed for that group and special populations.

As part of a developmental study of adolescents, Allen, Weissberg, and Hawkins (1989) used the Perceived Competence Scale for Children and other assessments to study the relationship between values and social competence in early adolescence. The meaning of "social competence" was explored for a group of normal teens, looking for areas of overlap and conflict in peer influence and adult influence. Their results support research findings that attaining autonomy from parents while staying connected to them is an important developmental task for adolescents.

The Problem Inventory for Adolescent Girls (MC-PIAG) is a 23-item multiple-choice assessment that asks the frequency of performance of illegal activities (Gaffney, 1984). It reflects the trend in recent years to include scales for specific populations in wider research studies. It is based on the PIAG, a longer questionnaire that measures social competence in adolescent girls by asking them to rate their own behavior in conflict situations on a 5-point scale. Social incompetence and low IQs correlate with delinquent activities in this group. The MC-PIAG may be a viable instrument for selecting girls for social skills training and identifying specific problem areas.

The Matson Evaluation of Social Skills with Youngsters (MESSY) (Matson, Macklin, & Helsel, 1985) has been used with adolescents whose physical handicaps cause them to be academically behind their age peers. Most research on social skills has been done on populations without major physical disabilities, although the physically disabled have a high rate of social and emotional problems. The MESSY consists of two similar parts: a 62-item self-report and a 64-item teacher-report questionnaire. Matson et al. (1986) found more evidence of inappropriate social behavior in "normal" than in visually handicapped subjects aged 9 to 22. Deaf children have been shown to have a high incidence of social–emotional problems, however, and there is a need for methods to evaluate and treat them. Using the MESSY, Matson found the hearing impaired to be less assertive than their peers regardless of age. Furthermore, the particular social skills that receive attention from researchers are not rated highly by deaf subjects as important (e.g., looking and smiling at people). This is a reminder to watch for a priori assumptions that are built into social skills assessments.

Self-report assessments of assertiveness have also been used to study the social behaviors of intellectually gifted students. The Social Performance Survey Schedule was standardized on college students but adapted for a group of early adolescent gifted students (D'Ilio & Karnes, 1987) to assess this group's positive and negative social behaviors. Conclusions indicate a need to foster growth in social skills in gifted boys but not girls.

In a study of gifted adolescents examining the internal barriers that block them from realizing their potential, a diverse group of high school sophomore girls were examined for nonassertiveness and self-perception of social competence as two barriers (Hollinger & Fleming, 1984). A prevalence of low social self-esteem was found in this group of girls.

Behavioral Measures

These methods of assessment are based on situational or functional analysis. They may consist of noting occurrence or nonoccurrence of behaviors in naturalistic environments, during performance of contrived tasks in a laboratory environment, or as responses to role plays or simulated interactions. Again, it is important to remember that "skill" is determined by the researcher's values and that similar behaviors might have different meanings in different situations. The observer must identify *critical* social tasks *situationally*.

Structured behavioral interviews have been used successfully to assess children's and adult's social skills. There is a need for such an instrument designed for adolescents. For example, the Children's Behavioral Scenario (Michelson et al., 1983) offers a script and a rating scale, but would be inappropriate for use with adolescents of average or above-average intelligence because the wording is too simplistic. The Personal Questionnaire (Shepherd, 1984) has been developed as a structured assessment interview to elicit symptom statements from adults in clinical settings but requires clients to verbalize cognitions that are difficult even for adults to identify. Therefore it is not recommended for use with adolescents.

Role Play

Assessment by observation of behavioral role play offers trained observers the chance to see social behaviors that may not occur often. Role plays are meant to be analogs of real-life, natural situations. Especially among adolescents, natural behavior is often inaccessible to adult observers. Having teenagers role play actually demonstrates enactment, and is controlled and inexpensive. It may also be more ethical and time saving than observations in natural setting.

However, Bellack, Hersen, and Lamparski (1979) have questioned the validity and utility of role-play tests with college-aged subjects. They found that comparing taped role plays with taped "naturalistic" interactions (using decoys) yielded equivocal results. They warn that, although there could be several explanations, role-play assessments are often imprecise, and they urge caution when interpreting research based on role-play procedures. Furthermore, role plays with children do not correlate well with naturalistic behavior, nor with sociometric, self-report, or teacher ratings (Gresham & Elliott, 1984). It has also been found that the type of assessment used influences the behavior displayed and therefore the treatment (Beck, Forehand, Neeper, & Baskin, 1982). The role-play method was used less often in the 1980s than in the 1970s.

Calvert (1988) highlighted another variable to be considered. He described the importance of physical attractiveness and its influence on raters, confederates, and social competence itself. Because physically attractive adolescents are viewed by their peers as more socially competent, it may be important to measure the influence of physical attractiveness on adult raters as well. This knowledge is currently more important than it was in the past, with the trend to more global and intermediate ratings (e.g., facial expression) rather than to molecular ratings (e.g., number of smiles).

Vignettes

Solicitation of verbal responses to hypothetical situations can be less global and therefore more evaluative of a person's behavior rather than of the person. This method is also likely to elicit less bias among judges. As with other methods, however, it does raise the question of who will judge and who will select situations to be used as stimuli. Of course, appropriate verbal responses do not guarantee appropriate behavior. Teenagers can be quite savvy in this regard.

The Adolescent Problems Inventory (API) developed in 1978 (Hunter & Kelley, 1986), consists of 44 situation descriptions (vignettes) that are read to subjects individually. Their answers are taped and rated according to the manual. The API measures social competence in situations related to antisocial behavior in adolescence. One situation, for example, describes the subject as a visitor to a new place who is deliberately bumped in the street by another teenager he does not know; what would he do? The API was administered to incarcerated juvenile delinquents to see if it differentiated the severity and extent of antisocial behavior in this population. It was concluded that *in vivo* observation may be necessary to measure behavior. The vignettes were too verbal and excluded nonverbal behavior.

The simulated Social Interaction Test (Curran, 1982) was devised for use with adults, but the situations it describes are applicable to older adolescents. Usually, trained judges view videotaped performances, but sometimes significant others in natural settings are the observers. Developed for use with psychiatric patients, the instrument asks for a response to each of eight brief situation descriptions. The situations include the following categories: disapproval or criticism, social assertiveness or visibility, confrontation and anger expression, heterosexual contact, interpersonal warmth, conflict with or rejection by parent or relative, interpersonal loss, and ability to receive compliments.

The Problem Inventory for College Students was developed to test the hypothesis that deficits in interpersonal competence and problem-solving skills are related to nonclinical depression (Fisher-Beckfield & McFall, 1982). A role-play measure of interpersonal competence, it was validated on a group of college men. Fifty-two items written in the form of vignettes describe problem situations, calling for the subject to either role play his response (what he would say) or describe his response (what he would do). Judges evaluate the responses on a 5-point scale using a manual containing item-specific criteria. One question, for example, describes an evening during which a couple argues and asks the boy what he would say to his very sarcastic date. This assessment is an example of the trend toward the development and use of situational competence measures with target populations.

Observing that 12- to 14-year-olds form an important but overlooked age group, clinicians have focused on shyness in early adolescence (Christoff et al., 1985). A group of students labeled as "loners" was selected by referral from school staff. Once chosen for intervention, the individuals were asked to write the middle portion of four stories for which they were given a beginning and an end to demonstrate their problem-solving skills in social initiation. The written stories were rated on a scale by trained judges. To demonstrate conversational skills, students were audiotaped in 5-minute conversations in groups of two. Self-disclosures, questions, positive opinions, statements of fact, and comments were rated. The Social Interaction Survey was devised to measure the likelihood of initiating social interactions in various situations by observing in vivo interactions in the school cafeteria. Some of these assessments were repeated as follow-up measures 5 months after training.

For a study comparing the cognitive mediators of antisocial aggression in incarcerated adolescents with that of high- and low-aggressive high school students, Slaby and Guerra (1988) used several forms of written and behavioral assessment. To select and categorize the high school students, a 10-item teacher rating scale was created. Once subjects were selected, a social problem-solving questionnaire, the Interpersonal Problem-Solving Analysis, was administered: Subjects imagine they are in a situation and answer questions based on a variety of criteria. From the results, the researchers were able to theorize about the thought processes leading to aggressive behavior in adolescents.

Assessment Batteries

Researchers often use two or more kinds of instruments in one study. For example, in a study mentioned earlier on adolescent social cognition and competence (Ford, 1982), the Social Competence Nomination Form, the Interviewee Social Competence Rating Scale, the interviewers' judgment, a formal Empathy Scale, and a self-report questionnaire were all used. In a study of self-perceived competence (Cauce, 1987), the Social Competence Nomination Form and the Perceived Competence Scale for Children, and two methods of peer nominations were used. To study cognitive strategies as part of social competence in adolescents (Meyers & Nelson, 1986), naturalistic observations, interviews, and scaled ratings were used. Young male adolescents conversed with female adolescents who were trained confederates. The male adolescents then viewed a videotape of the conversation and reported their thoughts during it, as well as their conversational strategies. Trained judges then rated the interview transcripts.

In the field of school psychology, projective techniques and self-report inventories have traditionally been the methods of choice for assessment (Goh & Fuller, 1983). Although procedures based on observable behavior are being used increasingly in research, there is little published evidence that school psychologists have changed their methods in practice. There is a growing interest in behavior rating scales, but school psychologists may be unfamiliar with the variety available, untrained in their use, or lack the desire to include them in their batteries.

AREAS FOR FUTURE RESEARCH

This survey revealed many unresolved issues in the assessment of social skills and the delineation of specific aspects of social skills and assertiveness. First, the adolescent group itself must be more clearly defined in terms of age. Developmental factors need more consideration as well. There is a need for research on specific social skills norms for the adolescent age group overall. Particularly, we should know which skills are important in early and late adolescence. Certain behaviors may be related to the personality characteristics of adolescents, and these need to be accounted for when assessing and labeling.

In addition to looking at distinctions among age subgroups in adolescence, there is a need for research regarding sex, socioeconomic, racial, cultural, and geographical differences. Should the same scales be used with white and nonwhite, lower and upper socioeconomic status, southern and midwestern teenagers, for example? Perhaps there is a need for social competence norms for this age group by sex, locale, and so on.

There are many ways in which the boundaries of assessment measures themselves can be better drawn. Often the purpose of assessment is not made clear—whether for classification, treatment, planning, treatment evaluation, or validation of another assessment. Researchers and clinicians could benefit by some guidance on what kind of tests are best to use for different purposes. They often need to clarify the goals of both assessor and subject. These may not be the same.

There is little agreement, and less information, about what method of assessment is best to use with adolescents. Subjects are rarely given an opportunity to explain their responses, but such an opportunity might be very helpful. Rating scales, for example, ignore the fact that assertive behavior can be situation specific; the global scores they yield omit important information.

Researchers are currently interested in the cognitive influences on social behavior. There is a need for more research on the relationships among self-judgments, peer judgments, and adult judgments of social skills, and between perceived and actual socially competent behavior. Clarifying cognitive content areas related to assertion might help psychologists develop more sensitive assessment instruments, allowing them to specify better the relationship between cognitions and assertion (Mizes, Morgan, & Buder, 1987). There is a need for reliable assessments of social cognition for adolescents in particular. One specific question to be answered is: Because childhood patterns continue, when does a person's cognitive pattern (e.g., for aggression) become stabilized? Knowing this would help in timing preventive interventions. Another question is: What characteristics can be identified in teenagers that contribute to both cognition and social competence? If identified, they could be nurtured to foster competent adults.

Because the many different social skills scales have been shown to comprise different factors, there is a need to enumerate the factors and clarify what they are. Writers of assessments also need more information about which skills can be grouped together and which need further breakdown. This information would be helpful in designing interventions. For example, because aggressive behavior is usually more obvious, many tests emphasize it. Research on which passive behaviors predict later psychological problems would be helpful. Along similar lines, there is a need to know which specific social skills deficits among teenagers need immediate attention, which do not, and which are most problematic for the long term.

To answer some of these questions, we need to develop better procedures for identifying individual tasks. We need to find more age-appropriate tasks to test, for example: persuasion of peers, entry into groups, and response to peer provocation. Research in this area might be part of the larger issue of the causes of and correlations between lack of social skills and "abnormal" behavior of "special" groups.

Ultimately the goals of assessment are to identify problematic behaviors and to measure change following intervention. To assess change in adolescents effectively, however, we need to know more about which behaviors predict what outcomes; which behaviors predict peer and adult acceptance; and what outcomes are important to teenagers. Without a clear idea of what is socially valid for adolescents, we may obtain more information without necessarily achieving revelation or change.

REFERENCES

Achenbach, T. M., & Edelbrock, C. S. (1979). The child behavior profile: 2. *Journal of Consulting and Clinical Psychology, 47*, 223–233.

Allen, J. P., Weissberg, R. P., & Hawkins, J. A. (1989). The relation between values and social competence in early adolescence. *Developmental Psychology, 25*, 458–464.

Beck, S., Forehand, R., Neeper, R., & Baskin, C. H. (1982). A comparison of two analogue strategies for assessing children's social skills. *Journal of Consulting and Clinical Psychology, 50*, 596–598.

Bellack, A. S., Hersen, M., & Lamparski, D. (1979). Role-play tests for assessing social skills: Are they valid? Are they useful? *Journal of Consulting and Clinical Psychology, 47*, 335–342.

Calvert, J. D. (1988). Physical attractiveness: A review and reevaluation of its role in social skill research. *Behavioral Assessment, 10*, 29–42.

Carolson, C. L., & Lahey, B. B. (1983). Factor structure of teacher rating scales. *School Psychology Review, 12*, 285–292.

Cauce, A. M. (1987). School and peer competence in early adolescence: A test of domain-specific self-perceived competence. *Developmental Psychology, 23*, 287–291.

Christoff, K. A., Scott, W., Owen, N., Kelley, M. L., Schlundt, D. B. G., & Kelly, J. A. (1985). Social skills and social problem-solving training for shy young adolescents. *Behavior Therapy, 16*, 468–477.

Connor, J. M., Dann, L. N., & Twentyman, C. T. (1982). A self-report measure of assertiveness in young adolescents. *Journal of Clinical Psychology, 38*, 101–106.

Curran, J. P. (1982). A procedure for the assessment of social skills: The Simulated Social Interaction Test. In J. P. Curran & P. M. Monti (Eds.), *Social skills training: A practical handbook for assessment and training*. New York: Guilford.

Del Greco, L., Breitbach, L., Rumer, S. McCarthy, R. H., & Suissa, S. (1986). Further examination of the reliability of the Modified Rathus Assertiveness Schedule. *Adolescence, 21,* 483–485.

Dickson, A. L., Hester, R. F., Alexander, D. H., Anderson, H. N., & Ritter, D. A. (1984). Role-play validation of the assertion inventory. *Journal of Clinical Psychology, 40,* 1219–1226.

D'Ilio, V. R., & Karnes, F. A. (1987). Social performance of gifted students as measured by the Social Performance Survey Schedule. *Psychological Reports, 60,* 396–398.

Dodge, K. A., & Murphy, R. R. (1984). The assessment of social competence in adolescents. In P. Karoly & J. Steffen (Eds.), *Adolescent behavior disorders: Foundations and contemporary concerns.* Lexington, MA: D. C. Heath.

Edelbrock, C. (1983). Problems and issues in using rating scales to assess child personality and psychopathology. *School Psychology Review, 12,* 298–298.

Fisher-Beckfield, D., & McFall, R. M. (1982). Development of a competence inventory for college men and evaluation of relationships between competence and depression. *Journal of Consulting and Clinical Psychology, 50,* 697–705.

Ford, M. E. (1982). Social cognition and social competence in adolescence. *Developmental Psychology, 18,* 323–340.

Furnham, A., & Henderson, M. (1983). Assessing assertiveness: A content and correlational analysis of five assertiveness inventories. *Behavioral Assessment, 6,* 79–88.

Gaffney, L. R. (1984). A multiple-choice test to measure social skills in delinquent and nondelinquent adolescent girls. *Journal of Consulting and Clinical Psychology, 52,* 911–912.

Galassi, J. P., DeLo, J. S., & Bastien, S. (1974). The College Self-Expression Scale: A measure of assertiveness. *Behavior Therapy, 5,* 165–171.

Gambrill, E. D., & Richey, C. A. (1975). An assertion inventory for use in assessment and research. *Behavior Therapy, 6,* 550–561.

Goh, D. S., & Fuller, G. B. (1983). Current practices in the assessment of personality and behavior by school psychologists. *School Psychology Review, 12,* 240–243.

Goldfried, M. R., & D'Zurilla, T. J. (1969). A behavioral-analytic model for assessing competence. In C. D. Spielberger (Ed.), *Current topics in clinical and community psychology* (Vol. 1). New York: Academic Press.

Gresham, F. M., & Cavell, T. A. (1986). Assessing adolescent social skills. In R. G. Harrington (Ed.), *Testing adolescents: A reference guide for comprehensive psychological assessments.* Kansas City: Test Corporation of America.

Gresham, F. M., & Elliot, S. N. (1984). Assessment and classification of children's social skills: A review of methods and issues. *School Psychology Review, 13,* 292–301.

Harter, S. (1982). The perceived competence scale for children. *Child Development, 53,* 87–97.

Hedlund, B. L., & Lindquist, C. U. (1984). The development of an inventory for distinguishing among passive, aggressive, and assertive behavior. *Behavioral Assessment, 6*, 379–390.

Hollinger, C., & Fleming, E. (1984). Internal barriers to the realization of potential: Correlates and interrelationships among gifted and talented female adolescents. *Gifted Child Quarterly, 28*, 135–139.

Hunter, N., & Kelley, C. K. (1986). Examination of the validity of the Adolescent Problems Inventory among incarcerated juvenile delinquents. *Journal of Consulting and Clinical Psychology, 54*, 301–302.

Jacob, T., Grounds, L., & Haley, R. (1982). Correspondence between parents' reports on the Behavior Problem Checklist. *Journal of Abnormal Child Psychology, 10*, 593–608.

Kimble, C. E., Marsh, N. B., & Kiska, A. C. (1984). Sex, age, and cultural differences in self-reported assertiveness. *Psychological Reports, 55*, 419–422.

Knoff, H. (1986). Behavior rating scale approaches. In H. Knoff (Ed.), *The Assessment of Child and Adolescent Personality*. New York: Guilford Press.

Lee, D. Y., Halberg, E. T., Slemon, A. G., & Haase, R. F. (1985). An assertiveness scale for adolescents. *Journal of Clinical Psychology, 41*, 51–57.

Matson, J. L., Heinze, A., Helsel, W. J., & Kapperman, G. (1986). Assessing social behaviors in the visually handicapped: The Matson Evaluation of Social Skills with Youngsters (MESSY). *Journal of Clinical Child Psychology, 15*, 78–87.

Matson, J. L., Macklin, G. F., & Helsel, W. J. (1985). Psychometric properties of the Matson Evaluation of Social Skills with Youngsters (MESSY) with emotional problems and self concept in deaf children. *Journal of Behavior Therapy and Experimental Psychiatry, 16*, 117–123.

McNamara, J. R., & Delamater, R. J. (1984). The Assertion Inventory: Its relationship to social desirability and sensitivity to rejection. *Psychological Reports, 55*, 719–724.

Meyers, J. E., & Nelson III, W. M. (1986). Cognitive strategies and expectations as components of social competence in young adolescents. *Adolescence, 21*, 291–303.

Michelson, L., Sugai, D. P., Wood, R. P., & Kazdin, A. E. (1983). *Social Skills Assessment and Training with Children*. New York: Plenum Press.

Mizes, J. S., Morgan, G. D., & Buder, J. (1987). *Global versus specific cognitive measures and their relationship to assertion deficits*. Paper presented to Association for the Advancement of Behavior Therapy, Boston.

Quay, H. C. (1983). A dimensional approach to behavior disorder: The revised Behavior Problem Checklist. *School Psychology Review, 12*, 244–249.

Rathus, S. A. (1973). A 30-item schedule for assessing assertive behavior. *Behavior Therapy, 4*, 398–406.

Shepherd, G. (1984). Assessment of cognitions in social skills training. In P. Trower (Ed.), *Radical approaches to social skills training*, London: Croom Helm.

Slaby, R. G., & Guerra, N. G. (1988). Cognitive mediators of aggression in adolescent offenders: 1. Assessment. *Developmental Psychology, 24*, 580–588.

Snyder, J., Dishion, T. J., & Patterson, G. R. (1986). Determinants and consequences of associating with deviant peers during preadolescence and adolescence. *Journal of Early Adolescence, 6,* 29–43.

Tremblay, R. E., LeBlanc, M., & Schwartzman, A. E. (1988). The predictive power of first-grade peer and teacher ratings of behavior: Sex differences in antisocial behavior and personality at adolescence. *Journal of Abnormal Child Psychology, 16,* 571–583.

Waksman, S. A. (1985). The development and psychometric properties of a rating scale for children's social skills. *Journal of Psychoeducational Assessment, 3,* 111–121.

Walker, H. M. (1986). The Assessment for Integration into Mainstream Settings Assessment System: Rationale, instruments, procedures, and outcomes. *Journal of Clinical Child Psychology, 15,* 55–63.

Wills, T. A., Baker, E., & Bovin, G. (1989). Dimensions of assertiveness: Differential relationships to substance use in early adolescence. *Journal of Consulting and Clinical Psychology, 57,* 473–478.

Part II

Ethical and Sociocultural Aspects of Adolescent Assertiveness and Social Skills Assessment and Training

Introduction

Iris G. Fodor

In this section, ethical and sociocultural aspects of adolescent assertiveness and social skills training are addressed. Implicit in the notion of assertiveness and social skills training is the concept of the appropriately assertive, effectively social skilled, or socially competent adolescent. The question that must be asked is who decides what is "appropriate" or "effective" in our culture. Most adolescents whose behavior is targeted as maladaptive will be referred by some agent of the school or society. Given our culturally diverse society, we might ask whose norms or values are given preference. Rena Schwartzbaum's chapter on ethical issues frames these topics. She presents a strong case for the value-laden nature of social skills training. In reviewing the history of social etiquette training she puts contemporary training in its historical context. In past centuries, the more privileged classes decided what was socially appropriate. She concludes with a plea for sensitivity to these ethical issues and presents guidelines for such work.

Given that assertiveness and social skills training programs were primarily developed by white, middle-class psychologists with mainstream American values for mostly white middle-class American populations, it is important that we begin to address the appropriateness of our assessment and training programs as we apply these procedures to multicultural populations. By the year 2040, it is estimated that white Anglo–Saxon Americans will be in the minority in the United States. The three remaining chapters in this section address the application of assertiveness and social skills programming for culturally diverse populations. Obviously, each population group has its own specific concerns. The chapters in this section cull the authors' personal and professional work with these diverse groups of adolescents who make up most of the inner-city school population. We have singled out for discussion the three most representative populations black Americans, Asian American, and Latinos. We begin with Tulsa Knox who reviews the literature on black Americans' experience. She then raises questions about the suitability of programs developed in a Euro-American culture to meet the needs of at-risk black adolescents. Next, Catherine Hsu discusses assertiveness training for Asian American populations. She focuses on the diversity of this group, stressing that we need to be sensitive to generational and gender differences in working with this population. We end with a chapter by Diana Planells-Bloom who discusses assertiveness and its applicability for the Latino culture. In particular, she focuses on issues of assessing assertiveness for Latina adolescents.

4

Social Skills Training: Ethical Issues and Guidelines

Rena C. Schwartzbaum

Till at last the child's mind is these suggestions, and the sum of the suggestions is the child's mind. And not the child's mind only. The adult's mind too—all his life long. The mind that judges and desires . . . made up of these suggestions. But all these suggestions are our suggestions. (Huxley, 1946, p. 19)

Novelists, philosophers, historians, educational theorists, and psychologists, among numerous others, have struggled over the centuries with ethical issues in the context of social control. Partly because of recent advances in behavioral psychology, including improved techniques for modifying targeted behaviors, along with developments in technology applied to educational settings, such as computer-assisted instruction and standardized programmed learning packages, ethical concerns continue to arise regarding the balance between individual rights and the desire for improved methods for effective socialization of the young. This is particularly true in the field of social skills training with children and adolescents. Surprisingly, however, with a few notable exceptions, there have been limited attempts to provide practitioners with guidelines for employing social skills training in an ethical manner.

This chapter attempts to assist the practitioner by exploring some of the ethical issues involved in social skills training. It begins by describing the objectives and justifications for teaching social skills, and then presents a philosophical and historical backdrop. This leads into a discussion of ethical concerns relevant to social skills training, with an emphasis on the clinicians' use of personal values in their work. The chapter concludes by reviewing previous ethical principles, and then presents new guidelines for social skills training that the practitioner can employ to foster ethical practice.

OBJECTIVES AND JUSTIFICATIONS FOR SOCIAL SKILLS TRAINING

The aim of social skills training is to broaden the clients' repertoire of behavior, across different social situations, as part of an interactional process where they feel comfortable with themselves and in their relationships with others. It is based on the notion that social skills, like any other skills, are learned, and can be taught where lacking (Trower, 1984). Social skills training programs have been developed for a wide range of populations including, among others, children and adolescents, learning disabled, gifted, psychotic, inpatient and outpatient, the elderly, and divorcees. It shares, with numerous other therapeutic and educational schools, a goal of the remediation of psychological problems, an enhancement of interpersonal effectiveness, and a general improvement in the quality of life (L'Abate & Milan, 1985). The most comprehensive and therefore theoretically satisfying views of social behavior address both the cognitions and emotions of the client as well as the overt behavior (Gambrill, 1984).

Social skills training differs from other therapeutic modalities such as psychoanalytical and humanistic approaches in several ways. For example, proponents of social skills training view dysfunctional behavior as a skills deficit resulting from faulty learning rather than as symptomatic of misdirected or unresolved unconscious conflicts (Bagarozzi, 1985). Radley (1985) maintains that social skills training, more than other approaches, depends on social norms and values to guide its application. According to Radley, the therapist, in conjunction with the client, must decide which behaviors are "appropriate" and which are in need of remediation. No matter how objective the clinician hopes to be, however, he or she must ultimately employ personal value systems. Radley also asserts that this reliance on personal meanings is what differentiates the social skills trainer from the teacher of other more concrete skills. At the same time, the employment of an approach that relies so heavily on the intrinsic value system of the clinician has generated some ethical concerns from both proponents and critics of social skills training.

Social skills training for children and adolescents can be viewed as one possible response to society's failure to produce desired social behavior in its young. The process of socializing youngsters has long been recognized as crucial for the effective functioning of society. Socialization is the process of learning how to play social roles effectively. Through this process, children acquire the knowledge, skills, motives and attitudes necessary for playing these roles. No society can survive without transmitting its preferred patterns of behavior to its young. The notion of social shaping, however, is not confined to our times. Societies have always been involved as social shapers. What is changing, however, is that schools, rather than families or other social institutions, have been assigned or forced to assume increasing responsibility for the direct and systematic transmission of "appropriate" social behaviors to the next generation.

HISTORICAL ROOTS

Etiquette

It would be short-sighted to assume that the analysis of social acts into their component parts, as is required before commencing a social skills intervention, is an achievement restricted to 20th-century psychology. Numerous writings on etiquette during the 17th century and the Enlightment depict societies as being more concerned with social conduct than is in evidence today. "Etiquette" often referred to prescribed sets of polite or appropriate behaviors. What was deemed "appropriate" was strongly influenced by one's social class or standing, and it appeared that the higher one's socioeconomic status, the greater the concern for proper behavior. The relationship between class standing and the concern for proper behavior continues today with the recent proliferation of the "Miss Manners" books and columns, which address such status-related issues as proper business correspondence, tipping while vacationing, and evening attire for formal parties (Martin, 1982).

Social Skills Training

As in etiquette training, the acquisition of appropriate behavior and the relationship between targeted behaviors and social class are central features of social skills training. According to Radley (1985), however, what distinguishes social skills training from etiquette classes, from a psychological standpoint, is the use of scientific methodology in the analysis and assessment of behavior in the former. An additional distinguishing feature is that etiquette training is more concerned with conforming the individual to a societal norm without regard for the impact that this might have on emotional health. Without a solid professional code of ethics from which to draw, the etiquette trainer is at a greater risk for undermining the best interests of the client.

The social skills training movement is the product of numerous disciplines and individuals. Larson (1984) traces its beginnings to the shift from clinical to public health–education models, from predominantly professional to paraprofessional workers, and from remedial to preventive methods of intervention. With the development of the community mental health movement, the focus shifted away from the medical model, with its emphasis on psychopathology and deficits, to greater concentration on life stress and competencies. To achieve greater efficiency and effectiveness, in response to governmental cutbacks to social service agencies, more systematic approaches to treatment developed in the form of skills training (Gazda & Brooks, 1985).

One of the early skills training modalities to receive much attention was assertiveness training, which has its roots in behavior therapy and the women's movement. Assertiveness behavior is defined as "That complex of behaviors, emitted by a person in an interpersonal context, which expresses that person's feelings, attitudes, wishes, opinions or rights directly, firmly and honestly, while respecting the . . . rights of the other person(s)" (Alberti, 1977). The assertiveness training movement represented the first of many single-focus, skills training approaches and produced a significant change in how social abilities would be conceptualized (Gazda & Brooks, 1985). For the first time, they would be thought of as similar to academic or social skills that could be improved through instruction, practice, and feedback (Rathjen, 1984).

PHILOSOPHICAL PERSPECTIVE

Because social skills training can be used to foster a full spectrum of behavior, it should not be viewed as inherently "good" or "evil." The ultimate evaluation of its merits, regardless of the clinician's theoretical orientation, is therefore dependent, in large part, on who is practicing it and to what ends. For example, a female teacher who is uncomfortable with aggression based on familial and societal influences might be intolerant of developmentally appropriate rambunctious boys, whereas another female teacher who was exposed to different influences would see the boys' behavior as annoying yet not abnormal. The value system that governs the application of the treatment inevitably emerges from the practitioner (Fischer & Gochros, 1975). Given the primacy of personal values in social skills training, a philosophical perspective might be helpful in providing the clinician with a framework for clarifying some of the broader underlying issues.

Philosophers have grappled over the centuries with conceptions of good and evil. Plato, for example, posited that only knowledge can prevent evil acts. He asserted that if one really knows what is right, one will do it. In the *Protagoras* (Hubbard & Karnofsky, 1982), Plato argued against the popular misconception that anger, pleasure, fear or pain can be a stronger guiding force than knowledge. He viewed knowledge alone as capable of controlling man, such that "If a man knew what is good and bad, nothing could overpower this knowledge or force the man to do anything other than what it dictates" (p. 54). The "good" clinician should always take a questioning stance with his work and that of other professionals, in trying to become as knowledgeable, and therefore competent, as possible.

Another way of examining the subject of good and evil is to look at absolutist and relativist perspectives. An absolutist position holds that the measure of good and evil is inherent in the nature of the universe. Good and bad, right and wrong, are absolute and apply in all situations and at all times. A relativist approach, in contrast, always looks at the particular situation involved. Time and place are seen as necessary and sufficient determinants of good and evil. The relativist position determines the ethical quality of an act in terms of the life of society, the good of the whole (Frost, 1962).

Pragmatists, whose views underlie the tenets of modern behavioral psychology, represent one example of the relativist approach. They hold that what is deemed good must undergo change as society changes and as knowledge of the physical environment increases. The noted pragmatist John Dewey maintained that "There are periods in life when a whole community finds itself in the presence of new issues which old customs do not adequately meet. The habits and beliefs which were formed in the past do not fit into the opportunities and requirements of contemporary life" (Dewey, 1960, p. 5).

Though the often rigid and unyielding stance of an absolutist value system is more susceptible to attack given the typical dogmatic nature of the position, a pure relativistic approach can be more chronically dangerous. There are some who interpret relativism as "anything goes." They hold that no person has the right to alter the behavior of another or to teach children about values; they presume that children will acquire these on their own as they mature. The question is: Will children automatically incorporate belief systems acceptable to their parents and society? In the meantime, the children have grown up without direction from their parents who have, in the name of permissiveness, refrained from imparting their values. They must therefore be willing to accept that the children may have developed their own moral code, which may make it difficult for them to live among others (Steininger, Newell, & Garcia, 1984).

ETHICAL CONCERNS

There are numerous ethical issues that confront practitioners when first considering whether or not to use social skills training with children and adolescents. These preliminary concerns include the basis for selecting targeted behaviors, consideration of possible negative consequences, the determination of which skills are important for whom, the right of children and adolescents to refuse participation, and the right of parents to prevent their child's participation in treatment (Michelson, Sugai, Wood, & Kazdin, 1983). Social skills assessments and interventions are inextricably embedded in cultural norms, and therefore must address a multitude of divergent value systems depending on the client's background.

Let us assume though, for the moment, that remediation has been justified. The practitioner must then determine the basis for selecting which social skills are to be targeted. Wolf (1978) identifies social validity as a criterion for determining which socially significant problems are appropriate for change efforts. She writes that social validity can best be specified by representatives of the community according to whether the behaviors have social significance regarding goals desired by the community (relevance), whether the procedures to be used are acceptable (ethics), and whether the results of the behavior change are satisfactory to the clients or referral source (effectiveness).

Basing an intervention plan on the basis of social validity is of questionable ethical practice as it may overvalue the community at the possible expense of the client. This approach may undermine the importance of accepting atypical patterns of culturally appropriate social behaviors and interactions, such as the expression of affect, speech modulation, and cultural differences in nonverbal communication. The social validity approach contains a potentially serious deficiency given the pluralistic society in which we live. Furthermore, Ysseldyke (1982) states that societal values are never static; as a result, the goals and objectives of many agencies are in a constant state of flux. Without always giving priority to the best interests of the client, based on a professional code of behavior, the practitioner risks subjecting him or her to treatment based on a passing community fancy.

According to Bagarozzi (1985), some critics of social skills training, though apprehensive about clinicians drawing from idiosyncratic personal value systems, are even more concerned about the larger issue of whether they have the right to impose any values at all. He cites, for example, a criticism that fostering prosocial behavior can be seen as an attempt to impose white, middle-class standards of behavior on ethnic and racial minorities. It can be perceived, he continues, as a means of social control—a way of maintaining the economic repression of the poor and disadvantaged.

A related concern is the issue of autonomy, or self-determination. Succinctly stated, the principle of autonomy states that people should be free to act according to their own beliefs and principles provided that, in doing so, they do not interfere with the ability of others to do the same (Steere, 1984). Social skills trainers, although hoping to broaden and enhance social repertoires, may concurrently restrict their clients' self-determination.

According to Williams (1976), ethical issues often appear as relative questions that weigh the good of the individual, of those immediately concerned with him or her, and of society in general. It is not uncommon for conflicts of interest to occur between these groups. For whom, then, is the social skills trainer to go to bat? In other words, who is the client?

L'Abate and Milan (1985) write that social skills training is considered one of the most widely used intervention strategies currently deployed in the delivery of mental health services. It is also rapidly becoming incorporated into school curricula. Though the ethical concerns of social skills training per se have yet to be directly addressed, one only has to turn to the more general literature on behavior modification to understand some of the issues and concerns that may emerge. Kelman (1965), for example, writes that it is conceivable that the day will come when the science of behavior modification will have developed to a point where the conditions necessary for producing a specific change in behavior can be carried out with relative precision. This notion of precise behavioral control is viewed by some, in the scientific and literary communities, as potentially damaging to the very core of our individuality. Sullivan (1975) writes, "Behavior modification should be seen as a threat to progress and to educational revolution because it does not question the system but implements the goals of the existing system" (p. 19). In *Brave New World*, Huxley (1946) expresses similar concerns in describing the socialization of infants into passive, unwitting pawns in a power-oriented, stratified society.

Skinner maintains that a technology of behavior is "ethically neutral" depending on whether it is used by "villain or saint" (1971, p. 143). In the literature on the ethics of behavior modification, however, a recurrent theme of concern is that clients will be forced to engage in behaviors that conform to the standards of the modifier rather than be helped to behave in ways consistent with their own goals (Fischer & Gochros, 1975). This is an issue of protecting the client's self-determination. Holland (1975) writes that the fear of manipulative control is well founded if a professional–client relationship is lacking. In this case, an elite stratum could set the goals and dole out reinforcers to a less powerful group, solely to exploit them for personal gain.

Kelman (1965) does not agree with Skinner's villain–saint dichotomy, regarding as ethically ambiguous any action that limits freedom of choice. Even the saint—the well-intentioned, unselfish controlling agent—can be tempted to ignore individual differences while doing what he or she deems good for others rather than what clients might consider advantageous for themselves. Free choice, according to Kelman, is a vital and necessary protection against tyranny.

In the literature on behavior modification in the classroom, some educators have expressed concern that the use of behavioral techniques could undermine the self-determination of children by fostering a homogeneous environment that would foster compliancy. Winnett and Winkler (1971), in an attack on the use of behavior modification in schools, charge that the educational system is being used to train docility and adherence to routines. They argue that behavior modifiers have developed techniques for increasing target behaviors, like sitting still, so that children will conform to existing educational systems, without examining the types of systems into which the children are being asked to adjust. In summary, they take a hard look at the desirability of the "appropriateness" of the behaviors that professionals are called on to modify.

In a rejoinder to Winnett and Winkler (1971), O'Leary (1971) defends that behavior modification is the victim of mass overgeneralization. He holds that a goal of behavior modification in the classroom is typically not reducing disruptive behavior to a "zero level" but generating behaviors that would make academic progress more likely; he sees it as a way of opening up options for the child by teaching alternative means of gaining positive feedback.

Others address the issue of possible violation of client self-determination more directly. Fischer & Gochros (1975) state that the very strength of behavior modification—the clarity and explicitness of its procedures—bring the ethical issues involved in its use into sharp focus and thus makes it especially vulnerable to attack. They maintain that it would be naïve to assume that insight-oriented approaches are any less of a threat to self-determination than thoughtfully practiced behavior modification, though they agree that the influence of the former may be subtler. Moreover, they suggest that use of the "less explicit" technologies may well be even more of a threat because they provide the illusion of self-determination, when in fact it may not exist.

Steininger et al. (1984) take a stand against those who oppose all forms of behavior control. They state that some form of control is a prerequisite for both individual survival and social functioning. They differentiate, however, behavior control, which is based on methodically implemented scientific theory, employed by competent professionals, from the use of manipulative measures designed to change behaviors irrespective of the client's best interests. Most psychologists reject using the latter as a matter of moral principle, and their professional codes prevent them from using clients for their personal gain, regardless of theoretical orientation.

As social skills training has many of its roots in behavior modification, it may be subject to many of the criticisms noted earlier. For practitioners to address these concerns by approaching this issue nondefensively, what is needed is a set of principles to aid in the establishment of ethical practice.

PRINCIPLES TO FOSTER ETHICAL PRACTICE

A recurrent theme of this chapter is that judicious use of professional guidelines can ensure that clinicians are sensitive in the assessment and implementation of social skills training programs that serve their client's best interests. These guidelines aim to protect the welfare of those who seek our professional services. The American Psychological Association (1981), for example, in its guidelines, addresses several issues especially pertinent to those considering the practice of social skills training. These include, but are not limited to, issues of professional competency and responsibility, client confidentiality, and the general welfare of the consumer. For example, in conducting social skills assessments, the competent trainer recognizes both personal limitations as well as the limitations of this technique in remediating certain psychological disorders, such as hyperactivity, learning disabilities, psychosis, and organic brain syndrome. Clinicians should show a willingness to consult with specialists of other orientations, when in doubt, regarding the appropriateness of using social skills training versus a different, possibly more comprehensive, therapeutic modality. This is not to say that social skills training cannot be employed with these difficult populations but rather that clinicians need to seek additional support when necessary (Michelson et al., 1983).

Beyond matters of professional competency, issues of responsibility and accountability also come into play. Psychological services are reaching greater segments of the population through schools, clinics, and the media. Though some believe that this movement will engender positive changes, especially in the realm of preventative mental health, others are concerned that trainers will also take on the burden of overwhelming responsibility or, conversely, delegate their work in an irresponsible manner. Psychologists, for example, may overextend themselves in implementing programs that require more supervision time than they can possibly provide. There is a risk that insufficiently trained staff, who are not sensitive to the issues raised in this chapter, will be assigned to run groups or to teach social skills as part of routine class work, in the name of reaching populations that would otherwise have no services at all (Larson, 1984).

Another ethical principle that is relevant to social skills training concerns the welfare of the consumer. Psychologists, for example, are to inform clients as to the purpose and nature of an assessment or treatment, and must acknowledge that clients have the right to refuse participation. Additionally, when an organization pressures a psychologist into violating ethical principles, the clinician must clarify the nature of the conflict, inform all parties of a psychologist's ethical responsibilities, and take the appropriate action. What happens, then, when a conflict of interest occurs between the client and the institution that has hired the clinician? Ethical problems can arise when psychologists find themselves doing behavioral interventions that reflect the demands of their hiring institutions, or of an oppressive environment, rather than conducting interventions that address the client's best interests (Fischer & Gochros, 1975). Trachtman (1980) defines this as an issue of "who's the client?"—a question he thinks our profession has never addressed satisfactorily. He states that it is difficult for psychologists, who have moral commitments to their clients, to be reminded in their everyday functioning that they are hired, and fired, by their organizations. There does not appear to be an ethical guideline that would be appropriate for all dilemmas of this nature. Instead clinicians must attempt to clarify the nature of their loyalities and proceed to keep all parties informed of their convictions and intentions.

The issue of establishing who is the client is especially problematic for professionals practicing in school systems. School psychologists are often torn between conflicting allegiances to the board of education, the principal, teachers, parents, and students. Holland (1975) warns that although behavior modifiers may see their intervention plans as benevolent, they all too often act on a passive acceptance of what their employers judge as the root of the "to-be-corrected behavior." What seems vital in these situations is a constant willingness to confront and accept responsibility for one's loyalities openly and to strive for an optimal balance between conflicting parties.

The professional standards manual of the National Association of School Psychologists (1984) is another valuable source for establishing guidelines. It urges, as an example, that professionals who work with children recognize the importance of parental support. It suggests maintaining direct parent contact before meeting with the student as well as frank and prompt reporting of results. Children and their parents should be informed of the nature of the training as well as its potential benefits and risks. Trachtman (1980) takes a similar, yet bolder stance, seeing schools as primarily serving parents, who have delegated responsibilitiy for the education of their children.

It is imperative that the professional maintain a keen awareness of the normal developmental processes of childhood and adolescence when assessing the appropriateness of social skills interventions. What is called deviant in latency may be equally troublesome, yet normatively appropriate, in adolescence. For example, a reasonable degree of rudeness toward authority figures or a moderate decrease in personal grooming would most likely be inappropriate grounds for social skills intervention if exhibited by an adolescent, whereas the same might not be true for a younger child.

Social skill trainers, particularly those working with culturally heterogeneous populations, must learn to recognize that individual family norms may differ radically from middle-class notions of appropriate social skills (Michelson et al., 1983). Adapting a pluralistic approach is necessary in a nation where people from diverse cultures are increasingly called on to interact. Those who dogmatically state their one and only truth will be surprised when they repeatedly encounter others with very different, equally valid truths (Steininger et al., 1984). An example of this, often encountered during assertiveness training with certain children from Asian cultures, is the equating of assertion with impetuosity. Though the well-intentioned trainer thinks he is expanding the child's social repertoire and ultimately increasing the child's personal freedom, this tactic may be at odds with the child's familial and cultural environment. Behavior that is adaptive at school may prove detrimental in other social environments.

Another helpful resource relevant to those concerned with the ethical practice of social skills training comes from the assertiveness training movement, and includes contributions from the following well-known innovators in the field: Alberti, Emmons, Fodor, Galessi & Galessi, Garnett, Jakubowski, and Wolfe (1977). These authors, among other early innovators in the field, became concerned that the rapid growth of assertiveness training, with the concurrent push to bring these techniques to the public as quickly as possible, might undermine ethical issues. Though they were primarily concerned with assertiveness training, many of their suggested principles are appropriate for the social skills trainer and for work with adolescents. For example, clients should be informed in advance of all procedures to be used, as well as to the education and experience of trainers. The goals and possible outcomes of assertiveness training, including potentially high levels of anxiety and negative reactions from others resistant to change, should be made explicit (this also holds true for social skills training). Clients should have the freedom to withdraw at any point in the intervention, regardless of the inconvenience to the clinician. Child and adolescent clients are equally entitled to these rights, and clinicians should be especially attentive to communicating them in a developmentally appropriate manner.

Alberti et al. (1977) concluded that the appropriate use of assertiveness training must be evaluated on a case-by-case basis. They developed a list of the following factors, also appropriate for social skills trainers, for clinicians to reflect on before commencing interventions:

1. Client's age, sex, ethnicity, capacity for informed consent, physical and psychological functioning, and so on
2. Identified problem and purpose for which intervention is sought
3. Professional and personal qualifications of the trainer including age, sex, ethnicity, training background, and so on
4. Characteristics of the setting for the intervention
5. Temporal issues
6. Proposed method of intervention
7. Outcome measures and follow-up procedures

Other than this early work developed by concerned innovators in the assertiveness training movement, practitioners of social skills training have been offered little assistance for fostering an ethical practice by way of ethical guidelines. In light of the issues raised throughout this chapter, it may now be appropriate to generate a list of ethical guidelines for implementing a social skills training program. Far from being a comprehensive and exhaustive list, however, it should be thought of as a starting point that will be expanded as the field continues to grow and mature. The guidelines are as follows:

1. Consult relevant professional guidelines including, but not limited to, American Psychological Association, National Association of School Psychologists, and assertiveness training guidelines.
2. Maintain a constant awareness that social skills training relies heavily on personal values. Be willing and ready to explore those values with colleagues and peers.
3. Be aware of cultural and racial biases that could serve to diminish rather than enhance client welfare. Recognize that there are several equally valid truths.

4. Maintain a keen awareness about issues of self-determination. Have the client's own values been given the utmost importance? Will imposing new social skills enhance client functioning and provide greater personal choice?
5. Clarify for oneself, and for others, who is the client. This is especially important when working in institutions. Should a conflict of interest emerge address it immediately.
6. Consider how targeted behaviors are being assessed. Consider issues of social class and normal developmental processes.
7. Avoid forming intervention plans on the basis of consensual validation, as it is of questionable ethical practice given that it may overvalue the community at the expense of the client.
8. Engage in rigorous and periodic self-inquiry so as not to lose sight of the magnitude of one's task.

WHERE DO WE GO FROM HERE?

Responsible clinicians cannot, in good conscience, abandon their professional obligation to help consenting clients mitigate their social deficits out of fear of limiting their personal freedom. Even in the case of certain children and adolescents who may be quite content with their social inadequacies, it is conceivable that their own values may be limiting their ability to maximize their personal freedom. A successful social skills intervention may, in fact, broaden their social repertoire to enhance their ability to choose more effectively. Though social skills training takes the clinician through difficult ethical terrain, an effective intervention should broaden, rather than limit, the patients' abilities to choose and use their own values. Clinicians who have the security of their ethical codes and guidelines, along with the flexibility to examine their values and motivations continuously, will be in a good position to help their clients as well as contribute to the knowledge base in a young and growing field.

REFERENCES

Albert, E., Denise, T., & Peterfreund, S. (1975). *Great traditions in ethics*. New York: Van Nostrand.

Alberti, R. E., Emmons, M. L., Fodor, I., Galassi, J., Galassi, M., Garnett, L., Jakubowski, P., and Wolfe, J. (1977). A statement of principles for ethical practices of assertive behavior training. In R. Alberti (Ed.), *Assertiveness, innovations, applications, issues*. San Luis Obispo, CA: Impact.

American Psychological Association. (1981). *Ethical principles of psychologists.* Washington, DC: American Psychological Association.

American Psychological Association. (1977). *Standards of providers of psychological services.* Washington, DC: American Psychological Association.

Bagarozzi, D. (1985). Implications of social skills training for social and interpersonal competence. In L. L'Abate & M. Milan (Eds.), *Handbook of social skills training and research.* New York: Wiley.

Cartledge, G., & Milburn, J. (Eds.). (1980). *Teaching social skills to children.* New York: Pergamon.

Dewey, J. (1960). *Theory of moral life.* New York: Holt, Rinehart & Winston.

Fischer, J., & Gochros, H. (1975). *Planned behavior change.* New York: The Free Press.

Frost, S. (1962). *Basic teachings of the great philosophers.* New York: Doubleday.

Gambrill, E. (1984). Social skills training. In D. Larson (Ed.), *Teaching psychological skills.* Monterey, CA: Brooks/Cole.

Gazda, G., & Brooks, D. (1985). The development of the social/life skills training movement. *Journal of Group Psychotherapy, Psychodrama and Sociometry, 38,* 1–10.

Holland, J. (1975). *Behaviorism: Part of the problem or part of the solution?* Paper presented to the American Psychological Association.

Hubbard, B., & Karnofsky, E. (Eds.). (1982). *Plato's Protagoras.* London: Duckworth.

Huxley, A. (1946). *Brave new world.* New York: Harper & Row.

Kelman, H. (1965). Manipulation of human behaviors: An ethical dilemma for the social scientist. *The Journal of Social Issues, 21,* 31–46.

L'Abate, L. & Milan, M. (Eds.). (1985). *Handbook of social skills training and research.* New York: Wiley.

Larson, D., (Ed.). (1984). *Teaching psychological skills.* Monterey, CA: Brooks/Cole.

Martin, J. (1982). *Miss Manners guide to excruciatingly correct behavior.* New York: Warner.

Michelson, L., Sugai, D., Wood, R., & Kazdin, A. (1983). *Social skills assessment and training with children.* New York: Plenum.

National Association of School Psychologists. (1984). *Professional conduct manual.* Washington, DC: National Association of School Psychologists.

O'Leary, K. (1971). Behavior modification in the classroom: A rejoinder to Winett and Winkler. *Journal of Applied Behavior Analysis, 5,* 505.

Radley, A. (1985). From courtesy to strategy: Some old developments in social skills training. *Bulletin of the British Psychological Society, 38,* 209–211.

Rathjen, D. (1984). Social skills training for children: Innovations and consumer guidelines. *School Psychology Review, 13,* 134–141.

Skinner, B. (1971). *Beyond freedom and dignity.* New York: Bantam.

Steere, J. (1984). *Ethics in clinical psychology.* South Africa: Oxford University Press.

Steininger, M., Newell, J., & Garcia, L. (1984). *Ethical issues in psychology.* Homewood, IL: Dorsey.

Sullivan, A. (1975). Don't move or I'll modify you. *Radical Education, 3,* 18–20.

Trachtman, G. (1980). On such a full sea. *School Psychology Review, 10,* 138–181.

Trower, P. (Ed.). (1984). *Radical approaches to social skills training.* London: Croom Helm.

Williams, C. (1976). *Ethical implications of behaviour modification.* Proceedings of the conference held at Lea Castle Hospital, Wolverley, Kidderminster.

Winnett, R., & Winkler, R. (1971). *Current behavior modification in the classroom: Be still, be quiet, be docile.* Unpublished manuscript, State University of New York at Stony Brook, Stonybrook, New York.

Wolf, M. (1978). Social validity: The case for subjective measurement or how applied behavior measurement is finding its heart. *Journal of Applied Behavior Analysis, 11,* 203–214.

Ysseldyke, J. (1982). The Spring Hill Symposium on the future of psychology in the schools. *American Psychologist, 37,* 547–552.

5

A Framework for Understanding High-Risk Black Adolescents' Social Interactive Issues

Tulsa Knox

We can, whenever and wherever
we choose, successfully teach
all children whose schooling
is of interest to us.

We already know more than
we need to do that.

Whether or not we do it must
finally depend on how we feel
about the fact that we haven't so far.

—Ron Edmonds (1979)

John has been practicing his cool walk and stand all weekend. The principal asked John to remove his hat when he entered the school. John positioned himself in a confrontational stance and asked, "Why don't you chill out?"

Preston is quite aware of the school rules regarding no fighting. He thinks it is more important, however, that his friends not perceive him as a "punk."

Michelle has been reprimanded by school officials for using profane language, dressing provocatively, and behaving improperly. To her, "they just don't get it."

It is common that black adolescents are likely to be referred to mental health clinics for maladaptive social behaviors (Gibbs, 1988). Statistics for 1985 reported by the President's Commission on Mental Health (1987) show that blacks under age 18 were more than twice as likely to be admitted to state and county mental hospitals as were Euro-Americans. According to 1980 census data, black children were placed in health, psychiatric, and foster care facilities at a rate about 75% higher than other ethnic groups. In addition, black adolescents were found in correctional facilities at a rate 400% higher than Euro-American adolescents (U.S. Bureau of the Census, 1985).

Sarason (1973) postulated that psychologists and educators must consider attitudes that are shaped by one's ethnic culture. He contended that people who are socialized in those cultures are imbued with attitudes and characteristics that are rooted in history. These characteristics, he indicated, are a kind of second nature, learned, absorbed and inculcated with all the force, subtleness, and efficiency of the processes of cultural transmission. Sarason (1973) further stated that "it is impossible to understand and evaluate intellectual or social performance without taking into account a group's historical attitude towards the activity." Finally, he predicted that this central psychological core of historically rooted groups cannot be changed in a lifetime.

Havighurst (1976) suggests that within a complex society, social class and ethnicity are two major ecological structures that produce diversity in human life-styles and development. He additionally stated that each social class consists of groups of people who possess a set of behaviors and attitudes that defines the group and separate it from other social classes. He concludes that "the system of ethnic groups consists of a group of people who each have a common history and a generally shared language, religion or racial identity."

At this moment in time, even what to call black people is in flux. In this author's lifetime, we have gone from Negro to black to Afro-American. Now, given the reemphasis in American society on multiculturalism and ethnicity, the term African American is now widely used. This changing of what black people are called perhaps adds to confused identity status. For the purpose of this chapter, because most of the recent literature refers to the black experience, we will use the terms *black* as well as *African American* to describe this population. Going beyond the uncertainty surrounding a unified label for ones' ethnic group, however, it is imperative that we embark on an understanding of the importance of an analysis of cultural and historical factors while assessing and formulating a psychological intervention.

This chapter explores some of the social, emotional, and cultural environmental factors relevant to black adolescents. In particular, I address these factors as background in considering how such adolescents have been singled out as having social skills deficits that require training. First I discuss the frame of reference needed to assess perceived social skills deficiencies, and then I make suggestions for the implementation of appropriate intervention strategies.

It is reasonable to suggest that the frequently perceived social skills deficiencies and misinterpretation of behaviors exhibited by this population may be reevaluated through an exploration of the preceding factors. Such considerations may also contribute to both effective assessments and to mutually productive therapeutic encounters. The goal of the chapter is to educate mainstream school psychologists who work in the inner-city school system toward a reevaluation of alleged social skills deficiencies for black youth. In addition, it is important to introduce the perspective that conceptualizes social skills behavior of black youth in neither a negative or pejorative manner. Instead, I view such behavior as an adaptive necessity developed to mediate between two cultures (i.e., mainstream culture and the community). It is hoped that a broader perspective on so-called social skills behavior will enable psychologists to communicate better with such youngsters and develop appropriate assessment and intervention strategies.

First, however, I must acknowledge that this population is not monolithic. The black adolescent population is quite diverse. Blacks have their origins in Caribbean, African, and African-American cultures. There are urban versus suburban, southern versus northern, urban versus rural and more. Furthermore, there are also vast socioeconomic differences among blacks. Some black Americans are quite affluent and share an elite status more like those of affluent Americans. Many blacks are middle class. Far too many are disadvantaged, however. Each diverse group of African Americans and each social class has its own set of issues. Certainly, being a minority group in an affluent culture has its own set of socially interactive issues for adolescents. For the most part, this chapter focuses on the at-risk adolescent, who has been singled out as "deficient in social skills," whose behaviors are often said to be problematic for acculturation, and who is failing to achieve either in school or in the community.

BLACKS' ENTRY INTO AMERICAN SOCIETY

Given that too many black youth fail to make it in mainstream American society and are said to have deficits in socialization, it is important to emphasize that African Americans have a unique history that needs to be considered for a fuller understanding of the context of black youths' plight.

Understanding the African-American view on acculturation depends largely on the factors surrounding this group's pilgrimage to the New World versus those of other ethnic groups. Most immigrants willingly settled in this country and as such were highly motivated. They conscientiously aspired to accept most of the values and social practices of American society readily. These characteristics significantly played a part in assimilating into the mainstream society and becoming an upwardly mobile group (Prudhomme & Musto, 1973).

African American's mistrust and reluctance to assimilate can be traced back to the slavery era. The notorious segregation period, the 1960s war on poverty, and the post–civil rights movement further reinforced notions of a racist society for blacks. Furthermore, mass migration of blacks between World War I and World War II from the rural South to urban areas resulted in the development of huge ghettos because of limited factory-related skills (Clark, 1965; Franklin, 1967).

Nevertheless, the civil rights movement and legislation allowed thousands of blacks in America to increase enrollments in college, and for some to become upwardly mobile and be somewhat accepted by mainstream culture (Chambers, 1968). These efforts, however, were only moderately successful before a widespread backlash ensued via governmental legislation (Omi & Winant, 1986). This more recent conservative change in governmental policy had a negative impact on black youth, as gains made in employment and in college enrollment rates achieved by the mid-1970s were virtually wiped out by the mid-1980s (Gibbs, 1988).

According to Glasgow (1981) and Wilson (1987) limited economic opportunities during urbanization laid the foundation for the "underclass" minority populations. This lack of fit between a largely unskilled black labor supply and the demands of a highly technical job market has aided in the creation of high rates of unemployment, poverty, and family dysfunction, which in turn contributed to increased levels of stress for black youth (Comer & Hill, 1985; Edelman, 1987; Wilson, 1987). Furthermore, these same factors are theorized to have significantly weakened the black family and major institutions of the black community, thus creating a hospitable environment for the development of social, psychological, and behavioral problems among black youth (Franklin, 1967; Omi & Winant, 1986; Wilson, 1987).

AT-RISK ADOLESCENTS

Black youth are more likely to live in deteriorating central inner-city neighborhoods and in substandard housing with poor sanitation, located in urban areas with depressed economics. In addition, they are less likely to have access to adequate health and mental health facilities (Children's Defense Fund, 1986; Kasarda, 1983; Schorr, 1985).

Researchers are in agreement that black adolescents experience increased difficulty assimilating into a mainstreamed educational–occupational milieu. For example, the high school dropout rates are conservatively estimated in the inner cities at 50%. According to the National Alliance of Black School Educators, however, the actual high school dropout rate is more like two thirds in those same cited areas (Reed, 1985). In July 1988 the unemployment rate for black teenagers aged 16 to 19 was 41.1%, more than twice the rate of white teenagers.

When looking at higher achievement, statistics also indicate that black students' enrollment in colleges are at an all-time low when compared with the pre–civil rights movement period. Given these factors there is no question that the black adolescent population is at extreme risk of becoming a permanent member of the underclass.

Present literature that addresses the black adolescent rarely takes into consideration the variables that directly impact on the overall functioning of this population. Most of the literature neither remedies nor provides a therapeutic framework from which to develop appropriate counseling strategies. For the purpose of this chapter, the discussion will focus on the black adolescent who is at risk: those who "inappropriately" act out community-oriented survival behaviors in the mainstream milieu. These youth are typically the target group for social skills intervention.

Factors that contribute to their at-risk status are as complex as any psychosocial phenomena. In addition to the traditional psychological upheavals characteristic of this developmental period, these youths must deal with mainstream expectations of adequate or appropriate behavioral functioning that are often at odds with the cultural context in which they live. For example, black youth are well aware that traveling in pairs or groups is frequently met with anticipation of delinquent criminal behaviors no matter how innocent their intentions. In addition to these factors, there are discrepancies in overall perceptions of the population. For example, tolerance for or interpretation of so-called adolescent acting-out behaviors are viewed quite differently depending on both the ethnic group and where the behavior occurs.

Black Adolescents in Schools

Abbott (1981) reported that race and other's perception of race may play a role in the self-appraisal process and thus may affect a student's achievement. Kifer (1975) linked the student's personality characteristics with academic achievement. Characteristics were defined as responses emanating from accumulated patterns of academic achievement. It is the student's history of consistent success or failure that is linked to effective personality traits (Kifer, 1975). A student's characteristics and race were shown to be deterministic of classroom interactional patterns.

The literature review of humanistic research by Roscoe and Peterson (1982) revealed specific characteristics of teachers and learning situations that facilitate the development of students as "total persons." They suggested that teachers should be interactive with students in a more genuinely accepting manner, which would enhance educational experiences. Unfortunately, many "at-risk" black adolescents are of the opinion that school officials do not understand them nor do they seek to try.

Brisson (1991) reported that a disproportionate number of black students are referred to special education. In a recent education report in New York, it was stated that for 1989–90 39% of the students placed in segregated or "self-contained" special education classes were black. Overall, minority students make up a whopping 59 percent of public school pupils who are sent outside of the classroom to learn. Furthermore, a recent New York City Board of Education memorandum reports that such programs are not effectively remediating targeted areas of deficiencies (Reed, 1988; Rivers et al., 1975). It is also important to note that, all too often, graduation from such classes only awards a certificate of attendance, which is not a diploma. Without a diploma not only is it difficult to obtain employment, but one is not even eligible to enter the armed forces. Furthermore a recent survey (*New York Times*, 1990) reported one in four black male adolescents have experienced some kind of involvement in the correctional system or have been incarcerated.

It is this school psychologist's contention that socialization as it is evidenced in the classroom, the willingness to seek counseling, variations in the use of verbal and body language, as well as discipline principles should all be aptly explored regarding cultural differences and subsequent impact on social behaviors. Defining what is meant by social skills, however, is crucial to ascertain an understanding of what is considered a deficit.

Generally there is agreement that social skills involve a complex of ability necessary for effective interpersonal functioning (Arggis, 1985; Argyris, 1965; Lewinsohn, Weinstein, & Alper, 1970; Weiss, 1968). Caldwell, Cobert, and Jenkins (1977) used the term *social skills* to refer to all interpersonal behavior, both verbal and nonverbal. The term *so-*

cial skill deficit has been used to pinpoint what is considered deficient in interpersonal behaviors.

Black adolescents are one of the groups frequently perceived by the dominate culture as exhibiting social skills deficits. Given the social cultural context described previously, we must question the uses of the typical social skills framing of "appropriate" and "deficit" to define behaviors of black adolescents. Questions should be deliberated on regarding the following: Appropriate and deficit to which culture? What is appropriate in the mainstream Euro-white culture may be inappropriate in the black ghetto culture. What is a deficit for Euro-white culture may be an adaptive behavior for black culture. One should not evaluate these behaviors without knowing the appropriateness and survival value of these behaviors for each community.

BLACK FAMILY'S ROLE IN ACCULTURATION

The extent to which a black family has assimilated and integrated into mainstream culture is correlated with black youth experiencing difficulty (Gibb, 1989). Adolescents with varying degrees of exposure to integrated neighborhoods and schools may present a different pattern of problem behaviors and acculturation issues (Gibbs, 1984, 1988; Powell, 1985).

It is my experience that too often black teenagers verbalize discontent regarding Black people's historical contributions being excluded from the traditional curriculum. Furthermore, they are treated differently from their majority counterparts in the traditional society and are well aware of this double standard. For example, a group of black students at an amusement park noted that they were followed by security whenever they entered a store. Teenagers of other ethnic groups (who were the actual shoplifters) were not perceived as probable perpetrators of crimes; as such they were not singled out for attention.

By common definition socialization refers to the preparation of children to take on adult roles and responsibilities (Baldwin, 1980). As Zigler and Child (1973) pointed out, socialization deals essentially with the practical problem of how to rear children so that they will become adequate adult members of society to which they belong. Young (1970) stated that this process is enacted principally through the teaching and learning of conventional beliefs, values, and patterns of behaviors.

According to Boykin (1985), the central, although surely not exclusive, responsibility rests with the individual's family. The authors further state that ideally socialization ought to be compatible with the initiatives and objectives attendant to family socialization and those of schools, the judicial system, work world, and the mass media. Afro-American parents, carrying out their responsibilities as value transmitters and socialization agents, do not have the same access to this mainstream socialization process as their Euro-American counterparts nor are they as committed to the process (Boykin, 1985). Consequently, the pervasiveness and degree of acculturation to the Euro-American ideal is lessened. Thus, socialization time must be shared with two other critical concerns: Black culture and one's minority status typically do not breed full acceptance of mainstream ideals. Hence, the authors conclude that Afro-American children are incompletely socialized vis-à-vis the Euro-American ethos; they develop a distinct repertoire rooted in their African lineage, which is culturally at odds with mainstream striving. They recommend that Afro-American children learn to cope with their racial and economic victimization within the American social order.

COPING BEHAVIORS OF BLACK ADOLESCENTS

Researchers have identified several coping styles that equip black youth to survive the experience of ghetto life but perhaps obstruct the potential of success in the mainstreamed society (Mancini, 1980; Myers & King, 1980). Some of these coping mechanisms are directly related to mannerisms used in communication patterns, body language, competition, and affect. For example, Levine (1977) offered an explanation for the persistence of black language styles despite mounting pressure to conform to standard English. He stated that living in the midst of a society that is hostile and repressive toward their ethnicity, black people found in language an important means of gaining pseudocontrol. In addition, blacks have learned to survive the high incidence of crime common in most ghetto neighborhoods via their ability to verbally plead their case in nonstandard English. Levine (1977) pointed out that, "while the appropriateness and usefulness of speaking standard English allows entry into the mainstream, there is often in the community an indirect reinforcement for speaking in the vernacular."

The use of humor also appears to be an important verbal coping tool for black adolescents (Gibbs, 1988). Kochman (1972) and Labov (1972) suggested that humor commonly is used for the purpose of reducing the tension generated by a society nonaccepting of its cultural attributes. Gibbs (1984) stressed that clinicians should be aware that language serves many symbolic functions for black youths, who use it artistically, as well as for verbal attack.

The research literature suggest that black adolescents usually pos-

sess good verbal skills. Youth raised in predominately black communities, however, too often interject nonstandard English throughout
verbal expression, thus contributing to pervasive miscommunication
with agents of society (Kernan, 1971; Kochman, 1972). For example,
Levine (1977) has descriptively identified what he characterized as an
important manhood rite in black communities called "playing the doz-
ens." The activity described by Levine (1977) usually involves male adolescents who in a playful spirit, engage in a verbal dual. A verbal dual is
defined by the author as the pseudohumorous expression of a barrage of
derogatory comments directed at each other or aimed at family members. In the context of a social gathering, the dueling opponents are
evaluated by the peer group, who serves to urge them on and determine
who was verbally outwitted. Levine (1977) cites the activity as an important rite for these youths because this type of verbal interchange
functions as a rehearsal in controlling one's emotions when depicted in
a derogatory fashion.

COMMUNICATION PATTERNS AMONG
BLACK ADOLESCENTS

Many linguists who work with disadvantaged blacks talk about a different linguistic culture. Lein (1975) conducted a study on speech behaviors and linguistic styles of black children. She found significant
differences in speech interactions at home and school. For example, in
many black homes emphasis is placed on spontaneity and general participation. In contrast, the school's linguistic environment is often characterized by long monologues with limited participation by others
(Lein, 1975). In addition, Lein (1975) observed that complexities in
speech patterns vary according to which environment the observation
occurred. For example, Lein (1975) reports that black children often
use their simplest speech for the classroom but are more prone to use
complex language with parents. Rationale offered by Lein (1975) for
differences in communication patterns relate to the experience of fear.
To Lein the fear is twofold, because it is experienced by the student and
the teacher. Black students commonly express fear of rendering a comment that is misinterpreted. For example, black adolescents typically
say, "Get off my case," meaning "I'm not prepared." In turn, teachers
not acquainted with culturally playful verbal argument styles, react in
a fearful manner toward the student. This social interchange is typically perceived by school officials as challenging authority (Lein, 1975).
    Furthermore, ethnographic studies suggest that in low socioeco-
nomic families, parent–child communication interactions are com-

monly authoritarian and confrontational (Bartz & Levine, 1978; Cahill, 1986; Peters, 1981). Oftentimes, conversation dialogue takes on the form of mutual teasing, sarcasm, and denigrating comments (Ladner, 1971; Schulz, 1969). For example, someone may be teased about their "big" lips. Again this type of social and verbal interchange may be linked to a historical experience and serve as a cultural preparation for later expected racial resentment. Unfortunately, long-term exposure to such patterns of communications may create certain difficulty in the acculturation process for the black adolescent. It is important to note that communication patterns among middle-class black families are commonly reported as more supportive and more like the American norm (Bartz & Levine, 1978; Peters, 1981).

BLACK ADOLESCENT THERAPEUTIC ENCOUNTER

It is well known within African-American communities that blacks are often hesitant about turning to mental health professionals for help. A common complaint among black parents referred to clinicians using traditional psychoanalytical techniques is the seemingly limited overt involvement of the therapist. Often, the traditional therapeutic interaction is misconstrued as a lackadaisical attitude on the part of the therapist. Furthermore, even after agreeing to participate in therapy, parents wonder why over a period areas of conflict remain unimproved. Too often, parents do not understand the complexity of psychological problems and the time required for its resolution. There is also a mistrust about how information given to the therapist will be used.

Because black families generally do not turn to mental health institutions for solution to emotional stress, black adolescents who exhibit emotional or behavioral difficulties are more likely to be referred to juvenile court or the social welfare agency (Franklin, 1982; Meyers & King, 1980). These blacks view such agencies as having a racist attitude toward their plight. Educated and uneducated blacks are quite cognizant of having to have desegregation and antidiscrimination legislation mandated to ensure appropriate services and adequate education.

The black adolescent's expectation of therapy usually differs from that of the therapist. For example, adolescents often respond better to goal-directed, cognitive behavioral interventions as opposed to long-term explorative therapeutic approaches that emphasize early childhood experiences. There is much talk among black adolescents about the need for a crisis-oriented, goal-directed approach with emphasis on defining and remediating targeted emotional–interpersonal difficulties. Of major concern to black adolescents is that therapy appears related to disarming them in such a way that they no longer can function adequately in the community.

Frequently, within low socioeconomic communities, preventive services are nonexistent. Often, there are resources for rehabilitation but not for before problems surface. In addition, even if specific social skills need to be learned, there is limited access to appropriate role models. Unfortunately, such adolescents turn to television characters or mavericks who buck the system. Further exploration of possible role models, preventive resources, and the actual transference of skills learned in therapy seem essential to aid the black adolescent who is "at-risk."

SOCIAL SKILLS INTERVENTIONS FOR HIGH-RISK BLACK ADOLESCENTS

Gender Issues

Although there is not a literature that specifically addresses social skills interventions for black adolescents, we do find that within specific topic areas, disadvantaged adolescents have been targeted for training in specific areas, and there are gender differences in this targeting as well.

Euro-American culture has stereotypically portrayed the black male adolescent as "too aggressive." From preschool on, the black male child is referred in disproportionate numbers to school counselors and psychologists for aggressive behavior. The adolescent himself and his peer group are not complaining about these referred behaviors. The school, parent, and community are usually very concerned, however.

Likewise, there has been stereotyping in assessing social skills behaviors of female adolescents. For the most part, like Hsu notes for the Asian population, black female teenagers have an easier access to Euro-American culture and entry to the middle class. Of interest, few schools offer Euro-American middle-class value training, but female adolescents appear to have an easier time negotiating the two systems because perhaps they are not perceived as aggressive as the male adolescent.

Subgroups of high-risk female adolescents, however, are also referred for help. These are female teenagers who are perceived to be too sexually active or pregnant too early. Black adolescents tend to initiate sexual activity about 1 year earlier than other ethnic groups and are less informed about contraception, less positive about its use, and less effective about using it (Chilman, 1983; Gibbs, 1988). Consequently, black female teenagers have a higher rate of pregnancy and higher birth rates (Chilman, 1983). Attempts to cope with parenthood often result in psychological problems for both male and female adolescents (Chilman, 1983; Robertson, 1988). Because black female adolescents are often referred for issues of sexuality, pregnancy, and parenting, mental health professionals should be familiar with their cultural attitudes about premarital sex, contraception, and childbearing (Dougherty, 1978). (See the chapter by Vardi on pregnancy and teenaged parents and the chapter by Duggan-Ali on sexual assertiveness for further discussion of these issues.)

Hence in considering social skills intervention for black adolescents, we need to move beyond stereotyping. Rather, there is a need to move toward programs that will aid in negotiating two worlds, that can promote self-assertive behaviors and help eliminate maladaptive behaviors that are troublesome for the community.

Guidelines for Assessment and Intervention

What is most strikingly absent in the black social skills literature are programs geared toward most black youth in dealing with their own issues of assertiveness as well as training in social competencies needed to negotiate the dual systems they inhabit. Before we rush into such programs, however, the following must be addressed as crucial for assessing the social competencies of black youth and designing appropriate interventions geared to their needs and to further their development. Because the black community is responsive to short-term structured programming, well-designed social skills programs that promised some remediation of problems would have a positive reception.

Assessment

The following points pertain to social skills assessment:

1. Who are the trainers? Such professionals need to examine their own attitude toward so-called appropriate and inappropriate behaviors, and the role they themselves play as agents of acculturation. In particular, because teachers, psychologists, and counselors are mostly middle class, they tend to project middle-class values. They may genuinely not be aware of the complexities and issues related to the underclass.
2. Who is doing the referring? For whom are the behaviors problematic? The adolescent, teacher, school, parent, or peer? One needs to consider the cultural context of the referral process. Is a new principal determined that certain standards of behavior are

to be observed? Is a panicky teacher who cannot control adolescents in class too quick to define their behavior as inappropriate?

For each referral, the context of the problem needs to be assessed.

3. Given the lack of standard assessment for this population, are you prepared to either develop your own assessment geared to the needs of this population or to modify existing ones? (See chapters by Yarris, Planells-Bloom, and Barrish for issues related to construction of assessment for the special population.)

Intervention

The following points raise some important questions about social skills intervention:

1. What behaviors are being singled out for change? What is considered? Are adolescents with aggressive behaviors referred, whereas the shy and withdrawn are overlooked? Are male adolescents referred more than female adolescents?

2. What are the expectations for training? Is the adolescent's behavior seen as a deficit in acculturation or socialization? What are the consequences for the adolescent of such training for functioning in his or her own context?

3. In designing a program for change, how much is self-esteem, self-efficacy, and the adolescent's own desires for change considered? Is it as important to help adolescents negotiate both worlds as it is to have trainers themselves who are equally familiar with both worlds?

4. Are you willing to bring in appropriate role models, even if they are not trained mental health professionals? The psychologist–counselor might not be appropriate socialization agents to provide such training for high-risk adolescents. We may need to develop programs to train community leaders or role models to do intervention work. For example, bringing in sports figures, prominent television characters, or music groups may be effective.

5. How comfortable are you with aggression? Will you be willing to let go of your own value system and together with the group help them to define and differentiate appropriate aggressive and assertive behaviors?

6. Are you willing to help them develop assertive self-expressions and to channel their anger into social activism, so they can pro-

mote their issues and causes whether or not it meets the main-stream approval?

It is important that the school and classroom begin this work. Instead of singling out the adolescent with inappropriate behavior, the entire class could work together to deal with the many aspects of social competency and assertiveness required for optimal adolescent functioning. Such work could involve role plays with classes on the best ways of handling racist, sexist, and aggressive behaviors. Ideally, one should begin work on these issues in preschool, but given the lack of resources and other bureaucratic barriers, the junior high school most probably is the best place to initiate such interventions before such students drop out of school entirely.

REFERENCES

Acosta, F. X., & Yamamoto, J. (1982). *Effective psychotherapy for low-income and minority patients.* New York: Plenum.

Abbott, A. (1981). Factors related to grade achievement: self perception, class-room composition, sex and race. *Contemporary Educational Psychology, 6,* 167–179.

Allen, W. R. (1978). Black family research in the United States: A review, assessment and extension. *Journal of Comparative Family studies, 9,* 167–189.

Argyris, C. (1965). Exploration in interpersonal competence. *Journal of Applied Behavioral Science, 1,* 58–83.

Baldwin, A. (1980). *Theories of child development.* New York: John Wiley.

Bartz, K. W., & Levine, E. S. (1978). Childrearing by Black parents: A description and comparison to Anglo and Chicano parents. *Journal of Marriage and the Family, 40,* 709–719.

Billingsley, A. (1968). *Black families in white America.* Englewood Cliffs, NJ: Prentice Hall.

Bowman, P., & Howard, C. (1985). Race-related socialization, motivation and academic achievement: A study of black youths in three-generation families. *Journal of the American Academy of Child Psychiatry, 24,* 134–141.

Boykin, A. W. (1985). The triple quandary and the schooling of Afro-American children. In U. Neisser (Ed.), *The school achievement of minority children.* Hillsdale, NY: Erlbaum.

Brisson, P. "More Blacks steered to special ed." Gannett Westchester Newspaper/Tuesday, February 5, 1991.

Brown, S. V. (1985). Premarital sexual permissiveness among black adolescent females. *Social Psychology Quarterly, 48,* 381–387.

Brunswick, A., & Messeri, P. (1986). Drugs, life style and health. *American Journal of Public Health, 76,* 52–57.

Cahill, I. D. (1966). Child-rearing practices in lower socio-economic ethnic groups. *Dissertation Abstracts, 27*, 31–39.

Cause, A. M., Felner, R., & Primavera, J. (1982). Social support in high risk adolescents: Structural components and adaptive impact. *American Journal of Community Psychology, 10*, 417–428.

Chambers, B. (Ed.). (1968). *Chronicles of black protest.* New York: New American Library.

Children's Defense Fund. (1986). *Welfare and teen pregnancy: What do we know? What do we do?* Washington, DC: Children's Defense Fund.

Chilman, C. (1983). *Adolescent sexuality in a changing American society.* New York: Wiley.

Clark, K. B. (1965). *Dark ghetto: Dilemmas of social power.* New York: Harper & Row.

Comer, J. P., & Hill, H. (1985). Social policy and the mental health of black children. *Journal of the American Academy of Child Psychiatry, 24*, 175–181.

Davis, K., & Swartz, J. (1972). Increasing black student's utilization of mental health services. *American Journal of Orthopsychiatry, 42*, 771–776.

Dembo, R. (1988). *Delinquency among black male youth.* Dover, MA: Auburn House.

Dougherty, M. (1978). *Becoming a woman in rural black culture.* New York: Holt, Rinehart & Winston.

Edwards, R. (1979). Effective schools for the urban poor. *Education Leadership, 40*, 23–27.

Franklin, A. J. (1982). *Therapeutic intervention with urban black adolescents.* New York: Praeger.

Franklin, J. H. (1967). *From slavery to freedom: A history of American Negroes.* New York: Knopf.

Gardner, L. (1971). The therapeutic relationship under varying conditions of race. *Psychotherapy: Theory, Research and Practice, 8*, 78–87.

Gibbs, J. T. (1984). Black adolescents and youth: An endangered species. *American Journal of Orthopsychiatry, 54*, 6–21.

Gibbs, J. T. (Ed.). (1988). *Young, black and male in America: An endangered species.* Dover, MA: Auburn House.

Glasgow, D. (1981). *The Black underclass.* New York: Vintage Books.

Griffith, M., & Jones, E. E. (1978). Race and psychotherapy: Changing perspectives. *Current Psychiatric Therapies, 18*, 225–235.

Hall, L. E., & Tucker, C. M. (1985). Relationships between ethnicity, conceptions of mental illness and attitudes associated with seeking psychological help. *Psychology Reports, 57*, 907–916.

Havighurst, R. J. (1976). The relative importance of social class and ethnicity in human development. *Human Development, 19*, 56–64.

Hines, P. M., & Boyd-Franklin, N. *Black families.* New York: Guilford Press.

Kasarda, J. (1983). Urban change and minority opportunities. In P. E. Peterson (Ed.), *The new urban reality.* Washington, DC: Brookings Institution.

Kifer, E. (1975). Relationship between academic achievement and personality characteristics: A quasi-longitudinal study. *American Educational Research Journal, 12*(2), 191–210.

Kochman, T. (1972). *Fighting words Black and White*. Unpublished Paper, University of Illinois, Chicago.

Labov, W. (1972). *Language in the inner city: Studies in the black English vernacular*. Philadelphia: University of Pennsylvania Press.

Ladner, J. (1971). *Tomorrow's tomorrow*. New York: Doubleday.

Lein, L. (1975). Black-American migrant children: Their speech at home and school. *Council on Anthropology and Education Quarterly, 6*, 1–11.

Levine, L. W. (1977). *Black culture and Black consciousness*. New York: Oxford University Press.

Lewinsohn, P. M., Weinstein, M. S., & Alper, T. (1970). A behaviorally oriented approach to the group treatment of depressed persons: A methodological contribution. *Journal of Clinical Psychology, 4*, 525–532.

McAdoo, H. (1981). *Black families*. Newbury Park, CA: Sage.

Mancini, J. K. (1980). *Strategic styles: Coping in the inner city*. Hanover, NH: University Press of New England.

Myers, H. F., & King, L. M. (1980). Youth of the Black underclass: Urban stress and mental healthnotes for an alternative formulation. *Fanon Center Journal, 1*, 1–27.

Omi, M., & Winant, H. (1986). *Racial formation in the United States: From the 1960's to the 1980's*. Boston: Routledge & Kegan Paul.

Peters, M. F. (1981). Parenting in Black families with young children: A historical perspective. In H. McAdoo (Ed.), *Black families*. Newbury Park, CA: Sage.

Powell, G. J. (1985). Self concept among Afro-American students in racially isolated minority schools: Some regional differences. *Journal of the American Academy of Child Psychiatry, 24*, 142–149.

President's Commission on Mental Health. (1987). *Task panel reports*, Vol. 3. Washington, DC: Government Printing Office.

Prudhomme, C., & Musto, D. F. (1973). Historical perspectives on mental health and racism in the United States. In C. V. Willie, B. M. Kramer, & B. M. Brown (Eds.), *Racism and mental health*. Pittsburgh: University of Pittsburgh Press.

Reed, R. (1988). Education and achievement of young Black males. In J. T. Gibbs (Ed.), *Young, Black and male in America: An Endangered species*. Dover, MA: Auburn House.

Rivers, L. W., et al. (1975). Mosaic of labels for Black children. In N. Hobbs (Ed.), *Issues in the classification of children: A sourcebook on categories, labels, and their consequences. Vol. 2*. San Francisco: Jossey–Bass.

Roscoe, B., & Peterson, K. L. (1982). Teacher and structural characteristics which enhance learning and development. *College Student Journal, 16*(4), 389–394.

Sarason, S. B. (1973). Jewishness, blackishness, and the nature-nurture controversy. *American Psychologist, 28*, 962–71.

Schorr, A. (1985). *Common decency: Domestic policies after Reagan.* New Haven, CT: Yale University Press.

Schulz, D. A. (1969). *Coming up black: Patterns of ghetto socialization.* Englewood Cliffs, NJ: Prentice Hall.

U.S. Bureau of the Census. (1981). *School enrollment: Social and economic characteristics of students, 1980.* Current Population Reports, Series p–20. Washington, DC: U.S. Government Printing Office.

U.S. Bureau of Census. (1985). *Statistical abstract of the United States: 1986* (106th ed.). Washington, DC: U.S. Department of Commerce.

U.S. Department of Health and Human Services. (1986). *Health, United States, 1986.* Washington, DC: National Center for Health Statistics.

Weiss, R. L. (1968). Operant conditioning techniques in psychological assessment. In P. McReynolds (Ed.), *Advances in psychological assessment.* Palo Alto, CA: Science & Behavior.

Wilson, W. J. (1987). *The truly disadvantaged.* Chicago: University of Chicago Press.

Young, V. H. (1970). Family and childhood in a southern Georgia Community. *American Anthropologist, 72,* 269–288.

Zigler, E., & Child, I. (1973). *Socialization and personality development.* Reading, MA: Addison-Wesley.

6
Assertiveness Issues for Asian Americans

Catherine J. Hsu

Today's mental health workers and school staff are finding themselves faced with a new and growing population of students. These students carry with them a different culture and language and thus problems that are unique in some ways to them. This new population is Asian American.

In the United States, Asian and Pacific Americans constitute a substantial population of more than 7,000,000. This group is also growing at a rate faster than any other ethnic minority community. Within the past 10 years the number of Asians and Pacific Islanders living in the United States has doubled, and demographers have predicted that this increase will continue. According to the 1990 census, there are approximately 1,645,472 Chinese residing in the United States today compared with 806,040 in 1980. This is an increase of 104.1%. The number of Japanese residing in the U.S. increased from 700,974 to 847,562, and the number of Koreans increased from 345,593 to 798,849. (These figures do not include the other nationalities that fall under the Asian-American category.) Of the Asian-American population in the United States most are native born, whereas there is a growing number of foreign-born persons.

CONCEPTUALIZATIONS OF ASIAN AMERICANS

When working with Asian Americans there are many variables to consider. A common misconception is that Asian and Pacific Americans constitute a single homogeneous group with a single culture, appearance, and language. There are four geographical areas from which

Asian and Pacific Americans have immigrated. They are East Asia, South Asia, Southeast Asia, and the Pacific Islands. This chapter focuses on Eastern Asians—especially the Chinese and Japanese Americans. Social scientists have described Chinese and Japanese family structure and interaction patterns as being similar (Sue & Sue, 1973). There are important differences within these groups as well as across these groups, however.

Within each culture (ethnicity) there are further diversifications: date of arrival in the United States, generational status, first or second degree of assimilation and acculturation, age, sex, and so on. One possible way to conceptualize differences among Asian Americans was suggested by Green (1982). He identified three family life-style patterns regarding generational differences for Asian Americans.

1. Immigrant families (Chinese and Japanese Americans who arrived before the 1924 Exclusion Act, and Philipinos, Koreans, and others who came shortly afterwards)
2. American born (second or third generation of Asian Americans)
3. New arrivals (recent immigrants who came after the Immigrant Act of 1965 including recent Indochinese refugees)

Green (1982) suggests that the early immigrant families and the recent immigrant families can be considered "traditional." Their ethnic culture will be predominant and dictate their life-styles. This can be seen in the way they raise their children, the family structure, and so forth. The American-born families tend to be acculturated to American norms, however, and may live a life-style similar to the dominant culture or a bicultural life-style.

Another way to conceptualize differences in Asian Americans is the counseling model used by Kitano (1989) to measure the interaction of assimilation and ethnic identity. He differentiates assimilation and ethnic identity as follows: "Assimilation involves the process of acculturation and becoming 'Americanized'; ethnic identity refers to the retention of customs, attitudes, and beliefs of the culture of origin" (Kitano, 1989, p. 142). As the length of time in the United States increases, the ethnic identification will decrease.

From this model, Kitano (1989) identified four types of Asian Americans.

Type A: High in Assimilation, Low in Ethnic Identity

Individuals in this category are very "American." Their life-styles, values, language, and culture reflect the dominant culture. Ethnic identification has very little influence especially during adolescence. The generation and length of time in the United States greatly influence this category.

In general, type A individuals experience problems similar to those experienced by the dominant culture. Some of the issues addressed are interpersonal relationships, personality and intrapsychic problems, mobility, job opportunities, advancement, dating, intermarriage, child care, and lack of social skills.

Type B: High in Assimilation, High in Ethnic Identity

The individuals in this category are essentially bicultural. They are comfortable in both cultures. Few people fall into this category; examples of those who do are intellectuals and business people who have to deal with both cultures.

Type C: High in Ethnic Identity, Low in Assimilation

This category mostly comprises newly arrived immigrants and earlier immigrants who have socialized almost exclusively in their ethnic communities. According to the previous model, they are considered the "traditionalists."

Type D: Low in Ethnic Identity, Low in Assimilation

This category comprises those who are alienated from both their ethnic and the American communities. Also included are the mentally ill and those with severe problems stemming from their inability to accept either community.

Within each category, the person will experience different problems. Kitano (1989), however, emphasizes that these are "ideal types," and in actuality few neatly fit into one category.

Sue and Sue (1973) postulated yet another way to conceptualize Asian Americans. They conceptualized three different types of Asian Americans: the traditionalist, the marginal man, and the Asian American.

In all these models it becomes clear that there is much diversification within the Asian-American population and that the level of acculturation is important. When working with Asian Americans it is important to identify what values they hold important, that of the dominant culture or of their ethnic heritage.

ASIAN FAMILY

Within the traditional Chinese family there is a strong emphasis on the role of each family member, and his or her relationship to others (Shon & Ja, 1982). Emphasis is also placed on family needs (verses the individual) and adherence to the rules of behavior established by a vertical hierarchy. The family structure is arranged to maintain orderly functioning and minimize conflict. Any behavior that disturbs the order or causes conflict is discouraged through the use of guilt or shame.

Traditionally, the leader of the family is the father. He is the decision maker of the family, and his authority is unquestioned. In the eyes of the community, the success or failure of the family's character as a whole and of its individual members is the responsibility of the father (Shon & Ja, 1982). He is also expected to provide for the economic welfare of his family. The father's behavior in general is dignified, authoritative, remote, and aloof.

The traditional role of the mother is of the nurturing caretaker of the family. She is responsible for the emotional nurturance and the wellbeing of the family. She is also responsible to teach her children their social roles and responsibilities, and will frequently advocate and intercede with the father on the children's behalf.

Within the traditional family the sons are generally valued more highly than daughters. The most valued child is the oldest son. His responsibility to the family is great as is his preferential treatment. He is expected to be a role model of character for his siblings and carry out his father's responsibilities when his father is absent. Younger siblings are expected to follow the role provided by the oldest son and respect his authority throughout their entire lives.

In the United States, Chinese families, depending on their level of acculturation, continue to follow these roles but to a lesser extent. For example, female children now receive the same preferential treatment as male children. Also mothers are no longer restricted to the home and often have great influence on family decisions.

In the recent immigrant family, children may often have the additional role of translators and negotiators with the outside world. They are called on to perform a variety of tasks such as shopping, filling out forms and applications, and paying bills (Huang & Ying, 1990; Kitano, 1989). This changes the child's role and may result in role confusion and conflict.

In general, the primary family unit is strong and typically exerts great control over its members. Emphasis is placed on education, obedience, and enhancement of the family name. In addition, the Chinese learn strong patterns of self-control and have a great respect for their elders.

ASIAN-AMERICAN ADOLESCENTS

The period of adolescence can be difficult for any child. Students are contending with changes in their body, learning to take responsibility for developing relationships, and attempting to establish some autonomy from their parents. Common to many adolescents and their parents is a "generational" gap, in which adolescents think their parents do not understand what is important to them and vice versa. Among Asian-American adolescents there is an additional conflict, a "cultural" conflict, within their family. Often parents do not understand their child because they fall in one cultural category, whereas the child falls in another.

Adolescence is also a time of intense peer pressure for conformity. Many traditional Asian parents have little understanding of the American peer-oriented teenaged culture. They do not realize the importance that clothing, appearance, and peer approval have for adolescents. Many parents also view nonacademic courses and extracurricular activities as a waste of time, and children are often discouraged from participating in these activities. This cuts down on the amount of peer socialization available to the adolescent.

Grace, a Chinese-American–born girl as well as the eldest child, recalls when she was 15 years old fighting a lot with her parents to be allowed to go out at night to parties or the movies with her friends. Her parents could not understand why she wanted to go out at night because as adolescents in Communist China this was not allowed.

Searching for a self-identity is another major part of adolescence. Many Asian Americans feel torn between wanting to be accepted by their family as well as their friends and society.

One 18-year-old Korean-American female teenager reported that she struggled with her identity because she felt neither truly Korean nor truly American. When she meets a Korean person this teenager knows she is not like him or her because she thinks and views situations differently. When she is with her American friends, however, she feels that she is immediately labeled as "Korean/different," and ethnical generalizations are presumed. She cites as an example that because she is Asian she is immediately presumed to be smart.

Another Korean-American 16-year-old male adolescent named Tony reported that he identifies with his ethnic background. He stated that most of his friends are Asian-American and that the school he attends is predominantly Asian-American.

The determination of self-identity for many Asian-American adolescents will often depend on factors such as the number of Asian Americans in the school, the socioeconomic status of the family, and with which group the adolescent wishes to identify. For example, a Chinese male adolescent who attends a school in a predominantly white middle-class neighborhood will most probably want to and feel the need to conform to the dominant culture versus a Chinese male teenager attending a school in an ethnic-specific area where there are many other Asian students.

Socioeconomic status of the family will also determine how the adolescent views himself or herself as well as how great the cultural conflict will be. Parents who are college educated and are working within the dominant society will themselves need to acculturate to succeed professionally. Though there still may be some conflict between what the parents desire and the adolescent wants, the parents are still more familiar with the dominant culture.

Within a family the amount of conflict can vary depending on the family position of the adolescent. First-born Chinese-American boys are under tremendous pressure and are more vulnerable to psychological disorders than other siblings (Hisama, 1980). As stated earlier, his responsibility is great. He must be the role model for his younger siblings by being a dutiful son and achieve honors in school.

The youngest daughter also experiences a higher rate of psychopathology compared with other siblings (Huang & Ying, 1990; Lee, 1982). She may resent the responsibility of taking care of her parents as her older siblings leave home while at the same time not receiving the same treatment as her other siblings. As the youngest she is also probably the most acculturated, and experiences greater cultural conflict and disagreements with her parents.

In some families, however, the youngest may experience less conflict with the parents than the oldest. In many cases the parents begin to acculturate after the conflicts with the oldest child. By the time the youngest becomes an adolescent the parents may be tired of debating the same issues and have become more accepting of the dominant culture.

Grace, the Chinese-American female adolescent mentioned previously, has a sister 2-1/2 years younger. Grace, the oldest daughter, after fighting with her parents was able to obtain a curfew of 11 p.m. while in high school. Her younger sister, Christine, while in high school was often able to stay out until 2 a.m. without a quarrel. The parents stated that with their first daughter they did not know better and became more familiar with the culture afterward.

Asian-American Male Adolescents

The Asian-American male adolescent is usually smaller in stature and will experience very little secondary hair growth compared with the average Caucasian male. For a teenager where emphasis is on bodily change and sexual maturity this may be distressing. They may view themselves as unattractive or inferior, which might lead to various psychological problems.

One observation is that Asian-American male teenagers start dating and establishing relationships with women at a later age. This can be due to feelings of inferiority and not being able to compete with other Caucasian men. Another possibility is that many may not see themselves as able to assert themselves and ask female teenagers out on a date.

A factor to remember is that the Asian-American male adolescent is an honored position in the Asian family. The emphasis placed on a son by his family is education and showing a respectable image to the community by fulfilling his role as a dutiful son. Parents may not acknowledge or see their son's concerns about dating because they do not believe that it is important for their son at this age and that it might distract him from his studies.

Tony, mentioned earlier, confirmed that a lot of his friends do not tell their parents they are dating. They know their parents would disapprove of dating at this age.

Sue and Sue (1973) conducted a study of students seen at the Student Health Psychiatric Clinic at the University of California at Los Angeles. Their preliminary results based on the Minnesota Multiphasic Personality Inventory, and clinical impressions indicated that Chinese and Japanese male students exhibited severer problems than non-Asians. The profiles for the Chinese male students "indicated problems involving blunted affect, dependency, inferiority feelings, ruminations, somatic complaints, and lack of social skills" (Sue & Sue, 1973, p. 122). In this study, Asian female students exhibited less disturbance than Asian male students.

Asian-American Female Adolescents

Dating

As the process of sexual maturity occurs in adolescence, so to does the focus of the adolescent turn to dating and experiencing sexual activity.

Dating can be a source of stress and anxiety for many Asian-American male adolescents as stated earlier. It seems that Asian-American female adolescents are better accepted in society than Asian male teenagers. It is more common to observe a Caucasian male adolescent dating an Asian female adolescent versus an Asian male teenager dating a Caucasian female teenager. In recent years, however, it seems that the number of the latter group is increasing.

In an anthropological field study done by Weiss (1973) in a Chinese-American community, he revealed that many Chinese-American female adolescents viewed Chinese-American male adolescents as inhibited, passive, and lacking sexual attractiveness. Weiss thought that Chinese-American female teenagers were better accepted than Chinese-American male teenagers by American society and that the stereotyping of these male adolescents has been generally less favorable. As a result, Westernized female adolescents sought boyfriends that behaved boldly and aggressively. In this study, Chinese-American male teenagers "agree that they are more inhibited and less aggressive than Caucasian males, and admit to feeling uncomfortable, if not insecure, in racially mixed company and in predominantly Caucasian setting" (Weiss, 1973, p. 89).

Chen and Yang (1986) measured the self-image of Chinese-American adolescents, and concluded that with acculturation their attitudes and perceptions about themselves and dating were similar to the dominant culture. They were also able to hold onto their ethnic values of loyalty, conformity, and respect for elders.

NEW ASIAN-AMERICAN WOMEN

Asian women are no longer solely portrayed as reserved, passive, shy, and humble. Today, the typical Asian-American woman is highly educated, works, and holds positions of leadership. These women face many obstacles in becoming successful in the American culture. Not only is she a woman but a woman of an ethnic minority group. She must try to integrate the two cultures successfully (Fujitomi & Wong, 1973). Many members within her own ethnic group may be against her because of her aggressiveness, assertiveness, and visibility. These factors are necessary for Asian-American women to be effective and successful, yet they conflict with the traditional Asian values of passivity and submission, and of modesty and moderation (Fujitomi & Wong, 1973). It is not surprising that many women today continue to struggle with feelings of inferiority because of traditional thinking.

ASSERTIVENESS AND ASIAN AMERICANS

Popular stereotypes depict Asian Americans as passive, quiet, submissive, nonassertive, and so on. This may seem true especially when Asians are dealing with someone of authority. Authority figures are often equated with adults and the elderly for Asian children, and in the traditional family ancestors and elders are viewed and treated with great respect. Asian children are taught very early to listen to adults, especially parents and elderly people, and to obey their requests without question. They are also taught that family and adherence to the family structure and goals are highly valued. Often Asian children who do not follow their family's wishes are looked on with great disapproval by their family as well as the community.

Are Asian Americans as nonassertive, however, as stereotypes indicate? The research literature examining assertiveness in Asian Americans is limited. In general, Asian Americans have not been the focus of inquiry concerning mental health issues. In studies that have been conducted, the focus was on adults, and the results and conclusions varied. The notion that Asian Americans are globally less assertive and more passive has been supported by Johnson and Marsella (1978), who showed that third-generation Japanese Americans were more concerned with male dominance, female subordination, and propriety of conversation than the Caucasian group. The Japanese Americans retained the specific speech norms explicit in the Japanese language. In addition, they consistently chose less assertive responses in all the hypothetical situations.

Fukuyama and Greenfield (1983) also demonstrated a significant difference between full-scale assertion scores between Asians and non-Asians. Asian Americans showed overall lower levels of assertiveness. Fukuyama and Greenfield attributed this to the values found within the Asian culture. For example, expressing individual needs may be difficult for Asian Americans especially if they do not coincide with the group or family's need. Another aspect of assertiveness, accepting compliments, is often not seen because in accepting compliments they would violate cultural norms of maintaining modesty. Many children are taught to acknowledge compliments very passively. For example, if a young girl was complimented on her beauty, she would either make a small smile or respond in a way reflecting her modesty, "Thank you but I am not that pretty."

Fukuyama and Greenfield (1983) also found ethnic differences reflecting greater value placed on preserving harmony in relationships. Asians may feel more anxious and guilty because situations that require assertion usually involve some sort of social conflict and would constitute a threat to interpersonal harmony, regardless of whether the person is assertive or not. This would make it difficult to express feelings and make requests difficult.

Hsu (1970), conversely, had speculated that the behavior of Asians was more influenced by situational factors than non-Asians. This was supported by Sue, Ino, and Sue's (1983) finding that Chinese Americans were as behaviorally assertive as Caucasian Americans in many situations (e.g., with friends in informal settings or with members of their own race). They did experience difficulty in asserting themselves, however, with an authority figure such as a professor.

Zane, Sue, Hu, and Kwon (1991) examined cultural differences in assertiveness for Asian Americans. Their results also suggested that the cultural differences in assertiveness are situational. The outcome for both the Caucasian group and the Asian group, however, depended on self-efficacy and expected outcome. They also reported that Asians, in situations involving only strangers, felt less self-efficacious and reported less assertion than Caucasians.

CRITIQUE OF RESEARCH

There remains controversy over the validity of these results. Sue et al. (1983) suggested that the differences found in performance between the two groups may be the result of the specific measure used. The prior tests that have shown Asians to be globally passive and nonassertive were pen-and-paper tests. In the study by D. Sue et al. (1983) both a pen-and-paper test as well as behavioral ratings in role-playing situations were given. The pen-and-paper measure supported previous findings that Asians are passive, whereas the behavioral rating indicated no overall differences between the two groups, except for only one role-play situation. When speaking to a professor, an authority figure, the Asian-American students behaved less assertively than the Caucasian group. Also, brief role plays will demonstrate whether the person has the skills to act assertively, but they will not predict how the individual will act in a natural situation (Linehan, Goldfried, & Goldfried, 1979).

GUIDELINES FOR ASSESSING
ASSERTIVENESS TRAINING

There are various reasons why Asian Americans would seek or benefit from assertiveness training. When the book's editor, Iris Fodor offered social skills training at the university, many Asian-American male students sought such training. They wanted to start dating but did not know how to ask a woman for a date and feared rejection. Other issues raised in the group included a desire to assert oneself within their peer group, with teachers, employers, or even with their family.

In any case, the goal is to develop an understanding of your clients–adolescents and what it is they are seeking. It is important to determine whether assertiveness skills are what they really want. Therapist must consider the degree to which an intervention should be targeted at changing behaviors, which may be entirely appropriate in the dominant culture but maladaptive for functioning in the clients' ethnic circles. The therapist can provide clients with the power of choice, by providing adolescents with the skills necessary to decide when and how to act assertively. This can be done by providing them with an understanding of assertive behaviors in various cultural contexts to recognize cues that discriminate these different situations and to build an increased repertoire for responding effectively in each of these contexts (Caldwell-Colbert & Jenkins, 1982). While making assessments the counselor must consider that clients may fear conflict from friends and family is they are assertive, or may fear change.

Some important variables to remember in formulating your social skills assessment while working with Asian-American adolescents are the following:

1. Level of acculturation of the family and the individual. Is the family very traditional? How long have they been living in the United States? Was the child born in the United States or did she or he immigrate here? If so, how old was the child or adolescent when she or he immigrated? How many generations of family have been in the United States? What language is spoken at home? Does the adolescent speak his or her native language?
2. Time of immigration. The time of immigration as well as the history that precedes or follows the immigration is important. For example, many Chinese adults that came to the United States after 1965 (when quotas were eliminated) lived during the Cultural Revolution. During this time in China, to speak one's mind or demonstrate any behavior different from that expected by the Communist party, earned one hard labor, imprisonment, and even death. Many Chinese American parents remain passive (in the background), in order not to call attention to themselves. For these parents, the fear may still be with them, and they model this behavior as well. Another example is the Japanese Americans who faced internment in the United States during World

War II. The desire to acculturate is strong in order not to draw attention to themselves.

3. Place of adolescent in the family hierarchy. Is the adolescent male or female? Oldest, youngest, or in the middle?
4. Parents' socioeconomic status. Are the parents educated and working in the dominant society? Are they working in factories in ethnic-specific communities (i.e., Chinatown)? This will also give you an indication on how much contact the parents have with the dominant culture. Also with the lower socioeconomic group, families may need their children to work—especially male children.
5. People with whom the parents socialize. Do they socialize exclusively with Asians or mostly with Caucasians?
6. Desires of adolescents. Do they want to be more acculturated or to hold onto their ethnical backgrounds? What balance between the two are they seeking?
7. Adolescents' academic plans. What type of school or college does the adolescent plan to attend?
8. Desires of parents. What do the parents have in mind for the child? Do the parents pressure the adolescent into a specific career? Do the parents view nonacademic activities as frivolous? How much do the parents value adherence to their culture or wish their child to acculturate?

As a reminder, these answers will be different for each individual. It is important that counselors do not look for "typical" characteristics but instead observe for any Chinese, Japanese, or non-Asian characteristics depending on the ethnicity, and use them to formulate the background and orientation of the individual.

REFERENCES

Abbott, K. A. (1976). Culture change and the persistence of the Chinese personality. In G. A. DeVos (Ed.), *Responses to change: Society, culture, and personality* (pp. 74–104). New York: Van Nostrand.

Asamen, J. K., & Berry, G. L. (1987). Self-concept, alienation, and perceived prejudice: Implications for counseling Asian Americans. *Journal of Multicultural Counseling and Development, 15,* 146–160.

Caldwell-Colbert, A. T., & Jenkins, J. O. (1982). Modification of interpersonal behavior. In S. M. Turner & R. T. Jones (Eds.), *Behavior modification in black populations* (pp. 171–207). New York: Plenum.

Chan, S. (1991). *Asian Americans: An interpretive history.* Boston: Twayne (division of G. K. Hall).

Chen, C., & Yang, D. (1986). The self-image of Chinese American adolescents. *Pacific Asian American Mental Health Research Center Review, 3/4,* 27–29.

Crystal, D. (1989). Asian Americans and the myth of the model minority. *Social Casework: The Journal of Contemporary Social Work, 70,* 405–413.

Fried, M. H. (1976). Chinese culture, society, and personality in transition. In G. A. DeVos (Ed.), *Responses to change: Society, culture, and personality* (pp. 45–73). New York: Van Nostrand.

Fujitomi, I., & Wong, D. (1973). The new Asian-American woman. In S. Sue & N. N. Wagner (Eds.), *Asian-Americans: Psychological perspectives* (pp. 252–263). Ben Lomond, CA: Science and Behavior Books.

Fukuyama, M. A., & Greenfield, T. K. (1983). Dimensions of assertiveness in an Asian-American student population. *Journal of Counseling Psychology, 30,* 429–432.

Gim, R. H., Atkinson, D. R., & Kim, S. J. (1991). Asian-American acculturation, counselor ethnicity and cultural sensitivity, and ratings of counselors. *Journal of Counseling Psychology, 38,* 57–62.

Green, J. W. (1982). *Cultural awareness in the human services.* Englewood Cliffs, NJ: Prentice Hall.

Hisama, T. (1980). Minority group children and behavior disorders—the case of Asian-American children. *Behavioral Disorders, 5,* 186–196.

Hsu, F. L. K. (1970). *Americans and Chinese.* Garden City, NY: Doubleday Natural History Press.

Huang, L. N., & Ying, Y. (1990). Chinese American children and adolescents. In J. T. Gibbs, L. N. Huang, & Associates, *Children of color: Psychological intervention with minority youth* (pp. 30–66). San Francisco: Jossey-Bass.

Hwang, P. O. (1977). Assertion training for Asian-Americans. In R. E. Alberti (Ed), *Assertiveness: Innovations, applications, Issues* (pp. 129–134). San Luis Obispo, CA: Impact.

Johnson, F. A., & Marsella, A. J. (1978). Differential attitudes toward verbal behavior in students of Japanese and European ancestry. *Genetic Psychology Monographs, 97,* 43–76.

Kitano, H. H. L. (1989). A model for counseling Asian Americans. In P. B. Pedersen, J. G. Draguns, W. J. Lonner, & J. E. Trimble (Eds.), *Counseling across cultures* (pp. 139–175). Honolulu: University of Hawaii Press.

Kong, S. L. (1985). Counseling Chinese immigrants: Issues and answers. In R. J. Samuda & A. Wolfgang (Eds.), *Intercultural counseling and assessment, global perspectives* (pp. 181–189). Lewiston, NY: Hogrefe.

Kuramoto, F. H., Morales, R. F., Munoz, F. U., & Murase, K. (1983). Education for social work practice in Asian and Pacific American communities. In J. C. Chunn II, P. J. Dunston, & F. Ross-Sheriff (Eds.), *Mental health and people of color* (pp. 127–155). Washington, DC: Howard University Press.

Lee, E. (1982). A social systems approach to assessment and treatment for Chinese-American families. In M. McGoldrick, J. K. Pearce, & J. Giordano (Eds.), *Ethnicity and family therapy* (pp. 527–551). New York: Guilford.

Linehan, M. M., Goldfried, M. R., & Goldfried, A. P. (1979). Assertion therapy: Skill training or cognitive restructuring. *Behavioral Therapy, 10,* 372–388.

Nagata, D. K. (1990). Japanese American children and adolescents. In J. T. Gibbs, L. N. Huang, & Associates, *Children of color: Psychological perspectives with minority youth* (pp. 67–113). San Francisco: Jossey-Bass.

Shon, S. P., & Ja, D. Y. (1982). Asian families. In M. McGoldrick, J. K. Pearce, & J. Giordano (Eds.), *Ethnicity and family therapy* (pp. 208–228). New York: Guilford.

Sue, D. W. (1973). Ethnic identity: The impact of two cultures on the psychological development of Asians in America. In S. Sue & N. N. Wagner (Eds.), *Asian-Americans: Psychological perspectives* (pp. 140–149). Ben Lomond, CA: Science and Behavior Books.

Sue, D., Ino, S., & Sue, D. M. (1983). Nonassertiveness of Asian Americans: An inaccurate assumption? *Journal of Counseling Psychology, 30,* 581–588.

Sue, S., & Morishima, J. K. (1982). *The Mental Health of Asian Americans.* San Francisco: Jossey-Bass.

Sue, S., & Sue, D. W. (1973). Chinese-American personality and mental health. In S. Sue & N. N. Wagner (Eds.), *Asian-Americans: Psychological perspectives* (pp. 111–124). Ben Lomond, CA: Science and Behavior Books.

Sue, D., & Sue, S. (1987). Cultural factors in the clinical assessment of Asian Americans. *Journal of Consulting and Clinical Psychology, 55,* 479–487.

U.S. Department of Commerce, Bureau of Census. (1991, September). Census Bureau Press Release CB91–215. *Census and You, 26,* 3.

Weiss, M. S. (1973). Selective acculturation and the dating process: The pattern of Chinese-Caucasian inter-racial dating. In S. Sue & N. N. Wagner (Eds.), *Asian-Americans: Psychological perspectives* (pp. 86–94). Ben Lomond, CA: Science and Behavior Books.

Wood, P. S., & Mallinckrodt, B. (1990). Culturally sensitive assertiveness training for ethnic minority clients. *Professional Psychology: Research and Practice, 21,* 5–11.

Zane, N. W. S., Sue, S., Hu, L., & Kwon, J. (1991). Asian-American assertion: A social learning analysis of cultural differences. *Journal of Counseling Psychology, 38,* 63–70.

7

Latino Cultures: Framework for Understanding the Latina Adolescent and Assertive Behavior

Diana Planells-Bloom

Latinos are the fastest-growing minority group in the United States. Estimates suggest that by the end of the twentieth century, they will be the largest minority group on the U.S. mainland. Within the context of this chapter, the term "Latino/Latina" implies a person of Latin American origin or descent currently residing in the United States regardless of their generational status or length of residence. Although the terms Latino and Hispanic have been used interchangeably, there is controversy regarding their usage given the sociopolitical implications of each term. For purposes of this chapter, Latino will be used because it better describes the heterogeneous background of this population in contrast to Hispanic, which emphasizes their Iberian heritage.

Although Latinos do share some common cultural and linguistic characteristics, the umbrella term *Latino* in fact describes a group of people with distinct historical, political, economic, and racial differences. There is considerable intergroup diversity as well as intragroup heterogeneity. The backgrounds of the Latino population include native Indian, African as well as Iberian heritages. Many Latinos are "mestizos," which means that they are a product of racial mixtures. The immigration and migration processes of these groups also differ in many ways and for many reasons. These factors have a direct impact on the economic, social, and political characteristics of each group. It is particularly important to understand the needs of the Latino population in light of the limited existing information. Increased cultural sensitivity will enable us to recognize the changing roles and circumstances of Latinos because not to recognize their diversity will result in reinforcing the existing stereotypes (Amaro & Russo, 1987).

DEMOGRAPHIC DATA REGARDING LATINO POPULATION

Latinos living on the United States mainland have the following backgrounds: Mexican (61%); Puerto Rican (15%); Cuban (6%) and other Central and South American countries and Spain (18%) (U.S. Bureau of the Census, 1985). Unfortunately, demographic data are not consistently available on the latter groups. The actual number of Latinos living in the United States can be underestimated because of the large number of undocumented or illegal immigrants. The literature regarding the Latino population has generally focused on the Mexican American, Puerto Rican, and Cuban populations. Most of the demographic data that follow will reflect information regarding these groups.

In general, the Latino population is young, and their median age is below that of the general population with the exception of Cuban Americans. The low median age of Latinos in general is largely due to the high birth rates in the Mexican American and Puerto Rican populations (Zavaleta, 1981).

The socioeconomic status of Latinos varies considerably. The median number of years that Latinos attend school is lower than that of the general population and differs across the Latino groups. Mexican Americans and Puerto Ricans fare least well compared with Cubans and Central or South Americans who are typically better educated and have higher rates of labor participation and higher income levels.

IMPACT OF SOCIOECONOMIC FACTORS

As a whole, Latinos are overrepresented among lower socioeconomic classes and younger ages. It is important to control for these factors before attributing Latino and Anglo differences in attitudes and behaviors to differences in cultural values. Frequently, acculturation and Latino cultural values are used to explain behaviors without acknowledging the interactive force of economic, social, and other life-cycle variables that could be influencing the behaviors (Amaro & Russo, 1987). Not to address the impact of these interactions may result in overgeneralizations and simplifications. Members of the same ethnic group but of different social classes may share commonalities in terms of their historical identification but not necessarily share similar values or behaviors (Cafferty & McCready, 1985).

REVIEW OF MAJOR LATINO GROUPS IN
THE UNITED STATES

Most Latinos in the United States are concentrated in ethnically spe-cific pockets. Mexican Americans are principally concentrated in the five southwestern states and in the Midwest. Puerto Ricans reside prin-cipally in New York, New Jersey, and Pennsylvania, whereas Cuban Americans are concentrated in Florida, with a large number living in and around New York City. Central and South Americans have mostly settled in large cities, for example, New York City, Los Angeles, and New York State as well as the southwestern areas of the United States (Zavaleta, 1981).

Mexican Americans

Mexican Americans represent one of the largest ethnic minority groups in the United States. They are unique from a cultural, demo-graphic, and historical perspective, and represent widely varied back-grounds. The Mexican culture is a rich blend of the Indian and Spanish heritages, and most Mexicans are mestizos.

Long before the United States gained possession of the Southwest, the Mexican Americans inhabited this region, yet they have been segre-gated socially and economically for more than a century because their language, race, and culture are different from that of the Anglo main-stream society (Cafferty & McCready, 1985). This has created serious economic and social problems for the Mexican-American population.

As a result of both poor employment opportunities in Mexico and its proximity with the United States, Mexican immigrants represent a constant flow of low-skill labor. In contrast to the pattern of previous European immigrant groups, Mexican Americans have not moved up the occupational ladder at the same rate. They continue to hold inferior jobs in nearly every major occupation category, and their unemploy-ment rates continue to be consistently higher than the general popula-tion.

Mexican families are usually large and remain intact in comparison with Anglo-American families. As a result of the proximity between Mexico and the United States, the trips back and forth enable families to renew their ties and reaffirm their ethnic identity (Falicov, 1982).

Puerto Ricans

The Puerto Rican cultural ancestry is a mixture of different races and ethnic groups including African, Taino Indian, and Spanish. The Puerto Rican migration is unique in comparison with the other Latino immigrants because Puerto Ricans are U.S. citizens. Nevertheless, they experience some of the problems of other immigrants between cultures because they speak a different language and come from a different culture than that of the Anglo mainstream society.

Puerto Ricans constitute the predominant Latino group in New York City. The Puerto Rican population is characterized by a high degree of mobility between the island and the mainland, which results in the reinforcement of the Puerto Rican culture. The institution that has been most influenced by the migration to the mainland has been the family. One of the consequences that has resulted from the stress confronting the immigrant family is the family breakdown. This breakdown represents a disruption in the family organization and values that had previously served as a stabilizing force to the Puerto Rican family (Canino, Earley, & Rogler, 1980). Forty percent of the Puerto Rican families are female headed, which is significantly higher when compared with other Latino populations, for example, Mexican-American families (Ho, 1987). The declining labor-force participation of Puerto Rican women and the deteriorating economic situation of Puerto Rican female-headed families has contributed to the tenuous economic position of the Puerto Rican migrant population.

Cubans

The Cuban culture is a mixture of Spanish and African culture. Historically, Cuba has had a unique involvement with such powerful countries as the United States, the former Soviet Union, and Spain. These circumstances distinguish Cuba from other Latin American countries (Ho, 1987).

The first wave of Cuban immigration (1958–72) was perceived by the U.S. government as politically motivated and thus fundamentally different from that of other Latino groups. The U.S. government developed programs at the federal, state, and local levels to assist Cuban refugees. In contrast, immigrants who are perceived as economically motivated (e.g., Mexican Americans) have not received the same type of support programs. This perceived political dimension has been a factor influencing the adaptation and adjustment of Cuban immigrants in the United States.

This first wave of Cuban immigration included a large first-generation population with a significantly higher proportion of white middle- and upper-class individuals as compared with other Latino groups. In contrast, the more recent wave of Cuban immigrants (since 1972) has included an increasing number of nonwhite workers from a wide variety of educational, occupational, and socioeconomic backgrounds. This latter group has been treated quite differently in comparison with the first wave of Cuban refugees (Cafferty & McCready, 1985).

Central Americans

Central Americans represent a more recent wave of immigration compared with the Mexican Americans and Puerto Ricans. This group comprises a growing number of individuals from the Dominican Republic, El Salvador, Nicaragua, Honduras, and Guatemala, many of whom have emigrated for political reasons. These groups are not legally seen as refugees (as were the Cubans) and therefore are not entitled to the important support services provided to refugees. Many of the recent Central American immigrants originate from rural areas and have limited occupational skills; as a result they gravitate toward large cities where there is a higher demand for service workers (Leslie & Leitch, 1989). Central American immigrants report greater psychosocial stress and generalized distress regarding the immigration process compared with Mexican immigrants. Their stress ratings related to premigration trauma (e.g., experiencing civil wars) were also found to be significantly higher in comparison with Mexican immigrants (Salgado de Snyder, Cervantes, & Padilla, 1990).

Shared Latino Characteristics

Many Latino families are bicultural and bilingual to a greater or lesser degree (Gibson, 1983). The family may participate in both cultures simultaneously by retaining values and behaviors of the Latino culture while acquiring values and behaviors of the host society. This is a dynamic and complex process which occurs at both an individual and group level. There are many different dimensions involved in this process.

In the areas of language, religion, family structure, and sex roles. there are similarities across the various Latino groups.

Many Latino families, especially first generation, continue to maintain Spanish as their primary language at home (Gibson, 1983). In general children are more likely to know English because they are exposed to English when they reach school age. A positive relationship usually exists between use and knowledge of the language of the host society and degree of adaptation.

Latinos continue to be predominantly Catholic, although the number of Latino Protestants is also growing. Regardless of denomination, religion continues to be a central element within their culture. Many churches represent a strong community center and often provide an important network and support system for newly arrived immigrants. As

a whole, Latinos emphasize spiritual values, and folk religion is prevalent throughout the Latino community. Folk religion combines the
heritage of Spanish Catholic, medical, and religious practices with African and Indian belief systems.

A similarity that Latinos share is the importance of the family (Gibson, 1983). The "traditional" Latino family is depicted as a patriarchal
one in which male and female roles are clearly defined. The man is described as "macho," which means that he is authoritarian and governs
the household. In contrast, the woman is expected to stay close to the
home, and her main responsibilities include childbearing and raising
the family. The Latino family is characterized by the concept of the "extended family." Relations between grandparents and grandchildren
are very close as are relations with aunts, uncles, and cousins. The extended family pattern represents an important natural support network and encompasses more individuals than those related by blood
and marriage. The concept of "respeto" (respect within the context of
relationships) dictates the appropriate deferential behavior toward
others on the basis of age, social position, economic status, and sex. The
institution of "compadres" (companion parents) is a network of ritual
kinship whose members have a deep sense of responsibility to each
other including economic assistance, encouragement, and support. The
children are called "hijos de crianza" (a child reared by the extended
family). When one segment of the family has migrated, the hijo de
crianza may form a bridge between a widening gap in extended family
relations, for example, a child may be sent to live with relatives on the
mainland so that she or he can receive a better education (Gibson,
1977).

It is important to recognize that the traditional Latino family model
that is described in the social science literature appears to be based on
families of lower socioeconomic status. Existing cultural diversity and
socioeconomic differences are frequently not considered. There are
marked differences between lower and upper or middle socioeconomic
levels that influence family life and circumstances. These differences
should not be minimized. For example, in contrast to the traditional
Latino family, the middle-class Latino family is characterized by more
child-centered behaviors, more emphasis on the nuclear family, greater
female autonomy, and a decline of male authoritarianism. These values are also more similar to those of the Anglo majority culture, which
stresses the nuclear family over the extended family, and encourages
individual achievement and autonomy. Therefore, because much of the
existing research on the Latino family is drawn from families of lower
socioeconomic status, the findings may not necessarily be representative of the middle- and upper-class Latino families.

LATINA AND LATINO ADOLESCENTS

For the Latina and Latino adolescents, in addition to negotiating the developmental tasks of adolescence, they must also negotiate their biculturality. One of the most important determinants in the development of adolescents' self-concept is the extent to which adolescents are similar to their reference groups (Rosenberg, 1979). Thus, one's status as a minority group member is a significant factor (Lloyd, 1985). Latina and Latino adolescents deal with two cultural worlds, which at times may be in conflict with each other. Some of the culture-related differences that have been identified include family dynamics and sex role attitudes.

The contrast between the Latino and the American mainstream values and attitudes has had an impact on the migrant Latino family, especially the more traditional Latino family. The first-generation Latino family in particular may also experience intergenerational conflicts because the parents were raised in a distinct culture from that of their children. Because the child often assimilates a new culture at a faster rate than the adult, a cultural as well as a generational gap may result.

Within the Latino culture, sex roles have been described as rigidly defined and demarcated, although recent investigations have begun to challenge these traditional roles (Vazquez-Nuttall, Romero-Garcia, & DeLeon, 1987). Socioeconomic factors, level of educational attainment (for both parent and child), and urban background have been recognized as important factors that influence sex role behavior within the Latino families. Traditionally, Latinas have been depicted as passive, submissive, and self-sacrificing (Gibson, 1983). Latinos, conversely, are described as dominant, aggressive, and authoritarian. The more positive side of "machismo" that is less often discussed is the strong sense of respect toward both the family and friends as well as the importance of honor and pride. Within the Anglo culture the male–female sex role delineations are not as rigid and are not as overtly defined. There is an espousal of a greater equality within the male–female relationship, and sex role attitudes regarding women are more liberal. Differences in sex role behavior between the Anglo and Latino cultures may be in terms of degree and perhaps not so much qualitative differences.

Assertiveness

When the culturally prescribed values of the home differ from those of the society at large, the adolescent is faced with making choices and often resolving conflicts. The adolescent who is raised close to the parents' culture and adheres to their standards will experience greater conflict as compared with the adolescent whose family values are more similar to the Anglo mainstream culture. One of the important developmental tasks of adolescence involves working out a place for oneself within the family while also forming new relationships in a society that differs from her or his own family values and traditions. The development of assertive behavior may be a particularly important tool for the Latina or Latino adolescent in helping her or him effectively negotiate these differences. Assertiveness has been recognized as an important aspect of interpersonal communication because it represents an effective and direct means of expression. Because sex role socialization is intrinsically linked to the development of assertive behavior, one would expect that the sex role attitudes found within the Latino culture may impact on the Latina's or Latino's ability to act assertively.

Latina Adolescent

According to the sex role literature, Latina women traditionally have been socialized to be passive and submissive in their interpersonal communications and discouraged from being assertive (Comas-Diaz & Duncan, 1985; Soto, 1979).

The behavior that is considered acceptable within the traditional Latino family stands in contrast to the mainstream culture, which encourages the adolescent to become increasingly independent and autonomous. The Latina adolescent's attempts to express her developing sense of self and her parents' difficulties in accepting her assertive behaviors may result in feelings of alienation for both parents and their adolescent daughter. Her difficulties with expressing different feelings or opinions may adversely affect her developing sense of self. The mother–daughter relationship in particular is noted for being emotionally charged because being of the same sex sets the stage for competition and identification in a way that is not found to the same degree in the mother–son dyad (Fodor & Wolfe, 1977). As a result, the mother–daughter dyad is especially vulnerable to communication problems. Alienation from the family is stressful for the Latina adolescent for, although she may have a different perception of the family, family ties are still important to her (Gibson, 1983). Within this context, assertiveness can provide a way for learning the communication and negotiation skills that can enable the adolescent to relate more effectively (Danzinger, 1976).

The Latina adolescent's difficulties with acting assertively may limit her ability to negotiate cultural differences in her relationships with peers. Within the peer culture, there is often a heightened pressure for conformity such that self-esteem is influenced by one's acceptance by peer groups (O'Donnell, 1979). Peer group conformity can become negative when pressure is exerted toward self-destructive behaviors (e.g., school dropout, premature sexual activity, etc.). Difficulty with expressing herself in a direct and honest manner may manifest itself either through acting-out behaviors, or through passive withdrawal and submissive conformity (Hardy-Fanta & Montana, 1982).

Latina adolescents have been found to be disproportionately delayed in education and also have the highest rate of premarital births when compared with the non-Latina adolescent population (Darabi, Dryfoos, & Schwartz, 1986). Adherence to traditional sex roles has been found to affect educational attainment adversely (Cardoza, 1991). Exposure to the Anglo mainstream culture and economic opportunities are influential in reshaping sex role attitudes. These findings are particularly significant considering that education is one of the important avenues for gaining socioeconomic mobility and greater independence.

The degree of change in sex role attitudes has been found to be related to socioeconomic status with women in the category of lower socioeconomic status being more resistant to change. Along these lines, the Latina adolescent who comes from the lower socioeconomic groups is particularly at risk because her struggles will be accentuated by additional environmental stresses associated with being poor and female. The opportunities for her to develop more appropriate coping skills through education and appropriate role models are limited by her lack of exposure to the mainstream culture. Her lack of assertiveness may engender feelings of powerlessness and helplessness in her struggle to confront multiple discriminations. The cycle contributes to keeping the Latina adolescent from moving beyond her socioeconomic confines.

Latino Adolescent

According to the sex role literature, Latino men have traditionally been socialized to be aggressive and domineering. Literature regarding the assertive behavior of the Latino, specifically the male adolescent, is scarce.

One study that compared assertiveness of Anglo and Mexican American male college students found Mexican Americans to be less assertive than their Anglo counterparts in their interactions with parents, same-sex peers, and business relations (Hall & Beil-Warner, 1978). The Mexican values of respect in family relationships and with same-sex peers was supported by the data. In addition, the role of machismo in assertive behavior appeared to be situationally determined. The data from studies that have looked at the husband–wife relationship within Mexican-American families have not found support for the hypothesis of male dominance in marital decision making. Joint decision making by the husband and wife was by far more common (Cromwell & Ruiz, 1979).

The Latino adolescent, especially the Mexican-American and the Puerto Rican male teenager, is at a greater risk for dropping out of school as compared with the non-Latino population. This places significant pressures on these Latinos as they prepare to enter adulthood and obtain a job. The Latino faces additional stress because of the multiple sources of discrimination that confront him, particularly in the occupational domain, as a result of his ethnicity, class, and race. The self-concept toward which the Latino aspires (i.e., self-determination and independence) stands in contrast to the reality that may confront him in terms of limited opportunities and discrimination. This is especially true of the adolescent from lower socioeconomic standing whose education and skills are more likely to be limited. The resulting frustration and poor self-esteem may leave him feeling particularly vulnerable. Assertive behavior can help to empower him so that he experiences an increased sense of self-confidence and control over his life.

Inner-directed anger, which is found among minorities in the United States, has manifested itself in passive–aggressive or self-destructive behaviors such as alcoholism, drug abuse, domestic violence, teen pregnancy, and gang membership (Watson, 1989). The anger of minorities may stem from the attempts of the majority culture to impose its own values and behaviors on the minority culture. The majority culture may perceive the values and beliefs of the minority culture as negative and inferior. For the Latino adolescent, aggressive behavior may be seen as an acceptable outlet for channeling the underlying anger that exists both toward the mainstream society for being rejecting as well as toward his family for being different. Along these lines, the development of assertive behavior increases his repertory of communication skills and may therefore provide a more effective means for interacting with the majority culture.

Clinical Considerations in Working with Latina Adolescents

Although the literature suggests that assertive behaviors may clash with Latino culturally prescribed behaviors, there is limited research in this area (Comas-Diaz & Duncan, 1985; Soto, 1979). A major shortcoming in the assertiveness research with culturally and racially diverse groups has been that it does not consistently describe the specific characteristics of the groups being studied, and the instruments used have not been developed or standardized for these groups (Wood & Mal-

linckrody, 1990; Grodner, 1977). Given the fact that there is so little research in this area, an assessment scale is in the process of being
developed to study assertive behavior with New York City–born Puerto
Rican female adolescents (Planells-Bloom, in press). As a preliminary
to the development of this scale, discussion groups were formed as part
of a pilot study to identify issues that emerge within the context of situations that elicit assertive behavior. The participants in these groups
were first- and second-generation Puerto Rican female adolescents who
were born and raised in the New York City Metropolitan area. The participants came from varied socioeconomic backgrounds, and many of
them are of lower socioeconomic status or working class.

Several themes surfaced in group discussions with the participants
in this pilot study. Many of these themes, which are discussed herein,
represent typical adolescent concerns on the one hand and issues related to their biculturality on the other hand. Contrary to what the traditional literature would predict, several participants described that
they could openly communicate their feelings and thoughts to friends,
boyfriends, siblings, and to a somewhat lesser extent parents. These observations are in line with recent research that has identified a shift in
sex role behaviors with Latinas (Vazquez-Nuttall et al., 1987). This is
an important point because, at times, stereotypes mask unique and
valuable information about an individual or a group.

Negotiation of Parental Relationship

Some of the girls did experience difficulties asserting themselves with
their parents, particularly their mother. Along these lines, the assertiveness literature describes that women who come for assertiveness
training frequently complain about problems with parents, especially
mothers (Fodor & Wolfe, 1977). Several girls described that in comparison with American parents, their parents tended to be stricter in certain areas (e.g., staying over friend's house and dating). These
differences have been documented in the literature on Latino families
and may be viewed as the family's attempts to maintain control in the
face of their daughter's increased independent strivings. This point
also illustrates the cultural clash between the parents who uphold the
values of family cohesiveness and the adolescent who demands increased peer contact (Inclan & Herron, 1989). Many of the participants
thought that in general, their parents were also more protective of
them because they were girls. In contrast their brothers were given
greater freedom and independence. Several interesting points were
made. For example, one participant described how differently her
mother treats her brother because she lets him go out whenever he

wants without asking questions, yet whenever she wants to go out, her mother asks her numerous questions. Another participant described how upset she gets because her parents do not allow her to go any- where. Even when she cries and yells about this, she thinks that her parents do not care. As a result, she locks herself in her room and does not talk to them. Another participant described her mother as very strict about boys and dating, and "doesn't want to hear anything about it." So when she was asked on a date, she thought that she could not talk to her mom about this.

Negotiation of Peer Relationships

Another theme that surfaced involved problems with being assertive in peer relationships. A particular concern that emerged across both male and female relationships was hurting the other person's feelings, and how this made it difficult to express one's own feelings and opinions.

The participants described a wide range of problematic situations with their female peers. These situations included expressing differ- ences of opinions, dealing with criticism, and expressing disapproval. For example, one participant described how one of her girlfriends is al- ways giving an opinion about her (the participant's) relationship with her boyfriend. The participant explained that although she appreciated her friend's concern she was having a difficult time letting her friend know that she felt, at times, that she was imposing her opinion.

The problematic situations that participants described with their boyfriends often included negotiating differences in feelings about each other and dealing with sex-related concerns in the relationship. For ex- ample, one participant described that because she felt unable to tell her boyfriend that she did not want to go out with him, she started to treat him differently so that he would reject her first.

Culture-Related Themes

Another theme that surfaced, although to a lesser extent, was cultural differences in relationships. The participants described how their friends or parents disapproved of their relationship with someone from a different cultural background. In some cases, their disapproval placed additional pressure on the relationship and raised issues of loy- alty. This type of conflict may also result in questions about identity de- velopment because the adolescent is faced with developing her identity in two cultural worlds, which at times are in conflict with each other. Feelings of isolation and a sense of discontinuity within the family may surface as a result of this conflict. For example, one participant de- scribed that her friends did not approve of her dating a "white" guy. She described how much her friends' disapproval bothered her even though she did not agree with them. Their comments left her feeling confused and misunderstood.

Factors Impacting on Development of Assertive Behavior

In discussing with these girls why some of them found it easier to assert themselves, whereas others did not, several issues were raised.

Generational Status

Some girls believed that their capacity to be assertive had to do with generational status, that is, first-generation parents are more traditional than second-generation parents, although this explanation does not consistently hold true. In other words, girls from a first-generation family are less likely to assert their needs and ideas as compared with girls from a second-generation family. Another aspect of this issue is that the presence of extended family (e.g., grandparents) in the home resulted in the parents holding onto more traditional values. It is possible that if their parents are unable to assert themselves and separate from their own parents, they do not facilitate the development of assertive behavior in their daughters.

Education

Education was identified as playing an important role because it represents a way of getting ahead and having more choices in life. The assertiveness literature does predict that increased exposure to American values and increased levels of education are related to a higher degree of assertiveness (Soto, 1979).

Birth Order

A few girls described that as a result of being the oldest sibling in the family, their parents were stricter and less tolerant of cultural differences. In contrast, their younger siblings were frequently given more freedom and independence, and greater tolerance to assert their needs. Parents may be more invested in their older children carrying the bastion of the culture.

Gender-Related Differences

Many of the participants also thought that, in general, their parents encourage boys to be more assertive than girls. According to cross-cultural research (Block, 1973; Miller, 1976), there is a prevailing cultural disapproval of female adolescents expressing themselves in an honest and direct way.

CONCLUSION

In working with the Latina adolescent, it is crucial to assess each individual and her circumstances. In cases in which the adolescent describes her family as traditional, it is particularly necessary to understand whether she experiences conflict between her role within the family and her role outside of the family. Several factors appear to facilitate or interfere with the development of assertive behavior. Therefore, it is important to understand the impact and interaction of cultural issues, gender-related issues, socioeconomic factors, and parent–adolescent dynamics.

The following is a summary of the special considerations to remember when working with Latina adolescents to ensure a better understanding of her cultural background and its impact on her development:

1. Be careful not to make generalizations and cultural stereotypes because they contribute to overlooking individual needs. Instead, use information about cultural groups as an orientation and guide.
2. Be sensitive to cultural differences across the various Latin American countries.
3. Ask group members to question the significance of stereotypes, thus helping them understand how these stereotypes impact on their lives.
4. Do not impose your own views or make judgments about cultural values and attitudes that are different from your own.
5. Show respect for the client's cultural values and choices.

REFERENCES

Amaro, H., & Russo, N. F. (1987). Hispanic women and mental health. *Psychology of Women Quarterly, 11,* 393–407.

Block, J. H. (1973). Conceptions of sex roles: Some cross-cultural and longitudinal perspectives. *American Psychologist, 28,* 512–526.

Cafferty, S. J., & McCready, W. C. (Eds.), (1985). *Hispanics in the United States.* New Brunswick: Transaction Books.

Canino, I. A., Earley, B. F., & Rogler, L. H. (1980). *The Puerto Rican child in*

New York City: Stress and mental health (Monograph No. 3). Fordham University, Hispanic Research Center. Maplewood, NJ: Waterfront Press.

Cardoza, D. (1991). College attendance and persistence among Hispanic women: An examination of some contributing factors. *Sex Roles, 24,* 133–147.

Comas-Diaz, L., & Duncan, J. W. (1985). The cultural context: A factor in assertiveness training with mainland Puerto Rican women. *Psychology of Women Quarterly, 9,* 463–476.

Cromwell, R., & Ruiz, R. A. (1979). The myth of macho dominance in decision-making with Mexican and Chicano families. *Hispanic Journal of Behavioral Science, 1,* 355–373.

Danzinger, K. (1976). *Interpersonal communication.* New York: Pergamon.

Darabi, K. F., Dryfoos, J., & Schwartz, D. (1986). Hispanic adolescent fertility. *Hispanic Journal of Behavioral Sciences, 8,* 157–171.

Falicov, C. J. (1982). Mexican families. In M. McGoldrick, J. K. Pearce, & J. Giordano (Eds.), *Ethnicity and family therapy.* New York: Guilford.

Fodor, I., & Wolfe, J. L. (1977). Assertiveness training for mothers and daughters. In R. E. Alberti (Ed.), *Assertiveness: Innovations, applications, issues.* San Luis Obispo, CA: Impact.

Garcia-Preto, N. (1982). Puerto Rican families. In M. McGoldrick, J. K. Pearce, & J. Giordano (Eds.), *Ethnicity and family therapy.* New York: Guilford.

Gibson, R. W. (1977). Evaluation and quality control of mental health services. In E. R. Padilla & A. M. Padilla (Eds.), *Transcultural psychiatry: A Hispanic perspective* (Monograph No. 4, pp. 13–20). Los Angeles: University of California at Los Angeles, Spanish Speaking Mental Health Research Center.

Gibson, G. (1983). Hispanic women: Stress and mental health issues. In J. H. Robbins & R. J. Siegel (Eds.), *Women changing therapy: New assessments, values and strategies in feminist therapy.* New York: Hayworth.

Grodner, B. (1977). Assertiveness and anxiety: A cross-cultural and SES perspective. In R. Alberti (Ed.), *Assertiveness: Innovation, application, issues.* San Luis Obispo, CA: Impact.

Hall, J. R., & Beil-Warner, D. (1978). Assertiveness of male Anglo- and Mexican-American college students. *Journal of Social Psychology, 105,* 175–178.

Hardy-Fanta, C., & Montana, P. (1982). The Hispanic female adolescent: A group therapy model. *International Journal of Group Psychotherapy, 32,* 351–366.

Ho, M. K. (Ed.). (1987). Family therapy with Hispanic Americans. *Family therapy with ethnic minorities.* Beverly Hills: Sage.

Inclan, J. E., & Herron, D. G. (1989). Puerto Rican adolescents. In J. T. Gibbs, L. N. Huang, & Associates, *Children of color.* San Francisco: Jossey-Bass.

Leslie, L. A., & Leitch, M. L. (1989). A demographic profile of recent Central American immigrants: Clinical and service implications. *Hispanic Journal of Behavioral Science, 11,* 315–329.

Lloyd, M. A. (1985). *Adolescence.* New York: Harper & Row.

McGoldrick, M., Pearce, J. K., & Giordano, J. (Eds.). (1982). *Ethnicity and family therapy.* New York: Guilford.

Miller, J. B. (1976). *Towards a new psychology of women.* Boston: Beacon.

O'Donnell, W. J. (1979). Adolescent self-reported and peer-reported self-esteem. *Adolescence, 14,* 465–470.

Rosenberg, M. (1979). *Conceiving the self.* New York: Basic Books.

Salgado de Snyder, V. N., Cervantes, R. C., & Padilla, A. M. (1990). Gender and ethnic differences in psychosocial stress and generalized distress among Hispanics. *Sex Roles, 22,* 441–453.

Soto, E. (1979). *Sex-role traditionalism, assertiveness and symptoms in first- and second-generation women living in the U.S.* Unpublished doctoral dissertation, New York University.

U.S. Bureau of the Census. (1985). *Persons of Spanish origin in the United States: March, 1985* (Advanced Report) (Current Populations Reports, series P–20, No. 403). Washington, DC: U.S. Government Printing Office (cited in Amaro, Russo, & Johnson, 1987).

Vazquez-Nuttall, E., Romero-Garcia, I., & DeLeon, B. (1987). Sex roles and perceptions of femininity and masculinity of Hispanic women. *Psychology of Women Quarterly, 11,* 409–425.

Warson, V. M. (1989, November). Minorities and the legacy of anger. *APA Monitor, 20*(11), 30.

Wood, P. S., & Mallinckrody, B. (1990). Culturally sensitive assertiveness training for ethnic minority clients. *Professional Psychology: Research and Practice, 21,* 5–11.

Zavaleta, A. (1981). Variations in Hispanic health status. *Research Bulletin Hispanic Research Center, Fordham University, 4,* 1–6.

Zayas, L. N., & Bryant, C. (1984). Culturally sensitive treatment of adolescent Puerto Rican girls and their families. *Child and Adolescent Social Work Journal, 1,* 235–253.

Part III

Assessment and Training for Special Populations

Introduction

Iris G. Fodor

Longitudinal research suggests that children and adolescents with poor social skills are at high risk for serious emotional disturbance as adults. For too many adolescents, the lack of interactive skills contribute to unhappiness during the teen years and psychopathology (Dodge & Murphy, 1984; Ford, 1982). Adolescents who withdraw may become overly anxious, and inhibited about interacting, and be labeled as "shy" (Michelson, Sugai, Wood, & Kazdan, 1983). Others who withdraw may retreat into depression, and feel helpless and berate themselves (Hops, Lewinsohn, Andrews, & Roberts, 1990). Still others develop aggressive patterns that become entrenched, and they may be labeled as delinquent, aggressive, or acting out (Feindler & Ecton, 1986).

Adolescents who are different may also have special problems with social interactive skills (e.g., the physically handicapped or learning disabled). Because adolescence is a particularly difficult time for most people, not having the skills to turn toward peer culture for support and friendship makes adolescence even more stressful (Seltzer, 1989).

The chapters in Part III address assessment and programs designed for special populations. Laura Parsons begins with a chapter on depressed adolescents, highlighting social competency deficits as crucial. Next, Dianne Ollech follows with an overview of the social skills and assertiveness literature for aggressive adolescents. Ollech highlights the role of cognitions in the evaluations, maintenance, and escalation of adolescent aggressive responding. In this chapter she reviews the representative skills training and anger control treatment programs. Carol Lampert Barrish's, chapter reviews assessment issues for the adolescent who is learning disabled. Her chapter highlights the social cognitive deficits which hinder social skills development. She also describes the development of an assessment for this population. In the last chapter in the section, Yarris describes an assessment project for physically disabled adolescents, drawing on his experience in working with adolescents in wheelchairs.

REFERENCES

Ford, M. E (1982). Social cognition and social competence in adolescence. *Developmental Psychology, 18,* 322–341.

Hops, H., Lewinsohn, P., Andrews, J., & Roberts, R. (1990). Psychosocial correlations of depressive symptomatology among high school students. *Journal of Clinical Child Psychology, 19,* 211–220.

Feindler, E. L., & Ecton, R. B. (1986). *Adolescent anger control: Cognitive behavioral techniques.* New York: Springer.

Michelson, L., Sugai, D. P., Wood, R., & Kazdin, A. E. (1983). *Social skills assessment and training with children: An empirically based handbook.* New York: Plenum.

Seltzer, V. C. (1989). *The psychological worlds of the adolescent: Public and private.* New York: Wiley.

8

Social Skills Deficits and Depression in Adolescents

Laura Parsons

Jane is a black high school senior. She has no girlfriends and has never dated. Although she has maintained good academic standing Jane is involved in no extracurricular activities at school. Besides her studies and occasional television viewing Jane's only other interest is sleep. She experiences no difficulty falling asleep within a few hours after waking from a 14-hour sleep. She is lethargic and has a low energy level; she sometimes moves as if she is in slow motion.

Bob is a white ninth grader whose behavior has changed dramatically in the past few months. He is irritable, agitated, and cannot sleep for more than a few hours. He has withdrawn from all athletic activities, he has not done his homework for the past few weeks, and he cannot seem to concentrate. His teachers have noted that he has alienated most of his classmates because of his increasing inappropriate behavior in social interchanges.

Mary, a Hispanic high school sophomore, is viewed by her peers as only able to talk about herself and her problems. They find her difficult to be around because she is so self-absorbed and "depressed," and they are beginning to make excuses to leave when she enters the group. She sometimes talks about wanting to kill herself, but her peers believe she only is saying this to get attention.

These three profiles highlight what is now considered to be a factor common in adolescent depression: social incompetence and withdrawal. Many experts in adolescent depression believe that the developmental tasks of adolescence, because they require mastery of new social competencies, make this a particularly vulnerable time for the development of behavioral maladaptations, especially depression, and we do indeed see a dramatic rise in prevalence in this age group. Although the question remains as to whether the lack of social skills causes depression or depression results in social skills deficits there is no question that there is an interrelationship between social dysfunction and depression: social withdrawal and incompetence are hallmarks of depression. It has also been established that adolescents who have pathological symptomatology are at much higher risk for similar adult disturbance. Moreover, poor peer relationships in childhood an adolescence are a powerful predictor of later psychopathology (Harrington, Fudge, Rutter, Pickles, & Hill, 1990).

ADOLESCENT DEPRESSION

Depression in adolescents is increasingly being recognized as a significant mental health problem (Klerman, 1988; Rutter, 1988). Although prevalence figures show significant variance depending on the population studied and the diagnostic criteria employed in clinical samples the incidence has been established at more than 33%. In nonclinical populations a prevalence rate of 12% has been documented (Reynolds, 1990). Probably less than 10% of adolescents could be formally diagnosed with a major depressive disorder, however, because the prevalence of the disorder is dependent on the rigor with which the definition is applied (Kaplan, Hong, & Weinhold, 1984).

Criteria for diagnosis of a major depressive disorder according to DSM-III-R include feelings of dysphoria of at least 2 weeks with accompanying feelings of worthlessness, marked restlessness or lethargy, changes in appetite, diminished ability to concentrate, loss of interest in daily activities, sleep difficulties, loss of energy, and suicidal tendencies or repeated thought of death (see Table 8.1). A dysthymic disorder is less severe than a major depressive disorder, but has a significantly longer duration as the depressive or irritable mood manifests itself over a period of at least 1 year. Other reported accompanying symptomatology can include excessive guilt; bodily preoccupations; a sense of futility or hopelessness; diminished school performance; social withdrawal; low self-esteem; lack of self-confidence; social abandonment; acting out; depressive appearance; negative self-evaluation; lack of specific concern; indecision; self-reproach; demanding, manipulative behavior; hostility; anxiety; and separation anxiety (Reynolds, 1990). Hops, Lewinsohn, Andrews, and Roberts (1990) found depressive symptomatology in adolescents to be significantly correlated with anxiety, suicidal ideation, irrational beliefs, negative attributional style, nega-

TABLE 8.1   Symptomatology of Major Depressive Disorder

DSM-III-R criteria	Behavioral manifestations
Dysphoria[a]	Tearfulness, crying
Anhedonia[a]	Loss of interest in pleasurble activities Social withdrawal or abandonment
Sleep disturbances	Insomnia, hypersomnia
Diminished ability to concentrate and think	Indecisiveness Poor school performance Irrational beliefs, negative cognitions Negative attributional style Preoccupation with inner thoughts
Eating disturbances	Changes in appetite and weight, anorexia, bulemia
Loss of energy	Fatigue, change in appearance
Psychomotor retardation and Agitation	Slowed latency in responses or speech Excessive anger, hostility, irritability Difficulty with impulse control Acting-out behaviors
Suicidal ideation or Attempt	Hopelessness
Feelings of self-reproach worthlessness, and inappropriate or excessive guilt	Bodily preoccupations Low self-esteem Poor self-evaluation and self-monitoring Anxiety, separation anxiety

[a]One of these mood states must be present in combination with four other symptoms.

tive cognitions, and diminished ability to self-evaluate and monitor their own behavior. Most researchers agree that the preoccupation with self that accompanies depression and these concomitant behavioral manifestations of symptomatology result in diminished social competence for the adolescent.

Distinguishing between normal and abnormal mood states is a critical issue in the diagnosis of depression. Misery and depression in adolescents are especially difficult to differentiate as the meaning and context of the presenting symptoms are not always self-evident. The critical diagnostic differential should be that although a dysphoric mood is a necessary condition of a major depressive or dysthymic disorder it is not a sufficient condition for diagnosis (Rutter, 1988). Diagnostic issues have also been complicated by the use of self-report questionnaires to measure prevalence rates, and to document the existence and frequency of depressive symptoms in this age group. Unfortunately, this is the most widely used methodological tool to establish prevalence rates and diagnose adolescent depression. Because it has not been established that these tools can adequately distinguish between normal and abnormal mood states nor that they are able to ascertain with certainty that other reported symptomatology is associated with the depressed mood, the results obtained from these measures cannot be considered reliable. Although self-report scales can be a valuable screening device, the structured clinical interview is required to make a diagnosis (Reynolds, 1990). The mounting evidence of the prevalence of depressive mood in adolescents, based on these self-report scales, should nevertheless, alert mental health professionals to the gravity of the problem in this age group.

Gender Differences

There are significant gender differences in manifestation of symptomatology and prevalence rates. Female adolescents mirror their adult counterparts: Depression is more frequent in females, and this sex ratio change is thought to occur at puberty. The typical pattern of the externalizing–internalizing dichotomy between males and females has been documented in adolescents. Kurdek (1987) evaluated gender differences in the psychological symptomatology of 198 seventh and ninth graders and found that females were more likely to develop overcontrolled, internalizing disorders, whereas boys developed undercontrolled, externalizing disorders. This is consistent with the conclusion by Gjerde, Block, and Block (1988) that depression in young boys is often embedded in externalizing, conduct disturbances, whereas in young girls there is an internalizing and passivity. Baron and Joly (1988) in their study of 249 adolescents, ages 12 to 17, found that depressed adolescent females displayed symptomatology related to body image distortion, loss of appetite, weight loss, and change in mood and satisfaction while males were characterized by irritability, work inhibition, social withdrawal, and sleep disturbance. As the female adolescent responds to the demands of the environment by employing socially conditioned responses of overcontrol she typically manifests more passive, internalized symptomatology like eating disorders, social withdrawal, concern with self-adequacy and body image, and self-loathing. Male adolescents, conversely, tend to externalize their anxiety so conduct disorders, lack of anger and impulse control, aggression, and acting-out behaviors are more prevalent.

Ethnic and Class Differences

There is a paucity of information about the impact of ethnicity and social class on the interrelationship of adolescent depression and social skills. The literature on prevalence rates does not distinguish ethnicity or social class, nor are these distinctions factored into analyses of diagnostic issues. (Reference should be made to the chapter on ethnicity and social skills for comprehensive coverage.) Two articles were located that examined this topic. Gibbs (1985) used a self-report measure to examine psychosocial factors associated with adolescent female depression in a small sample of urban female adolescents. Depression was found to be significantly related to parental occupation, geographical mobility, and the number of self-reported problems in 11 areas of adolescent psychosocial functioning. Hardy-Fanta and Montana (1982) in a qualitative analysis of the powerful cultural expectations placed on first-generation Hispanic female adolescents concluded that depressed withdrawal or excessive conformity was the result placing these youngsters at high risk for depression. Although there is not yet an empirical base to account for ethnic and class impact on depression and social skills to guide diagnosis and treatment, the clinician should be sensitive to these factors.

INTERRELATIONSHIP BETWEEN SOCIAL SKILLS AND DEPRESSION

Theoretical Models of Social Skills Deficits in Depression

The impact of depression on the development and maintenance of social skills deficits has been conceptualized within four theoretical models that explain depression within the context of inadequate social functioning: (a) learned helplessness; (b) cognitive; (c) social learning; and (d) self-regulation theory. All of these models are based, in part, on the psychosocial interactions of the individual. Although these theoretical constructs are not mutually exclusive they are not yet fully integrated in the literature. Nevertheless, all of them address the impact of depression on the social competence of the individual by examining the interrelationship of depression and social skills. Developmental psychopathologists also provide an explanatory model of adolescent depression while drawing on some of these theories, broadening the conceptual base by incorporating the critical developmental challenges required of adolescents.

Learned helplessness explains depression in terms of motivational, cognitive, affective-somatic, and self-esteem deficits. Depressed individuals, as a result of these deficits, are thought to be impeded from learning adaptive coping responses to the challenges of the environment. An attributional style that believes failure to be the result of internal causes and success to be the result of external factors leads to feelings of helplessness and hopelessness. The extension of this perception of powerlessness to social situations potentially can effect the development and/or maintenance of social skills as the individual has a very low expectation for future success and also exhibits a very strong, negative affect (Oster & Caro, 1990; Seligman & Peterson, 1986).

Cognitive theory explains depression as the result of the interrelationship of the individual's negative view of self, their environment, and the future. These negative cognitions cause distorted thinking, and maladaptive behaviors result from the individual's inability to plan and implement more adaptive coping mechanisms. This model may be especially relevant to an understanding of adolescent depression because of the adolescent's propensity to think in all-or-nothing terms coupled with the thought–feeling connection teenagers experience as they confront the possibility of failure (e.g., exams, dating, friendship) (Oster & Caro, 1990). As in the learned helplessness model the cognitive model explains the social skills deficits in depressed adolescents based on the individual's inability to plan and implement adaptive behavior as the result of negative expectations.

Rehm's model of self-control (1981) postulates that every behavioral process as well as physiological and somatic–pathological factors that can influence the frequency of an operant performance act together in depression in a variety of combinations and emphases. This model emphasizes the maladaptive or inadequate self-regulatory resources the individual possesses to deal with stress. Behavior is the result of the individual's poor self-monitoring, self-evaluating, and self-reinforcing causing him or her to dwell on the negative aspects of his or her environment. As a result, behavioral expectations are too rigid and unrealistic, and short-term gratification replaces long-term success. Attributions, as in learned helplessness, tend to be external when success is realized and internal when failure results (Matson, 1989). Social skills deficits in depressed adolescents could be explained in this model in much the same way the preceding theoretical constructs apply as this model incorporates some aspects of both learned helplessness and cognitive theory.

Social learning theory assumes that psychological functioning is best understood in terms of continuous reciprocal interactions among cognitive processes and expectancies, and behavioral and environmental factors, all acting as independent determinants of one another. This model accounts for depression by assuming that maladaptive behavior occurs within a psychosocial and interpersonal context, and that the individual experiences a low rate of response-contingent positive reinforcement in his social interactions as a result of depressive behaviors like fatigue and lack of interest. Depression, therefore, results from a lack of socially relevant skills capable of obtaining reinforcement from the environment, and these social skills deficits lead to depression (Lewinsohn, Clarke, Hops, & Andrews, 1990).

Developmental psychopathologists explain depression in terms of the interaction of experience, stress, and age-related biological and psychological factors. Experts in this field are suggesting that adolescent depression may be the result of hormonal changes in adolescence, genetic factors that begin to be expressed at this age, the alteration in frequency of environmental stressors, developmental variations in vulnerability or protective factors, the possible role of learned helplessness, and developmental changes in attributional capabilities or concepts of emotions coupled with the adolescent developmental tasks of differentiation of self, establishment of self-esteem, and acquisition of social competence. Cicchetti and Schneider-Rosen (1984) speculate that because early social competence plays a role in the realization of later social competence the impact of a depressive episode on social competence is that the individual learns inappropriate or maladaptive interpersonal behaviors that result in social incompetence.

Social Skills Deficits in Depressed Adolescents

The nature of interpersonal relationships go through significant changes in adolescence. It is critical, therefore, for the adolescent to master these new social competencies to acquire the adaptive social skills necessary for the development of social competence and success. Inability or failure to adapt behavior to these changing social requirements has serious implications for the adolescent's mental health and well-being. Although there are sparse empirical data specifying what constitutes social competence in adolescence, and there is no generally accepted definition of social competence, there is agreement the effective peer relations and social interactions are its hallmarks and that it is acquired by exposure to skilled models (Connolly, 1989).

Although evidence is accumulating about the dysfunctional social aspects of adolescent depression (Rutter, 1988) empirical data specifically documenting social incompetence in depressed adolescents are sparse. It is well established, however, that peer status is stable over time, particularly for rejected children, and those who experience troubled peer relationships are at significantly greater risk for developing psychopathology (Peterson, 1986). The reasons for poor acceptance by peers are not well understood, although there is some evidence that deficits in social skills are responsible.

Unpopular children behave inappropriately and lack knowledge about what is appropriate in various social situations (Renshaw & Asher, 1982). The ability to engage in conversation with peers is a good example of a social behavior that encompasses diverse social skills. Frequently adolescents with poor peer relationships are deficient in the skills required for conversation. For example, one must exhibit nonverbal interest in the other person both to engage and maintain the dialogue. Knowing what to talk about, how much to talk, and how turn taking should flow are another subset of skills. Additionally, each partner in the conversation needs to be able to modulate tone of voice, know how to elicit their partner's viewpoint and be able to state their own opinion in ways that facilitate the conversation. When the socially proficient adolescent engages in conversation it appears as if it is effortless. For the adolescent with social skills deficits in this area, however, any one or a combination of these necessary skills can be missing or deficient, thereby resulting in an inability to engage and maintain peers in conversation appropriately. As the clinician considers adolescents who are having peer difficulty it is likely skill deficits in this area are present.

Depression is associated with poor social adjustment, and as stated earlier, social maladjustment is considered by many experts on depression to be a necessary condition for diagnosis of the disorder. Because social withdrawal, lethargy, psychomotor retardation, irritability, and loss of interest in pleasurable activities are hallmarks of a depressive disorder any one or combination of these symptoms would necessarily result in decreased peer interaction as the depressive symptoms would inhibit the initiation or maintenance of social interactions. Social interactions are central sources of positive reinforcement for human beings and because these interactions are reduced or nonexistent in depressed persons positive reinforcement is absent or significantly reduced (Kazdin, 1988). Depressed individuals not only experience difficulty in developing new social relationships, but their behavior potentially drives people away (Becker, Heimberg, & Bellack, 1987). An inverse relationship has been established between depression and peer involvement.

In the profiles of the depressed adolescents used at the beginning of the chapter peer relations are clearly problematic for each of them. Not only are all three unable to engage in conversations with peers effectively, but they exhibit many other self-defeating social skills deficits in interpersonal relationships. The social withdrawal and socially inappropriate behavior Jane, Mary, and Bob engage in cause them to have fewer and fewer positive peer interactions. This results in a continuing decrease in the opportunity to view skilled role models as well as few opportunities to gain positive reinforcement form peer interaction. This cycle, if not interrupted, can continue on its downward spiral until they are socially isolated and have no reason to try to engage in social relationships.

EMPIRICAL DATA ON SOCIAL SKILLS DEFICITS IN DEPRESSED ADOLESCENTS

Much of the literature about social skills deficits in adolescents experiencing behavioral maladaptation is correlative, based on self-report instruments or must be extrapolated from data obtained with children or adults. (For a fuller description of the problem see Koegel's chapter on assessment). Despite assessment difficulties studies of both depressed children and adults confirm the relationship between depression and social skills deficits. In the adult population, for example, Paykel and Weissman (1973) found that the social skills deficits apparent in depression remained after the depressive episode ended, although they were not as severe. Puig-Antich et al. (1985) established that deficiencies in social skills were hallmarks of the depressed children they studied, and improvement was only quantitative when the depression lifted.

In the few studies available of adolescent populations social skills deficit were correlated with depression. Wierzbicki and McCabe (1988) found that those children, ages 8 to 14, with a higher level of social skills such as skillful timing of social responses, activity level, interpersonal range, and rate of positive reactions reported lower levels of depressive symptoms. Garber, Kriss, Koch, and Lindholm (1988) in their longitudinal study of 20 adolescent psychiatric inpatients followed 8 years after hospitalization established that those diagnosed with a depressive disorder had significantly worse adjustment in areas of social and leisure activities and family relationships. John, Gammon, Prusoff, and Warner (1987) developed a social adjustment inventory for children and adolescents to assess both social competence and problem social behaviors. Psychiatric diagnosis reliably distinguished patterns of social functioning, and children with a diagnosis of dysthymic disorder displayed the poorest functioning in all areas. Fauber, Forehand, Long, and Burke (1987) found social competence and self-reported depression to be negatively correlated. It is also worth noting that many of the researchers pointedly comment that it is not clear whether the social incompetence they have found to be correlated with depression is the cause or the result of the depressive episode. Although most explanations of depression based on social competency assume a skill deficit, there is some evidence that it may be a lack of motivation rather than a lack of skill (Matson, 1989).

Specific social skills deficits were identified in adolescent psychiatric populations by Trower, Bryant, Argyle, and Marziller (1978) and Connolly (1989). Trower et al. (1978) evaluated 18-and 19-year-olds in a 14-bed psychiatric hospital for social adequacy and found that these subjects displayed too little use of prosocial behaviors. The variety of their facial expressions and body posture was minimal, and they made very little eye contact. The two behaviors that were found to be exaggerated were interest in themselves and talk about their feelings. Connolly compared two samples of high school students with a psychiatric inpatient adolescent group to develop a scale to measure self-efficacy for social action. The author speculated that part of the difficulty of the disturbed group originated with their lack of a clear notion of themselves as socially effective as they reported lower self-efficacy for successful behavior in interpersonal situations than did their peers.

The other empirical evidence for social skills deficits in depressed adolescents is based on social skills training programs for varied populations and their reported efficacy in obtaining improvement in social behaviors as well as depressive symptomatology. Rehm and Kornblith (1979), in their review of more than 50 studies of behavioral intervention with depressed individuals, note that the designs of these studies rule out the possibility of evaluating the contribution of social skills training to the changes in levels of depression. Although there is minimal documentation of specific social skills deficits in these studies, there is some evidence that social skills training in these different populations results in better social performance as well as being an effective treatment for the depressive episode (Bellack, Hersen, & Himmelhoch, 1983; Hersen & Van Hasselt, 1987).

Most of the identified interventions with depressed adolescents that address social skills deficits are based on very small sample sizes. Schloss, Schloss, and Harris (1984) demonstrated the effectiveness of a social skills training program that included modeling, behavior rehearsal, feedback, and contingent reinforcement in increasing appropriate interpersonal behaviors with three hospitalized male adolescents diagnosed with schizoaffective disorders. In 1989. Hansen, St. Lawrence, and Christoff reported on their training in conversational skills with inpatient children and adolescents who demonstrated deficiencies in this area. In 1987, Plienis et al. provided social skills training to three adolescents, one of whom was depressed, and found treatment resulted in more effective performance during unstructured practice conversations and during role plays of social problems as well as improved ratings of adjustment by self and teachers.

In a selected review of the literature Fine, Gilbert, Schmidt, Haley, Maxwell, and Forth (1989) identified only one group-treatment program, established by Lewinsohn et al. (1990), for depressed adolescents that included social skills and assertiveness training within a cognitive–behavorial model. These researchers found that there was significant improvement of depression in those adolescents treated with their Adolescent Coping with Depression Course. This is a psychoeducational intervention consisting of 14 2-hours sessions. Adolescents were taught to control their depressed mood by relaxing, increasing pleasant events, controlling negative thought, and increasing social skills. The course also teaches communication, negotiation, and conflict–resolution skills. There is a simultaneous course for parents to provide them with an understanding of the treatment for their adolescent as well as to teach them similar communication skills. Results of this intervention based on two studies involving 73 adolescents demonstrate significant improvement in depressive mood and behaviors whether or not parents were part of the intervention.

ASSESSMENT

The current limitations of our knowledge about adolescent depression and social competency combined with the wide variety of assessment tools now available may be somewhat bewildering to the practitioner in search of reliable, valid measures to use as diagnostic aids. Both Kazdin (1988) and Reynolds (1990) provide a good review of diagnostic instruments. The diagnosis of depression is optimally made on the basis of a clinical interview like the Schedule for Affective Disorders and Schizophrenia for School-Aged Children, Epidemiological Version (K-SADS-E; Orvaschel & Puig-Antich, 1986). This allows the clinician to distinguish between a depressive disorder and a depressed mood as well as to ascertain that DSM-III-R criteria are met. Self-report scales can be helpful in confirming the adolescent's perspective, but they should be used only in conjunction with the interview and behavioral observation.

The adolescent's social competency should be assessed through a combination of observed behavior in real-life social interactions, social skills assessment instruments, and through the format of role play (see Koegel's chapter for specific assessment instruments). The clinician should bear in mind that the more precise the description of the adolescent's specific social competencies as well as deficits the more effective and targeted the intervention can be.

INTERVENTION

As previously noted, the most comprehensive treatment model currently available is the The Adolescent Coping with Depression Course (Clarke & Lewinsohn, 1984). One of its advantages is that it is designed to be used with a group so that the development and practice of social skills are ecologically valid. Additionally, it is cost-effective and uses the clinician's time efficiently. During the course the adolescent is taught the interrelationship of feelings, behavior, and thinking, and is expected to practice self-assessment of all three. The adolescent is also expected to determine short- and long-range goals, and to work on accomplishing them. There are homework assignments to practice what is learned during the training sessions. Each session also allows the clinician to evaluate what the adolescent has learned not only through behavioral observation of directed exercises but also by short quizes that require mastery of the content of the session. The themes of the sessions include Depression and Social Learning, Starting a Conversation, Reducing Tension, How to Set Good Goals and to Implement a Plan for Change, Making the Pleasant Activity Plan Work, the Power of Positive Thinking, Disputing Irrational Thinking, Relaxation, How to be an Active Listener, How to Effectively Express One's Feelings, and Negotiation and Problem Solving. This course has the potential to adapt easily to the model of assessment-intervention-assessment so that the clinician can match the course to the pace of skill acquisition.

We can use our opening case illustrations to show how the clinician who works in the schools would intervene using this psychoeducational intervention. As the reader may recall all three adolescents are exhibiting behaviors indicative of depression as well as social skills deficits. Their social incompetence is not uniform; it stems from deficiencies specific to each. As the clinician proceeds with a diagnostic evaluation the adolescent's belief system as well as social behaviors are observed and evaluated to identify and isolate each adolescent's specific skill deficit accurately.

Jane is friendless and occupies her time outside of school with television viewing and sleep. The clinician has observed in her interview with Jane that she exhibits minimal eye contact and responds to conversational initiatives by staring at her hands and speaking in an inaudible voice. In the cafeteria she isolates herself from peers and displays no nonverbal behaviors that would invite peer interaction.

Mary is alienating peers with her self-absorbed behavior. She manifests different social skills deficits from Jane. In the diagnostic observation and evaluation the clinician notes that Mary begins talking immediately on entering a group and is seemingly unaware of nonverbal messages from peers like turning or looking away, or leaving as she arrives. She tells the clinician in the interview that she initiates all telephone contact with peers outside of school and invites herself to be a part of a social activity. Mary acknowledges to the clinician that peers seem to have a lot of excuses for why they cannot talk to her on the telephone or "hang out" with her.

Bob has experienced a dramatic change in behavior and is alienating his peers because of inappropriate social behavior. The clinician has noted that Bob tries to gain peer's attention with provocative behaviors like teasing or grabbing their belongings. He shows no apparent interest in what they have to say and frequently interrupts. In the interview he cannot sit still, and many of his responses are curt and provocative. He professes a complete disregard for the importance to him of peer relationships.

All three are self-deprecatory, expressing hopelessness about themselves and exhibit a loss of interest in pleasurable activities. Bob's attitude of total indifference contrasts with Jane's belief that she can never find a friend. Mary is only vaguely aware that peers are rejecting her and is totally unaware that her behavior might be causing peer rejection.

Although each of these adolescents clearly manifests depressive symptomatology they have very different social skills deficits. The clinician's skill will be challenged in making sure individual differences in needs are addressed. For example, the first session of this course is devoted to understanding the purpose of the course as well as to help the adolescent understand the connections between feeling, thinking, and behavior, and there is a get-acquainted activity to introduce the group members as well as to use for self-evaluation. The clinician helps each youngster identify what they did well as well as what they need to work on when talking to people based on the activity. The clinician would want Jane to recognize how her lack of eye contact interferes with social interaction, for Mary to identify how turn taking is critical for keeping two people engaged in conversation, and for Bob to use conversational initiatives to attract attention. In the same session the clinician helps the youngsters to understand how to begin to identify and control their depressive cognitions, feelings, and behaviors. They are asked to chart their mood during the week and to practice the social skill they want to improve.

By the fifth session the participants are asked to implement a plan to pursue social activities on a daily basis. In a previous session they have identified activities they find pleasurable that involve others. There is a discussion of how each can meet their own personal goals, allowing for individualizing of the course. They also focus on evaluating their cognitions as positive or negative, and learn to identify activating events that provoke negative thinking. For homework they are to meet their goals for pleasurable activities, and to keep a record of their negative thoughts and the activating events that cause them. By the end of the course the adolescents are being taught more effective problem-solving skills. They not only learn more positive ways to handle difficult situations but practice assertive social skills. Through repeated practice of challenging negative cognitions with positive ones and using social skills that elicit positive responses, all three adolescents would begin to receive more positive reinforcement from their environment, thereby reinforcing their efforts to engage in more pleasurable activities and more positive thinking.

CONCLUSION

Because it is only recently that depression has been acknowledged as a valid diagnostic category in adolescence, and that there is an interrelationship between depression and social competency, there are many issues that have yet to be addressed adequately. Research and diagnostic tools are in the beginning stages of development and do not yet take into account the many social, environmental, developmental, and intrapsychic variables known to be present in the adolescent. Although it is known that there are gender differences in prevalence and manifestation of symptomatology we know very little about why this is so. Ethnic and class differences are also implicated, but almost nothing is known about the relationship of adolescent depression and social skills deficits to these factors. There is a paucity of empirical data on interventions, and current theoretical models used to explain depression are limited in that they are not parsimonious or predictive. For example, although learned helplessness may be correlated with depression, it has not been demonstrated that it is a necessary condition of that disorder nor that it is exclusive to depression. The model of developmental psychopathology accounts for several variables, but the research base does not exist yet to substantiate these hypotheses. However, the adolescent coping with depression course developed by Clarke and Lewinsohn appears promising. Clearly more research is urgently needed so that effective preventions and interventions can be developed.

REFERENCES

Allgood-Merten, B., Lewinsohn, P. M., & Hops, H. (1990). Sex differences and adolescent depression. *Journal of Abnormal Psychology, 99,* 55–63.

American Psychiatric Association. (1987). *Diagnostic and statistical manual of mental disorders (3rd ed., rev.). Washington DC: American Psychiatric Association.*

Baron, P., & Joly, E. (1988). Sex differences in the expression of depression in adolescents. *Sex Roles, 18,* 1–7.

Beck, A. T., Rush, A. J., Shaw, B. F., & Emery, G. (1979). *Cognitive therapy of depression.* New York: Guilford.

Becker, R. E., Heimberg, R. G., & Bellack, A. S. (1987). *Social skills training treatment for depression.* New York: Pergamon.

Bellack, A. S., Hersen, M., & Himmelhoch, J. M. (1983). Social skills training for unipolar depression. *Psychotherapy in Private Practice, 1,* 9–13.

Blumberg, S. R., & Hokanson, J. E. (1983). The effects of another person's response style on interpersonal behavior in depression. *Journal of Abnormal Psychology, 92,* 196–209.

Brion-Meisels, S., & Seligman, R. L. (1984). Early adolescent development of new interpersonal strategies: Understanding and intervention. *School Psychology Review, 13,* 278–291.

Chartier, G. M., & Ranieri, D. J. (1984). Adolescent depression: Concepts, treatments, prevention. *Advances in Child Behavioral Analysis and Therapy, 4,* 153–193.

Cicchetti, D., & Schneider-Rosen, K. (1984). Toward a transactional model of childhood depression. In D. Cicchetti & K. Schneider-Rosen (Eds.), *Childhood depression: New directions for child development* (pp. 5–27). San Francisco: Jossey-Bass.

Clarke, G. N., & Lewinsohn, P. M. (1984). *The coping with depression course adolescent version: A psychoeducational intervention for unipolar depression in high school students.* Eugene: University of Oregon Press.

Connolly, J. (1989). Social self-efficacy in adolescence: Relations with self-concept, social adjustment and mental health. *Canadian Journal of Behavioural Science, 21,* 258–269.

Dodge, K., & Murphy, R. (1984). The assessment of social competence in adolescents. In P. Karoly & J. Steffan (eds.), *Advances in child behavioral analysis and therapy* (Vol. 3, pp 661–696). Lexington, MA: Heath.

Fauber, R., Forehand, R., Long, N., & Burke, M. (1987). The relationship of young adolescent children's depression inventory (CDI) scores to their social and cognitive functioning. *Journal of Psychopathology and Behavioral Assessment, 9,* 161–172.

Fine, S., Gilbert M., Schmidt, L., Haley, G., Maxwell, A., & Forth, A. (1989).

Short-term group therapy with depressed adolescent outpatients. *Canadian Journal of Psychiatry, 34,* 97–102.

Garber, J., Kriss, M. R., Koch, M., & Lindholm, L. (1988). Recurrent depression in adolescents: A follow-up study. *Journal of the American Academy of Child and Adolescent Psychiatry, 27,* 49–54.

Gibbs, J. t. (1985). Psychosocial factors associated with depression in urban adolescent females: Implications for assessment. *Journal of Youth and Adolescence, 14,* 47–60.

Gjerde, P. F., Block, J., & Block, J. H. (1988). Depressive symptoms and personality during late adolescence: Gender differences in the externalization-internalization of symptom expression. *Journal of Abnormal Psychology, 97,* 475–486.

Hansen, D. J., St. Lawrence, J. S., & Christoff, K. A. (1989). Group conversational-skills training with inpatient children and adolescents: Social validation, generalization and maintenance. *Behavior Modification, 13,* 4–31.

Hardy-Fanta, C., & Montana, P. (1982). The Hispanic female adolescent: A group therapy model. *International Journal of Group Psychotherapy, 32,* 351–366.

Harrington, R., Fudge, H., Rutter, M. Pickles, A., & Hill, J. (1990). Adult outcomes of childhood and adolescent depression: I. Psychiatric status. *Archives of General Psychiatry, 47,* 465–473.

Hersen, M., & Van Hasselt, B. B. (1987). *Behavior therapy with children and adolescents: A clinical approach.* New York: Wiley.

Hops, H., Lewinsohn, P. M., Andrews, J. A., & Roberts, R. E. (1990). Psychosocial correlates of depressive symptomatology among high school students. *Journal of Clinical Child Psychology, 19,* 211–220.

John, K., Gammon, G. D., Prusoff, B. A., & Warner, V. (1987). The social adjustment inventory for children and adolescents (SAICA): Testing of a new semistructured interview. *Journal of the American Academy of Child and Adolescent Psychiatry, 26,* 898–911.

Kaplan, S. L., Hong, G. K., & Weinhold, C. (1984). Epidemiology of depressive symptomatology in adolescents. *Journal of the American Academy of Child Psychiatry, 23,* 91–98.

Kazadin, A. E. (1988). Childhood depression. In E. Mash & L. Terdal (Eds.), *Behavioral assessment of childhood disorders* (2nd ed., pp. 157–195. New York: Guilford.

Klerman, G. L. (1988). The current age of youthful melancholia evidence for increase in depression among adolescents and young adults. *British Journal of Psychiatry, 152,* 4–14.

Kurdek, L. A. (1987). Gender differences in the psychological symptomatology and coping strategies of young adolescents. *Journal of Early Adolescence, 7,* 395–410.

Lewinsohn, P. M., Clarke, G. N., & Hoberman, H. M. (1989). the coping with depression course: Review and future directions. *Canadian Journal of Behavioral Science, 21,* 470–489.

Lewinsohn, P. M., Clarke, G. N., Hops, H., & Andrews, J. (1990), Cognitive-behavioral treatment for depressed adolescents. *Behavior Therapy, 21,* 385–401.

Matson, J. L. (1989). *Treating depression in children and adolescents.* New York: Pergamon.

McCartney, J. R. (1987). Adolescent depression: A growth and development perspective. *Adolescent Psychiatry, 14,* 208–217.

McCauley, E., Mitchell, J. R., Burke, P., & Moss, S. (1988). Cognitive attributes of depression in children adolescents. *Journal of Consulting and Clinical Psychology, 56,* 903–908.

Orvaschel, H., & Puig-Antich, J. (1986). *Schedule for affective disorder and schizophrenia for school-aged children. Epidemilogic version: Kiddie-SADS-E (K-SADS-E)* (4th version) (Tech. Rep.). Pittsburgh: Western psychiatric Institute and Clinic.

Oster, G. D., & Caro, J. E. (1990). *Understanding and treating depressed adolescents and their families.* New York: Wiley.

Paykel, E. S., & Weissman, M. M. (1973). Social adjustment and depression: A longitudinal study. *Archives of General Psychiatry, 28,* 659–663.

Peterson, A. C., & Hamburg, B. A. (1986). Adolescence: A developmental approach to problems and psychopathology. *Behavior Therapy, 17,* 480–499.

Plienis, A. J., Hansen, D. J., Ford, F., Smith, S., Stark, L. J., & Kelly, J. A. (1987). Behavioral small group training to improve the social skills of emotionally-disordered adolescents. *Behavior Therapy, 18,* 17–32.

Puig-Antich, J., Lukins, E., Davies, M., Goetz, D., Brennann-Quattrock, J., & Todak, G. (1985). Psychosocial functioning in prepubertal major depressive disorders: II. Interpersonal relationships after sustained recovery from affective episode. *Archives of General Psychiatry, 42,* 511–517.

Rehm L. P. (Ed). (1981). *Behavior therapy for depression: Present status and future directions.* New York: Academic Press.

Rehm, L. P., & Kornblith, S. J. (1979). Behavior therapy for depression: A review of recent developments. *Progress in Behavior Modification, 7,* 277–317.

Reinherz, H. Z., Stewart-Berghauer, G., Pakiz, B., Frost, A. K., Moeykens, B. A., & Holmes, W. M. (1989). The relationship of early risk and current mediators to depressive symptomatology in adolescence. *Journal of the American Academy of Child and Adolescent Psychiatry, 28,* 942–947.

Renshaw, P. D., & Asher, S. R. (1982). Social competence and peer status: The distinction between goals and strategies. In K. H. Rubin & H. S. Ross (Eds.), *Peer relationships and social skills in childhood* (pp. 375–395). New York: Springer-Verlag.

Reynolds, W. M. (1984). Depression in children and adolescents: Phenomenology, evaluation and treatment. *School Psychology Review, 13,* 171–182.

Reynolds, W. M. (1990). Depression in children and adolescents: Nature, diagnosis, assessment, and treatment. *School Psychology Review, 19,* 158–173.

Rutter, M. (1988). Depressive disorder. In M. Rutter, A. H. Tuma, & I. S. Lann (eds.), *Assessment and diagnosis in child psychopathology* (pp. 347–376). New York: Guilford.

Scholss, P. J., Schloss, C. N., & Harris, L. (1984). A multiple baseline analysis of an interpersonal skills training program for depressed youth. *Behavioral Disorders, 9,* 182–188.

Seligman, M. E., & Peterson, C. (1986). A learned helplessness perspective on childhood depression: Theory and research. In M. Rutter, C. E. Izard, & P. B. Read (Eds.), *Depression in young people: Developmental and clinical perspectives* (pp. 223–249). New York: Guilford.

Siegel, L. J., & Griffin, N. J. (1984). Correlates of depressive symptoms in adolescents *Journal of Youth and Adolescence, 13,* 475–487.

Simons, R., & Miller, M. (1987). Adolescent depression: Assessing the impact of negative cognitions and socioenvironmental problems. *Social Work, 32,* 326–330.

Strober, M., Green, J., & Carlson, G. (1981). Phenomenology and subtypes of major depressive disorder in adolescence. *Journal of Affective Disorders, 3,* 281–290.

Sullivan, W. O., & Engin, A. W. (1986). Adolescent depression: Its prevalence in high school students. *Journal of School Psychology, 24,* 103–109.

Teri, L. (1982). Depression in adolescence: Its relationship to assertion and various aspects of self-image. *Journal of Clinical Child Psychology, 11,* 101–106.

Trower, P., Bryant, B., Argyle, M., & Marziller, J. (1978). *Social skills and mental health.* Pittsburgh: University of Pittsburgh Press.

Wierzbicki, M., & McCabe, M. (1988). Social skills and subsequent depressive symptomatology in children. *Journal of Clinical Child Psychology, 17,* 203–208.

Wilson, R., & Cairns, E. (1988). Sex-role attributes, perceived competence and the development of depression in adolescence. *Journal of Child Psychology and Psychiatry and Allied Disciplines, 29,* 635–650.

Yanchyshyn, G. W., & Robbins, D. R. (1983). The assessment of depression in normal adolescents: A comparison study. *Canadian Journal of Psychiatry, 28,* 522–526.

9

Anger Control for Adolescents: Review of Social Skills and Cognitive Behavioral Interventions

Dianne Ollech

ADOLESCENT AGGRESSION

A school psychologist working in the inner city too often sees adolescents referred for aggressive behaviors. This chapter addresses assessment and treatment issues for aggressive adolescents. I begin by considering the following cases:

> Arthur is a 14-year-old male adolescent. In the classroom he refuses to do any work, follow instructions, or sit quietly. Aggressive incidents include provoking fights, kicking and punching peers, breaking a classmate's notebook, and calling his teacher names. Often, Arthur wanders the halls, pulling fire alarms. He is described as guarded, antagonistic, and rebellious by his teachers.

> Charles is a 16-year-old male adolescent of above-average intelligence who attends a high school for gifted students. He was referred for an inability to get along with teachers and peers. He regards teachers as fools and holds contempt for their authority. With his peers, Charles maintains a flip, sarcastic attitude, and constantly teases them. Charles expresses his anger by finding his way to the rooftops of buildings and throwing eggs and tomatoes onto passing pedestrians while shouting obscenities. He also likes to torment guards in public buildings and minority newsstand owners.

> Theresa is a 13-year-old female adolescent who is at ease in the classroom, but becomes aggressive with peers during unstructured social time. She frequently engages in pushing and shouting matches in the hallways and

cafeteria. Teachers report that she does not know what is expected of her in interpersonal situations and that she is at a loss when she must spontaneously interact with others.

TREATMENT ISSUES

Anger has a particular immediacy for adolescents. They are caught between the control of parents, teachers, and other adult authorities, and their own emerging autonomy and strivings (Berman, 1984). Anger is often related to resentment at being controlled by others, and is perpetuated by believing that it is an acceptable response, that it promotes self-esteem, and that the consequences suffered by the victim are minimal (Slaby & Guerra, 1988).

Aggressive adolescents are too quick to define the situation as provocative, ignoring additional cues. Furthermore, they often lack the ability to generate viable, nonaggressive alternatives to deal with such problems (Slaby & Guerra, 1988). In a 10-year longitudinal study of 875 children, Eron (1980) found that youths who are perceived as aggressive by their peers also evaluate their world as an aggressive place. Sarason and Sarason (1981) posit that an individual's analysis of a situation impacts on subsequent behavior, and report an association between interpersonal skills and general adjustment in adolescents.

There is general agreement that angry adolescents are often isolated, without meaningful peer relationships. Lacking viable means of meeting their interpersonal and affectional needs, they become angrier and more deprived. In assessing and designing programs for treating these adolescents, special attention has focused on the cognitive appraisals that trigger, maintain, and escalate anger.

Triggers

From the adolescent's viewpoint, the triggers, or antecedents, to anger are provoked directly, indirectly, overtly, or covertly. Indirect triggers include appraisals such as feeling at fault or unfairly judged. Direct anger antecedents are those provoked by another person, such as teasing or pushing. Environmental triggers are overt or covert. They range from being caught, late for school, on a slow subway train (overt), to internal states such as tiredness, hunger, or diffuse anxiety (covert). Although some confrontations are unanticipated, anger-prone individuals are provoked by familiar triggers that can be prepared for (Novaco, 1979). For example, the recurring pattern in perceived provocation and response can be seen in the cases of Theresa and Charles. Theresa was provoked by even mild teasing by peers or when others brushed up against her in a crowded hallway. Charles's anger was triggered when authority figures placed demands on him that he regarded as unfair.

Role of Cognition in Maintenance and Escalation

Cognitive treatments highlight three processes that catalyze and maintain anger: self-statements, memory, and attribution. Cognitive determinants of anger find their symbolic representation in the form of private speech called self-statements, or internal dialogues. Self-statements may trigger, sustain, and heighten the intensity of anger and aggression. For instance, when Arthur insulted his teacher, he thought, "She's gonna get it. I'll show her she can't treat me this way in front of everybody."

Memory is conceptualized as a sense of personal history that imbues the present and allows individuals to project the future. For angry adolescents, there is often a storehouse of anger accumulated from past provocations and wrongdoings (Baron, 1983). By tapping into memory and fixating on present angering circumstances, an adolescent may wrongfully predict an antagonist's intentions and behaviors. Thus, Theresa became very angry when peers teased her and called her names because, "I've put up with it long enough. If I don't do something to stop it, they'll just keep on. It's just not fair."

Baron (1983) conceptualized attribution as an interpretation of the motivations behind another's provocative or noxious actions. An angry response is more likely if provocation is perceived as intentionally activated by noxious traits, and less likely if antagonistic behavior is seen as mitigated by external circumstances. For example, Charles expressed his anger toward nameless pedestrians by saying to himself, "I hate them all, because they are hateful." Theresa's peers angered her because, "they're always trying to put something over on me." None of these cognitive processes operates in isolation; rather, hostile self-statements, memory, and negative attributions interact to serve as multifaceted stimuli for anger and aggression.

It is also necessary to recognize the role that feelings and behavior play in the maintenance and escalation of anger. Under the influence of strong feeling and its concomitant physiological arousal, cognitive controls and consideration of unfavorable consequences are temporarily ignored. Angry or aggressive behaviors act as feedback mechanisms to escalate emotions, overstep cognitive controls, and perpetuate maladaptive behavior patterns.

ASSESSMENT ISSUES

Whether they are juvenile offenders, or angry mainstream high school students, aggressive adolescents are typically assessed through interview techniques, direct observations by teachers or residential staff members, and self-report inventories. Goldstein, Glick, Reiner, Zimmerman, and Coultry (1987) used a Direct Situations Test in audiotaped form, consisting of 40 situations with which incarcerated residents must routinely cope. The number of adaptive responses is recorded and used as a measure of skill competence. Novaco (1975) employed a 90-item self-report Anger Inventory to determine the circumstances an individual finds most angering. Examples of Anger Inventory items are (a) someone blames a mistake on you (p. 90), and (b) being wrongly accused of cheating on a test (p. 92). Hart and Cardozo (1986) formulated a Stressful Situation Reconstruction Inventory, which, through open and closed questions, allows adolescents to describe the circumstances and characteristics of angering situations. Sarason and Sarason (1981) interviewed teachers and students to identify relevant problems and specific areas of skill weakness in aggressive adolescents. For a more extensive review of assessment and evaluation methods, see Feindler and Ecton (1986).

BEHAVIORAL TREATMENT PROGRAMS FOR ANGRY ADOLESCENTS

Although psychodynamic approaches have proven largely ineffective in fostering adolescent anger control, purely behavioral approaches have been criticized for not developing the alternative responses necessary to channel anger constructively. To address these criticisms, cognitive behavioral interventions have endeavored to deal with disruptive anger by focusing on the mechanisms of thought, the role of affect, and the manifestations of behavior. These interventions teach a combination of social skills, interpersonal problem-solving techniques, and methods of reducing and controlling arousal (Stern & Fodor, 1989).

INTERPERSONAL COGNITIVE PROBLEM-SOLVING TRAINING

Problem-solving techniques teach individuals to construe provocation as a problem that needs to be solved rather than an ego threat demanding offensive action. Individuals learn to generate alternative solutions to angering situations and to consider the consequences of their actions. Through problem-solving, adolescents are encouraged to distance themselves from immediate impulse and create solutions that will help them further personal goals. Thinking-ahead procedures are used to predict the consequences of behavioral choices. Covert consequences may include losing self-respect, friendship, or affection. Overt consequences could entail losing privileges.

SOCIAL SKILLS TRAINING

Social skills training programs assume that angry adolescents become embroiled in aggressive encounters because they have not developed alternative, adaptive behaviors. Baron (1983) noted their unproductive communications skills, irritating manner of self-expression, and insensitivity to others' feelings and moods. In addition, the angry adolescent's ability to use common social skills such as "making requests, engaging in negotiations, and lodging complaints" (Baron, 1983, p. 113) is often highly deficient.

Lacking the necessary skills for everyday social interactions means that chronically angry adolescents cannot assert or handle themselves when provoked by others. Implicit in assertion techniques is the assumption that anger is a legitimate response to provocation. Individuals have a right to their anger, and can express it in a manner that maintains others' integrity and leaves their self-respect intact.

Research on Skills Training

There are approximately 30 skills training programs that have been implemented with angry and aggressive adolescents. Although most research focuses on juvenile delinquents, a few studies have been carried out with nonoffending, high-risk high school students. Four representative studies will be looked at (see Table 9.1). These studies were chosen because they demonstrate the range of social skills training programs including educating, modeling, and rehearsing assertive behaviors; interpersonal problem-solving techniques; and discussion of problem areas. For a more comprehensive overview, the reader is directed to Goldstein and Pentz (1984).

Long and Sherer (1984) studied the effects that social skills training and discussion groups had on the self-esteem and locus of control of 30 adolescent male offenders. The skills training group analyzed skill components and used modeling, role play, and feedback techniques. Discussion group participants talked about feelings that arose in difficult situations and generated suggestions for appropriate behavior. Although self-esteem was not measurably influenced, locus of control

TABLE 9.1. Social Skills Training Research

Study	Subject & setting	Treatment	Target skill	Outcome
Long & Scherer (1984)	30 nonincarcerated adolescent male offenders	Structured social skills, less structured discussion group	Self-esteem, locus of control	Increase in locus of control for both experimental groups
Moon & Eisler (1983)	40 male undergraduates with anger-control problems	Stress inoculation, interpersonal problem solving, social skills	Anger reduction	SST and IPST groups reduced angry cognitions and increased assertive behavior, SI group reduced angry cognitions
Pentz (1980)	90 high school students	Structured learning (social skills) with varied trainers	Unassertive or aggressive interactions with teachers	SLT group demonstrated more assertive behavior than verbal instructions group; SLT teacher groups significantly more assertive in teacher interactions than SLT student or parent groups
Sarason & Sarason (1981)	127 high school students at high risk for delinquency and dropout	Instructions, modeling of behavior and cognitions, rehearsal, feedback, discussion	Response to problematic situations, job interview performance	Experimental groups increased problem-solving skills in difficult situations and handled job interviews better

Note: SST = social skills training; IPST = interpersonal problem solving training; SI = stress inoculation; SLT = structured learning training.

increased for both experimental groups, with high-frequency offenders benefiting from the more structured social skills group, and low-frequency offenders improving in the less structured discussion group.

Moon and Eisler (1983) investigated the differential effects of interpersonal problem solving, social skills training, and stress inoculation techniques on 40 male undergraduates, aged 18 to 23. Although stress inoculation reduced anger-provoking cognitions, this approach stimulated withdrawal from the environment. In contrast, problem-solving and social skills approaches encouraged assertive behaviors and reduced angry cognitions.

In a study of 90 adolescents who were unassertive or aggressive with teachers, Pentz (1980) studied the effects of different trainers on skills generalization. Although social skills and instructions conditions proved beneficial for participants, the greatest gains were found with adolescents who had teacher trainers. This latter group demonstrated more assertive behaviors with teachers than all other groups. This study suggested that the similarity of treatment conditions to those in the extratherapeutic environment facilitated generalization of skills.

Sarason and Sarason (1981) conducted a social skills program with 127 students from a high school with high dropout and delinquency rates. After training, adolescents who learned social skills through live and videotaped modeling techniques demonstrated better problem-solving skills, and presented themselves more competently in a job situation than the control group. After 1 year, the experimental group showed less tardiness, fewer absences, and a lower rate of referral for behavior problems.

APPRAISAL AND EVALUATION

After viewing these representative studies, it can be seen that

1. Social skills training programs with angry and aggressive adolescents demonstrated modest improvements in specific, targeted social and interpersonal problem-solving skills. No longitudinal research has been initiated, however, to ascertain whether genuine change occurred, that is, if skills generalized to often hostile extratherapeutic environments. It is also unknown whether the skills taught were actually relevant to the adolescents' living situations.
2. Discussion and attention groups were in some instances more effective than, or as effective as, social skills interventions for some participants. In addition, different trainers yielded differential

generalization gains. Thus, the question of, "which type of patient, meeting with which type of therapist, for which type of treatment, will yield which outcomes?" (Goldstein, Sherman, Gershaw, Sprafkin, & Glick, 1978, p. 87) was left unanswered.

3. Most skills programs with angry adolescents have been conducted with male teenagers. Although both male and female adolescents experience problems in anger control, the needs of female teenagers remain "other" and subordinate to those of male teenagers.

TREATMENT PROGRAMS

Deficits in the aforementioned studies also lie in not addressing the cognitive, emotional, and behavioral aspects specific to anger and aggression. Although interpersonal cognitive problem-solving training, and underlying cognitions are addressed, they are often secondary in skills training approaches. Novaco (1975), and, more recently, Feindler and Ecton (1986) and Goldstein et al. (1987) formulated comprehensive training programs that encompass social skills training, cognitive restructuring, interpersonal cognitive problem-solving techniques, coping with emotional arousal, and changing maladaptive behaviors. These intervention programs attempt to sculpt the thoughts, emotions, and behaviors constructively that accompany disruptive anger. Because these three programs build on each other, and contain many of the same elements, only two will be discussed.

Stress Inoculation Approach

Novaco (1975) built on Meichenbaum and Goodman's (1971) research with anxiety, which led to the development of his stress inoculation program. As applied to angry populations, stress inoculation is a method of exposing angry individuals to moderate provocation while teaching them cognitive, affective, and behavioral coping skills. Novaco originally formulated his program for individual remediation with angry adults, and delineated the intervention process into the three stages of cognitive preparation, skill acquisition, and application and training.

During cognitive preparation, individuals gain insight into their anger processes. The therapist aids them in differentiating between adaptive and maladaptive anger manifestations, and in identifying salient triggers. A hierarchy of angering events that are meaningful to the individual is constructed. For instance, in the previously mentioned case of Arthur, he would explicate what makes him angry and under what circumstances. Better ways of dealing with anger, other than pulling fire alarms and kicking classmates, would be explored.

During skill acquisition, clients cope with anger-producing appraisals and expectations by using a self-instruction process that is conceptualized as (a) preparing for provocation, (b) dealing with the impact and confrontation, (c) coping with arousal, and (d) reflecting subsequently. In the initial phase of skill acquisition, participants acknowledge the interpersonal demands of angering situations. For example, if after being bumped in the hallway Theresa felt her anger rising, she could say to herself, "this could be a rough situation, but I know how to deal with it" (Novaco, 1979, p. 269).

During the second phase of skill acquisition, self-instructions facilitate regulation. For instance, before verbally assaulting a newsstand owner, Charles might reflect, "You don't need to prove yourself. Don't make more of this than you have to" (Novaco, 1979, p. 269). Such statements permit the possibility of maintaining control over potentially escalating conditions.

Phase three provides instructional contingencies if participants find themselves resorting to familiar angry responses. With statements such as, "Time to take a deep breath. Let's take the issue point by point" (Novaco, 1975, p. 269), Arthur can actively rechannel his anger when a classmate acts like he "knows it all."

In the final phase of skill acquisition, the individual is provided with a means of coping with the inevitable failures that accompany attempts to change ingrained habits. With instructions such as, "Don't take it personally. It's probably not so serious" (Novaco, 1975, p. 269), ruminations are minimized. Participants can also reinforce partial success by reflecting, "I could have gotten more upset than it was worth" (Novaco, 1975, p. 269).

Because relaxation and anger arousal are mutually exclusive states (Davis, Eshelman, & McKay, 1988), individuals learn Jacobson's (1938) progressive relaxation technique to cope with emotional arousal. Relaxation training not only serves counterconditioning purposes but also acts as a preventive measure to enhance a person's awareness of somatic cues that signal anger escalation. The technique can also be used at other times to effect a calmer, baseline state (Howells, 1988).

In the final stage of stress inoculation, participants apply their skills in role plays, and in an imaginal hierarchy of provocative situations. Thus, individuals learn to manage anger through regulated exposure to the circumstances (triggers) that provoke it.

Novaco's (1975) original 34 subjects were college students and adults with self-admitted and therapist-assessed anger problems. Intervention conditions entailed a combination of cognitive restructuring with relaxation training, cognitive restructuring alone, relaxation training alone, and an attention control group. The combined treatment yielded the greatest positive effects, with a decrease in explosive incidents, and an overall improvement in anger management. Cognitive restructuring also effected positive outcomes in the same directions, although to a lesser degree.

Anger Control Training

Feindler and Ecton (1986) elaborated and extended Novaco's stress inoculation approach into an adolescent anger control treatment for the individual and small (8–12 participants) group. Their intervention has been implemented with hundreds of angry adolescents in primarily outpatient and inpatient clinical settings. The approach interweaves the three training stages of cognitive preparation, skill acquisition, and application and training into each session. Because Feindler's techniques are varied, personalized, and extensive, they facilitate adolescents' participation in their own treatment process. For change to occur, individuals must observe, think about, define, and take responsibility for their angry behaviors. Behavior options are continually emphasized.

Feindler conceptualized the anger process as consisting of antecedents, behaviors, and consequences. Anger situations are construed as problems and defined by the questions: "(a) What is the problem? (b) What can I do? (c) What will happen if. . . . (d) What will I do? (e) How will it work?" (Feindler & Ecton, 1986, p. 83). Participants learn that an initial angry reaction can provoke others, which can escalate the adolescent's anger in an "Angry Behavior Cycle" (Feindler & Ecton, 1986, p. 103).

To control behaviors, cognitions are restructured through the use of reminders such as "chill out," or "ignore this." With individual clients, Wolpe's (1973) thought-stopping technique and Ellis's (1977) cognitive restructuring are offered as ways to circumvent ruminations and faulty appraisals. As in stress inoculation, brief and extensive relaxation techniques are used to cope with emotional arousal.

In addition to social skills, the principles and specifics of assertion training are explicated. Adolescents record their anger incidents in hassle logs that they bring to the sessions. These incidents are used in videotaped role plays to rehearse anger-control skills, and to facilitate analysis and criticism of behavior. Participants are reminded that others may respond to assertiveness with anger or aggression. Such unanticipated outcomes should be considered and prepared for.

In their work with clinical populations of adolescents, Feindler and

Ecton (1986) report that they have applied adolescent anger control with success. They provide two case examples for illustration. They discuss how Eddie, a 16-year-old hospitalized male adolescent with intermittent explosive disorder, was able to control his outbursts after 15 individual training sessions and made a successful transition to an open residential school setting. They go on to show how Wendy, a 13-year-old female adolescent who was hospitalized for physically assaultive behaviors, reduced her aggressive outbursts from five per week before treatment to one per week posttreatment. The posttreatment incident consisted of losing control verbally, rather than physically, and Wendy was able to return to her previous open cottage setting (Feindler & Ecton, 1986). In following up more than 300 adolescents who received anger-control training, most were found to demonstrate positive control over maladaptive anger.

WHERE ARE WE NOW AND WHERE ARE WE GOING?

1. Even though treatment sessions offer options for learning social skills, role plays, modeling, and problem solving, the interventions discussed are essentially prefabricated. They may therefore not address the needs of some adolescents, who, for instance, cannot orient themselves to the program rationale, or who are unable to comprehend adequately the steps involved in the cognitive portions. For these clients, a more personalized approach is necessary, with a therapist who possesses the requisite skills.
2. For the most part, the treatment programs are oriented toward delinquent-prone male adolescents. Further study needs to be pursued to determine if these approaches are effective for gifted adolescents with anger problems, as in the case of Charles, or with female adolescents who are rageful but inhibit their anger expression. Such investigations could determine whether an adolescent such as Charles would benefit more from a psychodynamic approach, or individual cognitive therapy; or if a female adolescent who has problems expressing any anger could benefit from a program designed with acting-out male adolescents in mind.
3. Logic is also defied when one considers that many adolescents must return to extratherapeutic environments that virtually demand angry or aggressive responses. In some cases, an adolescent may play the role of problem child in the family, expressing

other members' taboo anger. In other cases, adolescents live in hostile or abusive family environments in which parents model aggressive behaviors and in hostile urban environments. Thus, for many adolescents some type of additional intervention in the family or community is crucial to the maintenance of newly learned behaviors.

CONCLUSION

Chronic anger and aggression detrimentally affect the lives of adolescents afflicted with these traitlike behaviors and also those who must bear the brunt of their intense affect and disruptive responses. In this chapter, representative social skills programs are reviewed, as are two cognitive behavioral approaches offering multichanneled interventions for maladaptive anger.

Although initial research supports the efficacy of these programs, additional investigations need to be undertaken to ascertain if aggressive adolescents from ethnically diverse backgrounds can grasp and relate to an intellectual approach laden with cultural values that may be alien to them. It is also uncertain whether female adolescents can profit from interventions oriented toward acting-out male adolescents. These are realistic concerns that can only be answered through application, with necessary modifications to the specific needs of the previously mentioned groups.

The interventions discussed in this chapter do not attempt to deny anger but to learn how to handle it. The next formulation in the management of adolescent anger and aggression might address the differential styles inherent in class and ethnic differences. Continued work along these lines will aid professionals and paraprofessionals in meeting the diverse needs of a growing population of angry and aggressive adolescents.

REFERENCES

Baron, R. A. (1983). The control of human aggression: An optimistic perspective. *Journal of Social and Clinical Psychology, 1,* 97–119.

Berman, S. (1984). The relationship of aggressive behavior and violence to psychic reorganization in adolescence. In C. R. Keith (Ed.), *The aggressive adolescent: Clinical perspectives* (pp. 3–16). New York: Free Press.

Davis, M., Eshelman, E. R., & McKay, M. (1988). *The relaxation and stress reduction workbook.* Oakland, CA: New Harbinger.

Elder, J. P., Edelstein, B. A., & Narick, M. M. (1979). Adolescent psychiatric patients: Modifying aggressive behavior with social skills training. *Behavior Modification, 3,* 161–178.

Ellis, A. (1977). Can we change thoughts by reinforcement? A reply to Howard Rachlin. *Behavior Therapy, 8,* 666–672.

Eron, L. D. (1980). Prescription for reduction of aggression. *American Psychologist, 35,* 244–252.

Fehrenbach, P. A., & Thelen, M. H. (1982). Behavioral approaches to the treatment of anger. *Behavior Modification, 6,* 465–497.

Feindler, E., & Ecton, R. (1986). *Adolescent anger control: Cognitive behavioral techniques.* New York: Pergamon.

Goldstein, A. P., Glick, B., Reiner, S., Zimmerman, D., & Coultry, T. M. (1987). *Aggression replacement training: A comprehensive intervention for aggressive youth.* Champaign, IL: Research Press.

Goldstein, A. P., & Pentz, M. A. (1984). Psychological skill training and the aggressive adolescent. *The School Psychology Review, 13,* 311–323.

Goldstein, A. P., Sherman, M., Gershaw, N. J., Sprafkin, R. P., & Glick, B. (1978). Training aggressive adolescents in prosocial behavior. *Journal of Youth and Adolescence, 7,* 73–92.

Goldstein, A. P., Sprafkin, R. P., Gershaw, N. J., & Klein, P. (1980). *Skillstreaming the adolescent: A structured learning approach to teaching prosocial skills.* Champaign, IL: Research Press.

Hart, K. E., & Cardozo, S. R. (1986, August). *Ways of coping in anger-provoking situations: Cognitive correlates.* Paper presented at the annual meeting of the American Psychological Association, Washington, DC.

Hazaleus, S. L., & Deffenbacher, J. L. (1986). Relaxation and cognitive treatments of anger. *Journal of Consulting and Clinical Psychology, 54,* 222–226.

Howells, K. (1988). The management of angry aggression: A cognitive-behavioral approach. In W. Dryden & P. Trower (Eds.), *Developments in cognitive psychotherapy* (pp. 129–152). Beverly Hills: Sage.

Jacobson, E. (1938). *Progressive relaxation.* Chicago: University of Chicago Press.

Long, S. L., & Sherer, M. (1984). Social skills training with juvenile offenders. *Child and Family Behavior Therapy, 6,* 1–11.

Lorenz, K. (1966). *On aggression* (M. K. Wilson, Trans.). New York: Harcourt, Brace & World. (Original work published 1963).

Meichenbaum, D. (1985). *Stress inoculation training.* New York: Pergamon.

Michenbaum, D., & Gilmore, J. B. (1984). The nature of unconscious processes: A cognitive-behavioral perspective. In K. S. Bowers & D. Meichenbaum (Eds.), *The unconscious reconsidered* (pp. 273–298). New York: Wiley.

Meichenbaum, D. H., & Goodman, J. (1971). Training impulsive children to talk to themselves: A means of developing self-control. *Journal of Abnormal Psychology, 77,* 115–126.

Moon, J. R., & Eisler, R. M. (1983). Anger control: An experimental comparison of three behavioral treatments. *Behavior Therapy, 14,* 493–505.

Novaco, R. W. (1975). *Anger control: The development and evaluation of an experimental treatment.* Lexington, MA: Lexington Books.

Novaco, R. W. (1976). The functions and regulation of the arousal of anger. *The American Journal of Psychiatry, 133,* 1124–1127.

Novaco, R. W. (1979). The cognitive regulation of anger and stress. In P. C. Kendall & S. D. Hollon (Eds.), *Cognitive-behavioral interventions: Theory, research, and procedures* (pp. 241–285). New York: Academic Press.

Novaco, R. W. (1985). Anger and its therapeutic regulation. In M. A. Chesney & R. H. Rosenman (Eds.), *Anger and hostility in cardiovascular and behavioral disorders* (pp. 203–226). New York: Hemisphere.

Pentz, M. A. (1980). Assertion training and trainer effects on unassertive and aggressive adolescents. *Journal of Counseling Psychology, 27,* 76–83.

Rule, B. G., & Nesdale, A. R. (1976). Emotional arousal and aggressive behavior. *Psychological Bulletin, 83,* 851–863.

Sarason, I. G., & Sarason, B. R. (1981). Teaching cognitive and social skills to high school students. *Journal of Consulting and Clinical Psychology, 49,* 908–918.

Slaby, R. G., & Guerra, N. G. (1988). Cognitive mediators of aggression in adolescent offenders. *Developmental Psychology, 24,* 580–588.

Spence, A. J., & Spence, S. H. (1980). Cognitive changes associated with social skills training. *Behavior Research and Therapy, 18,* 265–272.

Spence, S. H., & Marzillier, J. S. (1981). Social skills training with adolescent male offenders: II. Short-term, long-term and generalized effects. *Behavior Research and Therapy, 19,* 349–368.

Stern, J. B., & Fodor, I. G. (1989). Anger control in children: Behavioral approaches to dealing with aggressive children. *Child and Family Behavior Therapy, 11,* 1–20.

Wolpe, J. (1973). *The practice of behavior therapy* (2nd ed.). Oxford: Pergamon.

10

Assessment of Social Skills Problems with Learning Disabled Adolescents

Carol Lampert Barrish

The challenges and problem situations encountered by adolescents in a secondary school environment (e.g., negotiating required communication between teacher and student, interacting in peer social situations to develop and sustain friendships, increasing independence in dealing with other adults at home and at part-time jobs) can be particularly problematic for learning disabled (LD) adolescents. The cognitive difficulties that limit their academic performance may also affect their perception of social situations as well as the skill with which they respond appropriately to the demands of a particular situation. Accompanying behavioral immaturities may cause LD adolescents to be recipients of social rejection, isolation, and lowered self-esteem.

ADOLESCENTS WITH LEARNING DISABILITIES

It is well documented that LD persons, especially those with multiple learning disabilities, lack appropriate social skills (Osmond & Binder, 1982). Although LD adolescents' learning difficulties vary from one individual to another, five main areas of difficulty have been found to exert the greatest influence on social adjustment.

Poor Body Awareness

Learning disabled adolescents may lack a strong sense of body awareness and experience anxiety about keeping in control of their bodies. To compensate for this difficulty, these individuals may devote extra time and energy to finding their classrooms, lockers, or desks, and not bumping into people or objects in the process. Although this intense effort is occurring, anxiety may also surface around a concern that they may get lost or appear clumsy or foolish to peers. Hence, given this extra demand in trying to cope, LD adolescents may have little awareness left for processing social feedback from their peers or physical feedback from their environment (Bruinicks, 1978; Jackson, Enright, & Murdock, 1987). Thus LD students may clump loudly up or down the stairs, hug friends too tightly, fail to modulate their walk or the tone of their voice, or stand too close in proximity to a person to whom they wish to speak. Unable to assume the perspective of other individuals, LD adolescents may not change their behavior in the face of nonverbal negative cues from others. Several studies indicate that the immediate and recurring impression of LD children by parents, teachers, peers, and strangers is a negative one. When the impression is communicated to LD individuals with nonverbal cues, they may not recognize the meaning of this communication (Pearl & Cosden, 1982; Wiig & Harris, 1974). In fact LD adolescents are often unaware of the negative effect of their social behavior until it is too late to repair the damage. This lack of awareness increases the likelihood of their experiencing rejection from others.

Organizational Problems

A second area of difficulty relates to organizational issues. It is difficult for these youngsters to plan an activity that requires several interrelated procedures. For example, the steps involved in arranging a movie date with a friend may be so overwhelming that LD adolescents may choose to stay at home alone and watch television instead. These same problems relate to LD adolescents' difficulties detecting cause–effect relationships in social situations.

Social Sensitivity Deficit

Normal adolescents make predictions about future events in an attempt to understand them and decide on a future course of behavior. Learning disabled children who have a poor memory system and are generally disoriented have limited prior social experiences to call on as a guide to future behavior. As a result, they are less able to make inferences or predict future behavior of other peers. It becomes very difficult to see another individual's viewpoint concerning a particular issue (Bergmann, 1987). Thus, LD adolescents may approach someone whom they perceive to be a friend with no awareness that this individual may actually dislike them.

Problems Processing Language

LD adolescents may also have difficulties processing language. They may mishear or forget what people say, forget instructions that they are given, or get lost in the meaning when a conversation is lengthy. Furthermore, LD persons may not be aware of the guidelines that affect conversation with peers—they may not pick topics that are interesting to their listener; they may discuss a topic that is potentially embarrassing or inappropriate to their listener, or they may not understand the role of a listener and try to fill in all conversational pauses (Bryan, Sherman, & Fisher, 1980; Bryan, Donahue, & Pearl, 1981). During adolescence, a way of developing respect from peers is to be able to persuade others to adopt your viewpoint. Researchers have found that LD children are less persuasive than other children and are often more easily influenced by their peers, even if it concerns performing antisocial acts (Bryan et al., 1981; Bryan, Werner, & Pearl, 1982).

Social Problems

The myriad deficits described previously that may characterize learning disabled adolescents can cause them to experience problems of self-esteem, peer acceptance, and academic achievement that extend beyond the limitations imposed by any cognitive deficits they might have. Researchers have found that negative self-concepts for the LD can begin as early as grade 3 in school (Chapman & Boersma, 1979). At this time many of these youngsters begin to have poor performance in reading, spelling, and arithmetic. Their self-views in these narrowly defined areas generalize to academic ability in general and then to school. Not only do the LD have lower expectations of their academic performance, but studies indicate that teachers and parents often share this lowered set of academic expectations for them (Hiebert, Wong, & Hunter, 1982). This negative self-concept, reinforced by these students' school and home environment, often contributes to their image as poor students and undesirable playmates. Thus, LD children are at greater risk for social rejection than their non-LD peers (Dudley-Marling & Edmiaston, 1985).

When LD children reach adolescence, the need to be a part of the larger successful social scene takes on an even greater level of significance. Yet research indicates that LD students, their teachers, and parents view their chance for academic success more bleakly than that of normally achieving students. Furthermore, there is also a tendency for teachers to generalize from LD childrens' low academic achievement to less acceptable social behavior than their non-LD peers (Keogh, Tchir,

& Windeguth-Behn, 1974). These problems perpetuate a vicious cycle for LD adolescents. Because of their negative self-esteem, they rarely participate in school activities but function on the fringe of the school environment. This lack of involvement makes LD adolescents act as loners and lessens their opportunities to develop appropriate social relationships in the future. Hence, this group needs social skills training. This author, as a first step in designing a social skills training program, began a systematic assessment of the deficits in an effort to define problematic situations that could be used as the basis for developing training modules.

LD POPULATION

LD adolescents between the ages of 12 and 19 who attended a special high school were selected for the study. The students all had IQs within the normal range and no apparent physical deformity to distinguish this LD group visually from a non-LD student population.

Development of Behavioral–Analytical Assessment Measure

The need for this assessment tool arose out of a growing concern shared by personnel at the high school. Students were making satisfactory to excellent progress academically, yet many of them were still handicapped by an immature level of social skills that negatively impacted on all their interactions. Although school personnel dealt with their social infractions on an individual basis as they occurred, the staff was eager to develop an objective, quantifiable assessment measure to (a) identify readily specific social skills behavior in which their students were deficient, (b) identify which youngsters were deficient in these behaviors, and (c) use these situations in the later implementation of a treatment plan.

The immediate goal of this project was the development of an assessment tool to evaluate the effectiveness of LD adolescents' responses to a particular problematic situation in their environment. Although other assessment measures for the LD exist, none seems ideal. Behavioral codes and checklists provide measures of actual behavior, but they do not consider how others accept the LD individual. Conversely, sociometric measures and rating scales may provide an indication of social validity, but they do not measure specific social behaviors.

LD Assessment

The assessment procedure for this project was modeled after the design employed by Goldfried and D'Zurilla (1969) because of its applicability to a special population. The focus for this study dealt with problem situations experienced by LD adolescents. Because a high school student in an urban area is exposed to myriad social encounters, a decision was made to include three basic areas in which youngsters this age interact: their school, homes, and part-time jobs. The interactions to be studied included problems involving teachers, peers, parents, and employers.

Following the Goldfried and D'Zurilla (1969) model, the assessment procedure entailed five major steps: (a) a detailed compilation of situations that were characterized as problematic for the LD population being studied, (b) the generation of a series of possible responses to resolve each problem situation successfully, (c) an evaluation of the relative effectiveness of each of the proposed solutions on a most effective–least effective continuum, (d) the development of a measuring instrument format, and (e) an evaluation of the measure taking concurrent and predictive validity into account. This chapter discusses the first four steps of the assessment development. The last step, relating to an evaluation of the assessment's validity, has not yet been completed.

Situational analysis. The first phase of this project was to collect a large sample of representative problematic situations that were likely to confront adolescent LD students during the school year. These situations could be experienced at school, at home, or at a part-time job. They could involve parents, teachers, peers, or part-time employers; however, they had to be related to the student's learning disability. Because many of the students we sampled had varying degrees of language impairment that affected their ability to communicate ideas, a decision was made to have members of the teaching and administrative staff generate the problematic situations based on their experiences with the students during the current academic year. Each staff member who participated in this study was selected because of the close relationship that he or she had with the students at the school. Not only did the teacher instruct the students in academic subjects but this individual was also approached frequently by students for counsel regarding their personal problems as well as academic concerns. After the initial situations were generated by staff members, students were asked whether or not they had ever experienced this situation or a situation resembling it.

Eleven faculty members were asked to describe problem situations involving friends, parents, teachers, or part-time employers that came up in their students' daily lives that were exacerbated by their learning disabilities. In addition, they were asked to describe the background for the problem, a possible student response, and a probable outcome. Their responses were transcribed. This is an example of a situation reported by a teacher as it is rewritten by the interviewer in a standardized format:

> *Specific Problem Situation*: You have a crush on another classmate. While you rarely speak to this person in school, you phone this person frequently every night and weekends. Your classmate is not warm or pleased to speak to you on the telephone. In fact, your classmate's parents frequently get on the phone when you call and say that your special friend isn't home.
> *Background*: Student A constantly seeks approval from others; she often pushes people beyond their limits. She may phone a classmate 10–20 times a night or calls her teachers at their homes to discuss her personal problems. She cannot detect subtle social cues of rejection. When she is rebuffed, she may get embarrassed for a brief period but then resumes her pursuit.
> *Response*: You continue to pursue your classmate with many phone calls each night.
> *Probable Outcome*: Your classmate finally tells you off in a cruel and angry manner. You are devastated.

At the end of the interview process, 40 problematic situations were identified. At this point, the situations were edited so that redundant, trivial, or seldom experienced situations could be eliminated. The situations were then rewritten in a more appropriate form for assessment purposes. Each situation was made up of two components: one describing the background and the other the problematic situation. Care was taken to make the background general enough to relate to most students but specific enough to provide a clear context for the problem. Personal reactions such as thoughts and feelings were retained as much as possible. An attempt was also made to avoid rewriting the situations in such a way as to suggest an obvious solution.

To assess whether these situations had occurred at least once within our sample of LD adolescents, the students were asked during individual interviews whether or not they had ever experienced any of the situations read to them from the previously collected group or if they had experienced a situation similar to it. Situations were included in the later assessment form only if at least half of the students participating in the study had experienced the situations or similar ones. It was possible to retain a total of 30 problematic situations, each one having occurred at least once in the experience of 50% of the students surveyed.

Response enumeration. The goal in this phase of the assessment development was to obtain numerous different responses to each of the previously generated problem situations. The 30 problematic situations were separated into two questionnaires, each one requiring approximately 20 minutes to complete. The situations were presented to 25 students. Because of reading comprehension problems and related language difficulties that some of the students experienced, this phase of the study was conducted by individual interviews with the students. To reduce the possibility that error might occur because of fatigue or boredom, half of the subjects completed the second questionnaire first; they then went back and completed the first half of the questionnaire during their second interview.

Each student met with an interviewer who explained that the student would be presented with a series of problem situations. The student was told to imagine that he or she (or a friend) actually experienced these situations, and was asked to deal with them, giving at least four possible responses for each situation. A sample situation and sample set of responses were read to the student to provide a model of what was desired, with further explanation, if needed. On several occasions the situation was paraphrased for the student whose reading or language confusions interfered with a clear understanding of the presented situation. An example of one situation and the responses that were elicited by one student follow:

> You have some trouble with reading which makes you a slow reader. Your teacher is giving you an open book exam. He will ask a series of questions and you will have to find the answers in 15 minutes. You feel that you won't have enough time to finish the test. You could:
>
> 1. Take the bad mark on the test.
> 2. Do something stupid to get thrown out of the class and not take the test.
> 3. Ask to take the test after school with more time.
> 4. Tell your parents and ask them to ask the teacher to give you more time for the test.

Once the interview process with the students was completed, the responses were reviewed. Those situations that tended to elicit ambiguous responses, ones that were not clearly effective or ineffective in solving problems, were discarded. This was done because these situations were judged unlikely to discriminate appropriate social behavior later. After this rating process, 27 situations were retained for future use.

Among the 27 situations, it was possible to differentiate three distinct areas of concern that had been selected by study participants. These areas related to difficulties with problematic academic activities, peer relationships largely in the classroom, and situations in the outside world that were adversely affected by the LD adolescents' cognitive or perceptual deficits.

Five of the situations involved experiences with problematic academic activities. An example of one such situation follows:

> You received your homework back with a comment on it from your teacher that she couldn't read it. The teacher said that you must improve your handwriting if you want to pass her subject. You know that your handwriting can't be improved and you don't know how to type.

Fifteen of the situations were concerned with problematic aspects of interpersonal relationships. They included same-sex relationships, opposite-sex relationships, and relationships with teachers and parents. An example of this follows:

> You have a little trouble talking to other kids but you have managed to get some friends anyhow. People tell you that you have a good sense of humor and you enjoy the attention you get. One of the kids in your class talks in a strange way and is a little funny looking but this kid is pretty nice to you. You talk about sports with this person when no one else is around. The other kids don't seem to like this person. One day you are talking to a group of friends when this strange kid comes over.

Seven of the situations were nonacademic in nature but were nevertheless linked to limitations imposed by the students' cognitive or perceptual deficits. An example of this follows:

> You buy your lunch at a deli near your school. You always buy the same lunch. Lately you notice that you aren't getting enough change back after you pay for your lunch.

Response evaluation. The purpose of this step of the assessment procedure was to develop a rating scale discriminating levels of effectiveness for each of the responses previously obtained. Following the Goldfried and D'Zurilla (1969) model, school personnel were selected to judge the effectiveness of each student response and to rank these responses in a hierarchy from the most to the least effective.

The eight evaluators selected included the director of the high school, the assistant director, the school psychologist, and five classroom teachers.

These judges were provided with a compilation of problematic situations and related student responses. They were instructed to read each situation and its possible responses, and to then rate the effectiveness of each response on a scale from 1 (least effective solution) to 7 (most effective solution). The instructions given to judges are listed subsequently.

Based upon my interviews with staff and students, a number of problematic situations likely to confront LD adolescents as well as potential courses of action have been identified. I would like you to rate the effectiveness of each alternative for the students in this school.

By *effectiveness* I mean the response that would best resolve the situation and tend to maximize the positive consequences while minimizing the negative ones. Your personal opinion regarding the general effectiveness of the various alternatives for the population at school is sought because of your interest in student problems, your close contact with the students and the value students hold for your opinions.

Instructions for Rating

(1) Read each situation. (2) Read the possible responses listed. (3) Rate each response as to its effectiveness. (4) If you wish, you may add your own additional effective response on the reverse side of the sheet of paper.

A 7-point rating scale is to be used in judging the effectiveness of each alternative response.

inferior	fair	good	extremely effective

[___1___]___2___]___3___]___4___]___5___]___6___]___7___]

Guidelines for Ratings:
Inferior—use for the most inadequate response
Extremely effective—use for those alternatives which, considering the constraints of the situation, represent the best possible way to respond.

It is possible that you may judge none of the alternatives as "extremely effective." If that is the case, I hope you will be able to add responses which you feel would fall into the extreme categories of inferior and extremely effective.

To indicate your estimate of the effectiveness of each alternative, please write the number from the rating scale in the blank provided in front of the alternative responses.

The ratings from the eight judges were then compiled. Problematic responses were retained if there was a 50% consensus from the judges on the "most effective" response. If the evaluators were unable to agree, the situation was not employed.

The following is an example of one most effective–least effective response hierarchy as defined by the judges:

You have to take a math competency exam in order to get credit for the entire school year. While you know how to solve the problems, it takes you a lot longer to complete the work. The teacher has said that the test is timed

and you will have exactly two hours to complete the test. You fear you will
fail because you don't have enough time. You could:

Most Effective

    Ask your teacher for additional time

Moderately Effective

    Practice before the test and work on your speed

    At the end of the test, if you didn't do well, ask for a retest

Least Effective

    Only do a little of the test since you know you can't finish

    Cheat

The final assessment form was made up of 20 problematic situations
that were likely to confront adolescent LD students at least once during
high school. Each situation was paired with five possible responses.
These responses had been rated on a continuum from most effective to
least effective by a group of school staff members who were judged to
have a significant influence on the high school students' social behavior.

Development of measuring instrument format. Although the Goldfried and D'Zurilla (1969) model employed a format that required participants to write a detailed description of a likely response to a given
problematic situation, this approach was not suitable for a LD population with oral and written language problems. It was decided that a
multiple-choice response format would be best to employ. The student
was required to read the problematic situation as well as its proposed
solution. Care was taken that the passage was written in short, clear
simple sentences. The student was to put a "M" next to the response he
would "most likely" employ and a "L" next to the response that he felt
least inclined to follow.

Advantages of Measure

Although the assessment of deficient social skills is a necessary
requisite before the initiation of any social skills intervention program,
it still taps only one piece of the picture. Additional work needs to be
done using sociometric measures to get the perspective of others for a
true interpersonal assessment. A sociometric study of LD adolescents is
clearly the next stage of assessment.

The assessment tool described in this project offers several distinct
advantages. The situations it provides in the actual assessment scale
are developed directly from adolescents' daily life experiences and are
therefore representative of the current daily issues that perplex and
confound LD adolescents. These issues are described in specific behav-

ioral terms; this explicit format is easier for the LD population to understand and respond to when they are engaged in the assessment. The relative effectiveness of the solutions generated by the subjects was rated by the adults who interact with and influence the students' behavior, and hence provide some outside social validity. Finally, the assessment situations provide the framework for constructing behavioral modules for building social skills interventions for the learning disabled.

Appendix

Social Skills Assessment for Learning Disabled Adolescents

For each situation, write *M* next to the response you are most likely to use and *L* next to the response you are least likely to use.

1. You have some trouble with reading, which makes you a slow reader. Your teacher is giving an open book exam. He will ask a series of questions, and you will have to find the answers in 15 minutes. You feel that you won't have time to finish this test. You could

    _____ Try your best even if you think you won't finish
    _____ Ask your teacher for additional time if you need it
    _____ Skip the test
    _____ Tell your parents and ask them to ask the teacher for more time for you
    _____ Do chapter reviews and underline the main idea of each passage to prepare before the test

2. You don't have any friends in school or any special group to hang out with. One day you forget your homework and are told to stay in for detention at lunchtime. While you are sitting in detention, a few of the other popular kids are brought in for detention too. They start teasing the kids who regularly eat lunch in the lunchroom and are not on detention. They call these kids nerds. You think the whole thing is funny and start to join in on the teasing. One of the kids who is being teased starts to cry. You could

    _____ Stop the teasing
    _____ Tell the teacher in charge and get help
    _____ Ignore the situation entirely
    _____ Bug the nerds more
    _____ Say you are sorry to the kid without the other kids noticing

3. You have a lot of trouble understanding what you read. Your English teacher wants your class to read three chapters in a new book at home for homework. You start to read the first chapter, but it is too difficult for you. You put the book down after spending 10 minutes trying to understand the first three pages. You could

_____ Ask your teacher to go over the reading in class or at free time

_____ Tell your teacher you cannot do it and ask for an easier book

_____ Get notes on the book

_____ Not do the assignment

_____ Do the best you can

4. You get a job selling jewelry to make some extra money. You bring your jewelry case to school, leave it in your locker over the weekend, and find that it is gone on Monday. Your employer has called you several times to collect the money you have earned or to take back the unsold jewelry. You could

_____ Tell your employer exactly what happened and offer to pay for the jewelry

_____ Forget about it

_____ Try to find out who stole the jewelry yourself by asking others

_____ Tell your parents and hope that they have an idea

_____ Put up a sign to see if anyone in school saw the case

5. You went on a ski trip with other friends from your school. You did not know these kids well, but they were very popular. You thought they were accepting you as their friend when they invited you to share a room with them. The first night of the trip, your roommates brought in a bunch of kids for a "party." The rules regarding the trip clearly said no parties were to be held in the rooms, or the students would be sent home. You wanted all these kids to get out of your room so that you could get some sleep. You could

_____ Ask them to hold their party somewhere else

_____ Join them with their party

_____ Start yelling at them to leave

_____ Try to find one of the teachers to handle it

_____ Sleep in one of the other kid's rooms

6. You received your homework back with a comment on it from your teacher that she could not read it. The teacher said that you must improve your handwriting if you want to pass her subject. You know your handwriting cannot be improved and you do not know how to type. You could

   _____ Tell your teacher you cannot write well and ask her to help you
   _____ Take a handwriting class
   _____ Learn to type
   _____ Do nothing
   _____ Offer to give oral responses to your teacher

7. You have to take a math competency exam to get credit for your math work for the entire school year. Although you know how to solve the problems, it takes you a lot longer to complete the work. The teacher said that the test is timed, and you will have exactly two hours to complete the test. You fear you will fail because you do not have enough time. You could

   _____ Ask your teacher for additional time
   _____ Practice before the test and work on your speed
   _____ Only do a little of the test because you know you cannot finish
   _____ At the end of the test, if you did not do well, ask for a retest
   _____ Cheat

8. You are working in a coffee shop to make extra money for the summer. You have to answer the telephone and write down all the take-out orders. It is difficult for you to remember the customers' orders because they talk so fast. You could

   _____ Ask the customers to repeat their orders or speak more slowly
   _____ Stay with the job, hoping you get better
   _____ Hang up on the customers if they speak too fast
   _____ Ask your boss for a different job in the restaurant
   _____ Learn shorthand to write more quickly

9. Your friend has access to drugs, which he offered to sell to you. Your friend said that it would make you feel really good to get high. You know that several of your friends have tried drugs. You could

_____ Avoid seeing your friend for a few days

_____ Buy the drugs and throw them out later

_____ Act like you took drugs already so your friend will not give you more

_____ Tell your friend you are not interested

_____ Report your friend to a teacher or a policeman

10. Your teacher makes you stay after school for detention. You are supposed to meet your friends to go "hang out" after your class. Your weekly schedule is filled with after-school appointments every day except today. You were really looking forward to getting a chance to "unwind" with friends today. You could

_____ Ask to stay a different day

_____ Not show up and make an excuse the next day

_____ Serve your detention and meet your friends later

_____ Say you have a doctor's appointment, which is a lie, and not stay

_____ Ask your teacher if you can have extra homework instead so you can still see your friends

11. You came to school late for the third time this week. You got a late pass, went to your locker, and got your books for class. You hate to go to class late because you are confused about what to do. You could

_____ Go to the bathroom and stay there until class is over

_____ Go to class but ask the teacher what you missed as soon as you enter the classroom

_____ Go to class, do the best you can, and xerox your friend's notes after class

_____ Go to class and do the best you can

_____ Sit in class but do not pay attention

12. After school yesterday you saw two of your teachers walking off together. It seems to you that they must be out on a date. You really want to hear about the details of their after-school time together. You really want to know whether they like each other. The next day you see one of the teachers standing alone during morning break. You could

_____ Forget about your interest in their relationship

_____ Start a conversation with this teacher, hoping your teacher will say something

_____ Ask your classmates if they know whether these teachers are dating

_____ Follow them, watch how they act with each other, and draw your own conclusion

_____ Tell the teacher there is a rumor going around that this teacher is going out with the other teacher and see what the teacher says

13. During class, you have a bad habit of shouting out the first thought that comes into your mind. You have tried to control this problem, but it is very difficult for you. To make matters worse, you always get into trouble because of it. You have had detention once already. Your parents say that if you get detention again, you will not be allowed to go away with your friend and his family for a short vacation during the next school holiday. You could

_____ Ask your teacher to help you control yourself

_____ Don't say anything in class unless you are spoken to

_____ Raise your hand calmly to speak. If you are not called on, put your hand down and forget it

_____ Sit way in the back of the room so no one can hear your comments

_____ Sleep in class

14. You have a crush on another student in your class. You like to call this person after school and in the evening to talk about anything. You think that this person might begin to like you if you call a lot. In fact, you may call 5–10 times each night. Lately, whenever you call, your friend's mother or other family member says that your friend isn't home. In school other kids tell you that this person has another special person to date. It is 7 p.m., the time you usually start calling this person. You could

_____ Call the person

_____ Have a friend call the person and ask if this person likes you

_____ Accept the fact that this person has another to date and try to forget about it

_____ Ask if this special person wants to go out with you and a bunch of friends

_____ Speak to the special person at school and ask this person to call you about help with homework

15. You have been placed on detention at lunchtime instead of after school. You must wait for other students to buy your lunch for you, and you are very hungry. As you sit in the cafeteria, you see

the regular kids who eat lunch every day. They seem like nerds to you. You are angry that you must sit in the same room with them for your detention. You could

_____ Sit by yourself and eat your lunch
_____ Just walk out and forget about detention
_____ Ask to change your detention place
_____ Try to do some work because you must stay there
_____ Ask your teacher if you could have detention after school instead of during lunch

16. You do not feel comfortable around the opposite sex. A friend invites you to a big party in their honor, but you refuse. You know all your friends are going to this party. You cannot give a good reason for your refusal to go. Your friends as well as this person are angry and say you are a snob. You could

_____ Go to the party but avoid the opposite sex
_____ Tell your friends you are shy with the opposite sex, do not want to go to the party, and ask for their help
_____ Ask your parents to explain to your friends why you cannot attend
_____ Go to the party and try to have fun
_____ Say you are sick the night of the party

17. You buy your lunch at a deli near your school. You always buy the same lunch. Lately you notice that you are not getting enough change back after you pay for your lunch. You could

_____ Tell the cashier you are not getting the right change and ask for it
_____ Do nothing
_____ Go to a different deli for lunch
_____ Bring your own lunch
_____ Ask another person if they also got the wrong change

18. You have a half day of school before your final math exam. Your parents are concerned about your math grades. You are in danger of failing and having to go to summer school. You are finally with a group of kids that you like in school. They are popular and have a lot of friends. Your friends decide to take off from school and go to the beach that day. You want to go with them and study at night when you return from the beach. You could

_____ Stay at home and study
_____ Study at the beach

_____ Go to the beach, study at night, and hope for the best

_____ Do not tell your parents it is a half day and go to the beach

_____ If your parents say, "no," go anyhow

19. You just got your first job at the pizzeria. You have to use a time clock to keep track of the hours you work. On the second day of work, your boss tells you to punch out at 7 p.m. but to work until 8 p.m., 1 hour extra. You know they are cheating you of part of your salary. You could

_____ Ask the manager why he is cheating you

_____ Ask to be paid for the extra hour

_____ Quit

_____ Ask for a raise

_____ Just leave at 7 p.m.

20. Your classmate asks a question that seems ridiculous to you. You think the answer is obvious. You are annoyed that this kid is wasting class time with such nonsense. You could

_____ Ignore the entire situation

_____ Sit there and listen

_____ Tell your classmate to shut up

_____ Complain to the teacher that this kid always asks stupid questions

_____ Tell your classmate he is wasting class time, and everyone would like to get on with the lesson

REFERENCES

Bergmann, M. (1987). Social grace or disgrace: Adolescent social skills and learning disability subtypes. *Journal of Reading, Writing and Learning Disabilities International, 3*, 161–165.

Bruinicks, V. (1978). Actual and perceived peer status of LD students in mainstream programs. *Journal of Special Education, 12*, 51–57.

Bryan, T., Donahue, M., & Pearl, R. (1981). Learning disabled children's peer interactions during a small group problem-solving task. *Learning Disability Quarterly, 4*, 13–22.

Bryan, J., Sherman, R., & Fisher, A. (1980). Learning disabled boys' nonverbal behavior within a dyadic interview. *Learning Disability Quarterly, 3*, 65–72.

Bryan, T., Werner, M., & Pearl, R. (1982). Learning disabled students' conformity responses to prosocial and antisocial situations. *Learning Disability Quarterly, 5*, 344–352.

Chapman, J., & Boersma, F. (1979). Learning disabilities, locus of control and mother attitudes. *Journal of Educational Psychology, 71,* 250–258.

Dudley-Marling, C., & Edmiaston, R. (1985). Social status of LD children and adolescents: A review. *Learning Disability Quarterly, 8,* 189–204.

Goldfried, M., & D'Zurilla, T. (1969). A behavioral-analytic model for assessing competence. In C. D. Spielberger (Ed.), *Current topics in clinical and community psychology.* New York: Academic Press.

Hiebert, B., Wong, B., & Hunter, M. (1982). Affective influence on LD adolescents. *Learning Disability Quarterly, 5,* 334–342.

Jackson, S., Enright, R., & Murdock, J. (1987). Social perception problems in learning disabled youth: Developmental lag versus perceptual deficit. *Journal of Learning Disabilities, 20,* 361–364.

Keogh, B., Tchir, C., & Windeguth-Beth, A. (1974). Teachers' perception of educationally high risk children. *Journal of Learning Disabilities, 7,* 367–374.

Osmond, B., & Binder, H. (1982). *No one to play with: The social side of learning disabilities.* New York: Random House.

Pearl, R., & Cosden, M. (1982). Sizing up a situation: LD children's understanding of social interactions. *Learning Disability Quarterly, 5,* 371–372.

Wiig, E., & Harris, S. (1974). Perception and interpretation of nonverbally expressed emotions by adolescents with learning disabilities. *Perceptual and Motor Skills, 38,* 239–245.

11

Assessment of Social Skills of Physically Disabled Adolescents

Steve Yarris

The purpose of this chapter is twofold: (a) provide the reader with an illustration of how a behavioral assessment model can be adopted to the specific social skill deficits of special populations and (b) to detail the initial efforts at developing a social skills assessment measure for adolescents with a physical disability.

This work grew out of my counseling work at New York University's Upward Bound program which prepares the city's special education high school students for postsecondary education or vocational training. This program's particular emphasis was upon nurturing academic success within a population that, at a young age, has already encountered physical challenges in developing emotionally, socially, and academically. Thus, any efforts to improve academic functioning also required a sensitivity to the interpersonal skills that most nondisabled adolescents display as a standard part of their behavioral repertoire.

SOCIAL SKILLS OF PHYSICALLY DISABLED ADOLESCENTS: REVIEW OF LITERATURE

Initial research on the social development of physically disabled adolescents who have achieved academic success identifies a pattern of common challenges that have been encountered and successfully mastered.

They include issues of self-esteem, negative social stigma, and academic achievement (Winter & DeSimone, 1983; Wright, 1983).

Self-Esteem

The link between the acceptance of a disability, and levels of self-esteem and interpersonal skills among adolescents with physical disabilities has been well documented (Salzinger, Antrobus, & Glick, 1980; Wright, 1983). Studies draw strong parallels between how people perceive themselves, and how well they are able to provide for their own needs and take charge in socially difficult situations (Belgrave & Mills, 1981; Morgan & Leung, 1980). Because physically disabled students usually have had fewer numbers of positive social experiences to confirm their self-identity, they have a strong tendency to assume that their disabilities make others feel uncomfortable and that voicing their needs will create embarrassing social situations (Lipowski, 1970; Wright, 1983).

Negative Social Stigma

Fitting in socially and gaining confidence in one's physical capabilities are critical parts of adolescent development. Research indicates, however, that the physically disabled adolescent is viewed as an outsider, often subject to scapegoating and denied the social affirmations taken for granted by others in his or her age group (Gliedman & Roth, 1980; Westwood, Vargo, & Vargo, 1981). Numerous studies cite low levels of social interactions between the disabled and their nondisabled peers, particularly when visible disabilities are present (Featherstone, 1980). These findings are consistent with other studies citing negative reactions by the nondisabled to persons with physical disabilities (Westwood et al., 1981; Wright, 1983) and social stigmatization directly related to having a visible physical disability (Donaldson, 1980; Siller, 1970; Weinberg & Santana, 1978). Such interpersonal difficulties appear increasingly predictive of future limitations as children with poor interpersonal skills have been found to have a significantly greater likelihood of social adjustment problems as adults.

Academic Achievement

Physically disabled students have been shown to have a more difficult time adjusting to school social activities than their nondisabled peers (Flores De Apodaca, Watson, Mueller, & Isaacson-Kailes, 1985; Semmel & Cheney, 1979). Studies also indicate that socially stigmatized students tend to have relatively poorer academic records; more verbally and physically aggressive behaviors (Weintraub, Prinz, & Neale, 1978); and a greater likelihood of an adult life hampered by social adjustment difficulties and related mental health impairments (Cowen, Pederson, Babigian, Izzo, & Trost, 1973; McCandless, 1967).

THE SPECIAL NEEDS OF THE UPWARD BOUND STUDENTS

Most Upward Bound Students were in their junior or senior year of high school, with ages ranging from 16 to 21 years. These particular adolescents, because of a physical disability (such as cerebral palsy, muscular dystrophy, or other orthopedic limitations owing to birth defects, accidental trauma, etc.), are forced to rely on wheelchairs or crutches as part of their everyday routine. (These adolescents were otherwise fully capable in terms of physical stamina, and emotional and cognitive functioning.) Because of this reliance, they have a high level of visibility among the general school population and face unique social experiences as a part of their school life. (For example, they prompt a slowdown in hallway traffic; they limit the number of students that can squeeze into the school elevator; they can create classroom distractions with their entrance; and they frequently need assistance in the school lunchroom with trays and cause a subsequent slowdown in services.) Given the need to adapt to anxiety-provoking experiences that often result, many of the interviewed students reported a pattern of social avoidance. They would stay out of the hallways until their able-bodied peers were gone. They would avoid lunchrooms. They would refrain from asking for assistance, to "avoid causing problems."

During my counseling efforts, pervasive social skill deficits related to these unique day to day experiences became increasingly evident. Although they were attending several different high schools throughout the city, the reported problematic experiences were quite similar in nature and tended to involve insurmountable physical barriers, physically unmanageable academic activities, interpersonal difficulties stemming from behavioral limitations, or combinations of all three. (For example, difficulties in maneuvering through school hallways may result in missed learning activities as well as negative comments from interrupted classmates.)

LIMITATIONS OF A STANDARDIZED ASSESSMENT
AND INTERVENTION PROGRAM

When these social skill deficits were recognized, a social skills training intervention was formulated with the initial intent of using the assertiveness training modules designed by Michelson, Sugai, Wood, and Kazdin (1983).

Twelve physically disabled students were selected for this initial intervention. Four of the students used manual wheelchairs, one a motorized chair, two used crutches, and the balance had restricted levels of physical activities related to their disability (arthritis, cerebral palsy, orthopedic impairment). The sessions followed the prescribed format and included behavior-modeling activities between, and among, the trainers and the students; behavioral rehearsals using role playing, role reversal, and trainer feedback; classroom discussions; and "in vivo" homework assignments. Specific training modules used included "expressing and receiving complaints," "refusals or saying 'no'," "requesting favors," "asking why," "requesting behavior change,'" "standing up for your rights," and "conversations."

As the intervention progressed, however, the students' difficulty in identifying with, and responding appropriately to, the given scenarios became strikingly evident. Many of the students indicated that they had not encountered, and could not even imagine themselves involved in, the depicted scenarios. (For example, scenarios involved being asked by parents to wash dishes or being asked by a friend to help rake leaves.) Although the students were willing to dramatize the scenarios (such as being a store customer who had been shortchanged) most of them conceded that they had never even been in a store on their own. (Two of the students stated that they would not enter stores, even if they had the opportunity, because of their fears of "making a scene.") Along these lines, although students willingly play acted a scenario about introducing themselves to new classmates, several students indicated that they depended on others to make such introductions or altogether avoided situations in which introductions were necessary.

Thus, although the Michelson et al. (1983) training module initially appeared promising in the training of more assertive social behaviors, the unique nature of the social experiences of the physically disabled adolescents minimized the usefulness of such training in their everyday lives. (During the training, the students devised their own scenarios: "How do you handle a bus driver who wants you to leave your last period class early so that he can get home and watch soap operas?" and "What would you do if you were in the middle of the school hall and your motorized wheelchair stopped working?")

Development of Population-Specific Assessment Measure

Given the need to develop an assessment measure that could more appropriately address the everyday experiences of the physically disabled adolescent, the behavioral–analytical model of Goldfried and D'Zurilla (1969) appeared ideal, given its capability to be tailored to meet the needs of situation-specific problematic experiences. (See chapter by Koegel on assessment for further description of test techniques.) Because the Upward Bound program had academic success as a primary objective, problematic school situations were selected as the initial focus of the assessment measure.

As a means of further illustrating how the Goldfried and D'Zurilla (1969) model can be applied to the social experiences of special populations, the balance of this chapter will be devoted to an in-depth description of how the model was developed with the assistance of physically disabled adolescents, themselves, and the school staff who they interact with on a daily basis.

Application of Goldfried and D'Zurilla Assessment Model

The implementation of the Goldfried and D'Zurilla (1969) model called for a five-step process involving (a) a behavioral description of the most frequently encountered problematic situations; (b) the collection of possible alternative solutions; (c) a decision-making phase, involving the identification of the "most effective" alternative solution through an evaluation of possible social consequences; (d) the development of a standardized presentation format; and (e) the verification of the measure's statistical properties through a consideration of its concurrent and predictive validity.

The following describes the implementation of the first four steps with the Upward Bound students. (Because the sole purpose of this pilot study was the development of a population-specific assessment measure, the fifth step of statistical validation was not attempted.)

Situational analysis. The initial goal was to collect a large sample of detailed problematic situations that confront the physically disabled student in his or her everyday school activities. Four sources were drawn on: the students themselves; school personnel involved with the students on a daily basis; informal observation of the students in their school setting; and a review of the student files at the program.

Forty-three physically disabled students were mailed instructions and blank response forms with the promise of a small payment for their completion. They were instructed to give as many detailed descriptions as they could of problematic school situations that they felt were related to their having a physical disability. The instructions emphasized that problematic situations occurred to everyone and commonly happened whenever people spent time together.

This is an example of a situation reported by a student as rewritten in a standardized format.

> *Situation*: I only had a half hour for lunch and the cafeteria was really crowded. When I got on line, one of the school workers told me I would have to wait on the side because my wheelchair was getting in everybody's way. When I told my teacher why I was late, he said I should have brought my lunch, or planned my time better.
> *Background*: I don't like making my own lunch. I went to the lunchroom as soon as I could. The only way I could have gotten to my next class on time would have been to skip lunch.
> *Outcome*: The teacher thought I was not interested in learning and that I had an "attitude" problem.

The same blank forms and instructions (except that respondents were asked to describe problematic situations observed rather than experienced) were given to 15 high school faculty and school staff members selected because of their proximity to problematic social interchanges within the schools. Those selected included special education and mainstream classroom teachers, guidance counselors, bus matrons, elevator operators, and rehabilitation counselors. In addition, the author spent 4 days in different high schools informally observing the daily activities of physically disabled students. Folders of the students already enrolled in the program were also examined for references to specific problematic situations.

At the end of this process, 63 problematic situations had been generated, with 42 of those coming from the students. An initial editing for duplicate and seldom encountered situations left 40 problematic situations that had a good probability of occurring at least once in the experience of high school students with a physical disability. (Situations were only included if they had occurred at least once in the experience of 50% of the students surveyed, as in the Goldfried and D'Zurilla [1969] prototype.) Because the situations were still in a "rough" form, they were then rewritten in a more standardized and easily read format. The basic nature of the reported situation, as well as the expressed student concerns, were kept intact as much as possible.

Response enumeration. The main objective of this step was to obtain many different responses to the rewritten problematic situations. The situations were divided equally among 30 physically disabled students into two 15-item sections. Each situation was presented with spaces for written responses. The students were told that the situations had actually occurred, and that the author was interested in how they might respond to each situation. Students were instructed to list at least four possible responses for each situation. A sample situation with sample responses was included to provide a model of the description desired.

The following is an example of one situation and the responses that it prompted from one student:

> Because you can't fit comfortably into a regular desk, the teacher has given you a spot in the front of the room by her desk. All of your friends sit near the back, and every class you can see that they are having a good time.
>
> 1. Say,, "I'm uncomfortable up front. Can I move to the back?"
> 2. Tell the teacher, "I can't see the board from up front."
> 3. Try to get my friends to move up.
> 4. Do the boring thing, nothing.

Once gathered, the situations and the provided responses were reviewed, and those situations that consistently brought consistently ambivalent responses were discarded. As a result, of the original 40 situations only 25 were retained for future use. Among the 25, the three types of situational difficulties discussed earlier could be distinguished.

Eleven of the situations could be linked to physical barriers. One example follows:

> You are waiting for the elevator to go to your 4th period class. The elevator arrives and the operator steps out, saying, "This elevator is out of service. It's time for my break." Your class is three flights up, and there is no way you can climb the stairs.

Nine of the situations were primarily interpersonal in nature and concerned difficulties relating to, or asking assistance from, peers, school staff, and service aides. An example follows:

> For the past two weeks, everytime you need an attendant to help you during the school, they are nowhere to be found.
> When you have asked others for assistance, they do help you but give you an annoyed look while saying that you should really start to take care of yourself.

Five situations described experiences with inappropriate academic activities. An example follows:

> The teacher announces that you have an hour for the exam. You write slowly and by the end of the hour, your test is only half finished. The teacher asks for your paper, and when she sees it is only half complete says aloud: "You should have studied more."

Response evaluation. During this step, a most effective–least effective rating scale for the obtained responses was developed. As in the Goldfried and D'Zurilla (1969) model, the judges to develop this hierarchical ranking were selected from those seen as having significant influence over the student's academic or social achievements. Their relative rankings of the responses would decide the relevant behavioral norms, within which the social competencies of the physically disabled students would be evaluated. The 10 evaluators selected included school principals, special education coordinators, teachers, guidance counselors, elevator operators, and bus drivers. They were provided with a compilation of problematic situations and related responses, as well as instructions on how to rank the "most effective" and "least effective" responses. Rankings from the 10 evaluators were then compiled and averaged, and if at least 50% of the judges were unable to agree on the most effective response, the situation was discarded because of its presumed ambiguous nature and inability to elicit clearly discriminable responses (following the Goldfried and D'Zurilla [1969] model). Here is an example of one such most effective–least effective response hierarchy created by the judges.

> Your wheelchair breaks during the middle of the school day. The guidance counselor says that they don't have anyone available to help you around for the rest of the day, and that he has arranged for the bus company to take you home.

Most Effective

> Refuse the offer and ask if your assignments can be brought to the office.
> I would have the school call my mother and tell her that my wheelchair is broken, and ask if she can bring my spare chair.

Average

> Ask if I can stay in the library for the day.
> Ask if there is a spare wheel chair I can use during the day instead.

Least Effective

> Go home and contact friends after school about what I had missed.

The resulting form consisted of 25 problematic situations (see appendix) that were likely to occur at least once in the experience of a physically disabled student during high school. Each situation now had an accompanying range of five possible responses. Each of the responses had been assigned a relative "effectiveness" value by school personnel who regularly decided the behavioral appropriateness of high school students.

Development of measuring instrument format. The next step entailed developing a scale format to suit the administrative needs of the program. The initial request was for a screening device that allowed for the screening of many students by general staff and that would provide information on social skill deficits and interventional needs.

Although Goldfried and D'Zurilla (1969) used an observed role-playing format, this was rejected because of the number of students typically screened (30–40) and the anxieties raised in role-playing activities observed during the initial intervention. Instead a questionnaire, using a multiple-choice response format, was developed. The 25 problematic situations with accompanying responses were listed with instructions to respond with a *M* next to the response "most likely" to be given, and a *L* next to the response "least likely" to be given. Such a format, in addition to being easily administered by the general staff, also provided an assessment of general social competencies in relevant situation-specific scenarios.

CONCLUSION

This chapter provides school psychologists and special educators with a working model for developing a situation-specific assessment measure tailored to meet the unique social needs of special populations. It was based on the behavioral–analytical model of Goldfried and D'Zurilla (1969) and adapted to the problematic social experiences reported by a sample population of adolescents with a physical disability.

Appendix

Questionnaire Instructions

The following questionnaire has 25 different problem situations that have actually happened to students with disabilities while they were attending high school. Each situation has five different potential responses to the problem being described.

Please Note: There are not any "right" or "wrong" responses. Some responses, however, may be more effective than others in helping students meet their particular needs in a specific situation. Although a response may seem best for you, it may not be the best for another student who has a different social style and manner of acting.

You may not have personally experienced some of the situations that are being described. For the sake of this study, however, please imagine that you are involved in the situation, even if it does not apply to your particular disability.

For each of the twenty five situations

1.   Select one response that you would most likely make, and mark it *M* for "most likely."
2.   Select another response that you would be least likely to make, and mark it *L* for "least likely."

1.   You have a chance to sing in the school chorus. It meets after school, however, and the school bus driver says you have to be downstairs as soon as classes are over. You could

_____ Tell him to leave without you and take the city bus
_____ Write a letter to the Board of Education asking that another bus be assigned
_____ Tell the bus driver to go to hell
_____ Find a friend or relative to take you home
_____ Not join the chorus

2.   You are in a new school, waiting in line at the cafeteria. There is a section of hot foods that looks pretty good. You have trouble carrying a tray, however, and are afraid you might spill the food that you place on it. There are no school assistants in sight. You could

_____ Ask another student for help
_____ Bring sandwiches from home
_____ Be careful and carry it yourself
_____ Bring your lunch with you until you get to know someone who will help with your tray
_____ Not worry about spilling it

3.   The only accessible bathroom on your classroom's floor is usually locked, and you usually have to ask the teacher for the key. The teacher has been acting annoyed at having to walk down the hall and open the door. You are tired of having to talk to him so that you can go to the bathroom. You could

_____ Ignore the teacher's behavior and hope that he gets used to it
_____ Break the lock
_____ Ask the teacher to have a key made up for you
_____ Find someone else who has the key
_____ Try to be more polite in asking

4. Your teacher has begun pestering you about arriving late for class. There are only 5 minutes between periods, and you usually wait a few minutes until the hallway is not so crowded. The teacher says he does not want to hear any more excuses. You could

_____ Ask the teacher to be reasonable
_____ Ignore the teacher
_____ Have your guidance counselor speak to the teacher
_____ Find a friend to help push you through the crowd
_____ Give the teacher an angry look

5. You receive your homework back, and the teacher has written a note across the top saying that you better improve your handwriting, or get a typewriter. You know your writing cannot be improved, and you cannot afford a typewriter. You could

_____ Tell the teacher you have a writing problem
_____ Have someone write your homework while you dictate it
_____ Not hand in any more homework
_____ Tell the teacher that it is the best you can do
_____ Try doing better in class so your homework does not count as much

6. The school elevator has a "broken" sign on it when you arrive at school. Most of your classes are on the top floor, and there appears to be no other way upstairs. Your bus driver suggests going home. You could

_____ Call the teachers and ask that they send down your class work
_____ Call your mother and say that you will be coming home early
_____ Go home and watch television
_____ Tell the bus driver that you want to stay
_____ Agree to go home but first have someone go to the classes and explain your problem while getting the homework assignments

7. The bus driver has asked you to begin bringing your crutches with you because the wheelchair lift has to go in for "maintenance" work, and you will have to climb a few steps to get on the replacement bus for the time being. The bus driver asks you not to "make a big deal about it." You could

_____ Tell the bus driver that you were not planning to make a big deal about it

_____ Agree with him and change the subject
_____ Ask the bus driver if he can get another wheelchair-lift
bus
_____ Get the parents together to write a petition
_____ Make a scene and embarrass the driver

8. Your guidance counselor has just told you that you cannot graduate in June as you have planned. He says that he has looked through your records, and that you have been absent for several classes. He says that there is nothing he can do, but that he will go over the records with you when you return next September. You could

_____ Try to explain it to your parents
_____ Threaten to report him to the Special Education Department
_____ Go above the guidance counselor and talk to the assistant principal
_____ Check the records to see what you are missing
_____ Say nothing and walk away

9. This is your first year of mainstream classes. On the first day, the teacher says that anyone coming late on a regular basis will fail the course. When you speak with her after class, she says that if you cannot make it to class like everyone else you do not belong in a mainstream class. You could

_____ Try to make it to class on time
_____ Try taking a special education class instead
_____ Yell at the teacher about being unfair
_____ Have your parents talk to the teacher
_____ Ask the teacher to talk to the one you have before her class about letting you out early

10. In crossing the hilly street to school, you are faced with people darting in front of your wheelchair as the light changes, with cars honking at you. The crossing guard has warned you to speed up. You could

_____ Try crossing at another corner
_____ Ask the crossing guard to come across with you
_____ Try to speed up your wheelchair
_____ Continue at the pace you are going and not say anything
_____ Slow down even more

11. For the past two weeks, everytime you need an attendant to help you during school, they are nowhere to be found. When you

have asked others for assistance, they do help you but give you an annoyed look while saying that you should really start to take care of yourself. You could

_____ See if you can do without the coat

_____ Thank them again and go on your way

_____ Ask your teacher to get an attendant

_____ Ask your mother to call the school and get an attendant

_____ Say to them, "If the situation were reversed, I wouldn't help you either"

12. During the first week of school, a new teacher asks why it takes so long for you to complete classroom assignments. You try to explain about your disability, but the teacher interrupts you and says that unless you speed up you could fail the course. You could

_____ Try to explain some more to the teacher about your disability

_____ Pretend you do not know what he or she is talking about

_____ Get a tutor to work with you on assignments

_____ Ask your teacher if you can stay after school to complete the assignments

_____ Talk to the other students about the problem

13. You have just received your report card, and you have received a *C* for your first-period class. When you approach the teacher, he says it is because you are always late in the morning. You try explaining that the school bus is always arriving late, even though you are waiting outside your house on time. The teacher says that you better shape up or next marking period, you will receive a *F*. You could

_____ Tell the teacher to talk to the bus driver

_____ Say, "It's not my fault, the bus is always late"

_____ Learn to take the city bus to school

_____ Call the bus company yourself and complain to the dispatcher

_____ Have your parents call the teacher

14. Because you cannot fit comfortably into a regular desk, the teacher has given you a spot in the front of the room, by her desk. All of your friends sit near the back, and every class you can see that they are having a good time. You could

_____ Ignore your friends

_____ Cause scenes in class until the teacher moves you

_____ Tell the teacher that you do not feel comfortable in the front of the class, and ask if an accessible desk could be put in another part of the classroom

_____ Ask one of your friends to sit in the front with you

_____ Tell the teacher that the student next to you is bothering you and ask to sit somewhere else

15. Your wheelchair breaks during the middle of the school day. The guidance counselor says that they do not have anyone available to help you around for the rest of the day, and that he has arranged for the bus company to take you home. You could

_____ Ask if there is a spare wheelchair you can use during the day instead

_____ Refuse the offer and ask if your assignments can be brought to the office

_____ Tell the counselor, "Thanks for nothing"

_____ Go home and contact friends after school about what you have missed

_____ Ask if you can stay in the library for the day

16. There is someone in your class that you would really like to meet. The trouble is that you usually do not get to school early, and the school bus driver gets annoyed if you do not come right outside after your last class. Still, you would like a chance to talk to this attractive person. You could

_____ Threaten to get the bus driver in trouble unless he or she cooperates

_____ Ask the bus driver to pick you up earlier in the morning

_____ Talk to the special person after school and give the bus driver an excuse

_____ Take the city bus to school

_____ Just hope that you will have a class together

17. You are waiting for the elevator to go to your fourth-period class. The elevator arrives, and the operator steps out saying, "This elevator is out of service. It's time for my break." Your class is three flights up, and there is no way you can climb the stairs. You could

_____ Tell the operator it is his or her responsibility to operate long enough for you to get to class

_____ Speak to the guidance counselor about assigning another operator during the break

_____ Run the wheelchair over the operator's foot
_____ Tell friends to speak up when this happens to them
_____ Stay in the hallway and talk to friends

18. On the first day of school, you find that your first class is only accessible by climbing a flight of stairs. You somehow manage the first week (by getting some help, if necessary) but cannot see yourself doing this week after week, even if people are willing to help you. You could

_____ Go to the lunchroom during that period
_____ Ask the teacher to get your class changed
_____ Ask your parents to call the principal about having a ramp installed
_____ Complain out loud during the class
_____ Get a friend to take notes for the missed classes

19. The sidewalk outside of school is particularly bumpy and broken up with cracks. In your wheelchair, you made it across safely the first week, but the ride was really rough. There are 39 more weeks of school left, and a lot more trips across that sidewalk in the future. You could

_____ Start riding in the street
_____ Have someone help you across
_____ Tell your parents that you fell over in your chair
_____ Try to find a back exit to use
_____ Fake a fall and get time off from class

20. The teacher announces that you have an hour for the exam. You write slowly and by the end of the hour, your test is only half finished. The teacher asks for your paper, and when she sees it is only half complete says aloud, "You should have studied more." You could

_____ Tell the teacher before the test that you have trouble writing and need more time
_____ Yell at the teacher that it was wrong for him or her to say what he or she said outloud
_____ Tell the teacher that you did study
_____ Ask the teacher if you could finish it for homework and bring it back tomorrow
_____ Do not say anything

21. In using the school library you realize that some of the books you need are beyond your reach, because of your disability. You ap-

proach the librarian, but she says there is nothing she can do. You could

_____ See if your parents will take you to a nearby library to help you finish your work
_____ Plead with her by stressing in a nice way that it was her job to help people
_____ Ask someone else in the library to help get the book
_____ Try doing without the book
_____ Knock books off the shelf until you get help

22. In the school hall, on your way to class, your wheelchair suddenly stops working and you cannot move. People are rushing past you to get to their classes. You could

_____ Ask someone passing by to help you
_____ Yell for help and create a scene
_____ Sit there and mutter to yourself
_____ Ask someone to call the guidance counselor about your problem
_____ Read a book

23. To save time getting home, the bus driver has been asking you to leave classes a few minutes early. Your last class is one you really enjoy, but if you stay until the end, the bus driver complains for the entire trip home. You could

_____ Try to get the bus driver to understand your situation
_____ Leave the class early but get someone to take notes for you
_____ Start arriving later and later for the bus
_____ Report the bus driver to the dispatcher
_____ Ignore the bus driver and hope he or she gets used to it

24. Because your speech is sometimes difficult to understand, you need extra time to ask questions in class. At first, your teacher gave you that time in class. Now, however, you realize that the teacher ignores you when you raise your hand. You could

_____ Ask the teacher why she is ignoring you
_____ Have a friend ask the teacher why he or she never calls on you when you raise your hand
_____ Call out, "Hey, how about calling on me?"
_____ Have your counselor speak to the teacher about paying more attention to you in the classroom
_____ Have someone in class ask your questions for you

25. Though there are two elevators in your school, only one is in service during the day. As a result, everyone tries crowding into one elevator, some people try walking up the stairs, and others just accept being late for all of their classes. You could

_____ Learn how to run the elevator by watching the operator
_____ Get a pass from the guidance counselor explaining why you are late for class
_____ Try using the teachers' elevator
_____ Say nothing until the teacher brings up your lateness and then explain the situation
_____ Get the students together to complain to the principal

REFERENCES

Belgrave, F. Z., & Mills, J. (1981). Effect upon desire for social interaction with a physically disabled person of mentioning the disability in different contexts. *Journal of Applied Social Psychology, 11*, 44–57.

Cowen, E. L., Pederson, A., Babigian, H., Izzo, L. D., & Trost, M. A. (1973). Long-term follow-up of early detected vulnerable children. *Journal of Consulting and Clinical Psychology, 41*, 438–446.

Donaldson, J. (1980). Changing attitudes toward disabled persons: A review and analysis of research. *Exceptional Children, 46*, 504–514.

Featherstone, H. (1980). *A difference in the family: Life with a disabled child.* New York: Basic Books.

Flores De Apodaca, R., Watson, J. D., Mueller, J., & Isaacson-Kailes, J. (1985). A sociometric comparison of mainstreamed, orthopedically handicapped high school students and nonhandicapped classmates. *Psychology in the Schools, 22*, 95–101.

Gliedman, J., & Roth, W. (1980). *The unexpected minority: Handicapped children in America.* New York: Harcourt Brace Jovanovich.

Goldfried, M. R., & D'Zurilla, T. J. (1969). A behavioral-analytic model for assessing competence.. In C. D. Spielberger (Ed.), *Current topics in clinical and community psychology.* New York: Academic Press.

Lipowski, Z. J. (1970). Physical illness, the individual, and the coping process. *Psychiatric Medicine, 1*, 91–102.

McCandless, B. R. (1967). *Children: Behavior and development.* New York: Holt, Rinehart & Winston.

Michelson, L., & Wood, R. P. (1982). Development and psychometric properties of the Children's Assertive Behavior Scale. *Journal of Behavioral Assessment, 4*, 13–14.

Michelson, L., Sugai, D. P., Wood, R. P., & Kazdin, A. E. (1983). *Social skills assessment and training with children.* New York: Plenum Press.

Morgan, B., & Leung, P. (1980). Effects of assertion training on acceptance of disability by physically disabled university students. *Journal of Counseling Psychology, 27,* 209–212.

Roff, M., Sells, S. B., & Golden, M. (1972). *Social adjustment and personality development in children.* Minneapolis: University of Minnesota Press.

Salzinger, S., Antrobus, J., & Glick, J. (1980). *The ecosystem of the "sick" child.* New York: Academic Press.

Semmel, M., & Cheney, M. (1979). Social acceptance and self-concept of handicapped pupils in mainstreamed environments. *Education Unlimited, 1,* 65–68.

Siller, J. (1970). *The structure of attitudes toward the disabled* (U.S. Public Health Service Publication No. RD 707-1967). Washington, DC: U.S. Government Printing Office.

Weinberg, N., & Santana, R. (1978). Comic books: Champions of the disabled stereotype. *Rehabilitation Literature, 39,* 327–331.

Weintraub, S., Prinz, R. J., & Neale, J. M. (1978). Peer evaluations of the competence of children vulnerable to psychopathology. *Journal of Abnormal Child Psychology, 6,* 461–473.

Westwood, M. J., Vargo, J. W., & Vargo, F. (1981). Methods for promoting attitude change toward and among physically disabled persons. *Journal of Applied Rehabilitation Counseling, 12,* 220–225.

Winter, M., & DeSimone, D. (1983). I'm a person, not a wheelchair! Problems of disabled adolescents. In R. L. Jones (Ed.), *Reflections on growing up disabled* (pp. 27–33). Reston, VA: Council for Exceptional Children.

Wright, B. A. (1983). *Physical disability: A psychosocial approach* (2nd ed.). New York: Harper & Row.

Part IV
Assertiveness and Social Skills Programs in Schools

Introduction

Iris G. Fodor

Following the psychoeducational model, school personnel are increasingly involved in working directly with adolescents on assertiveness and social skills issues within the schools. Such programs range from communication training and enhancement of social competence in normal adolescents to development of therapeutic interventions for problematic adolescent groups. Most school psychologists, counselors, and teachers customize the standardized assessments and treatments for their particular school population. Others develop their own curriculum.

The chapters in Part IV were written by psychologists and psychologists–teachers drawing from their experience in schools serving diverse populations. All the authors used some of the standard modules described by Goldstein, Sprafkin, Gershaw, and Klein (1980) and Michelson, Sugai, Wood, and Kazdin (1983), but adapted these programs to the needs of their particular group.

Marilyn Bernstein Shendell, in the opening chapter, describes her project with a rap group for suburban junior high school female adolescents. She used key features of Goldstein et al.'s (1980) structured learning for her students. Additionally, she emphasized communication and self-expressive skills that fit her model of expanding social skills to the emotional domains outlined in her chapter. Diane Duggan-Ali, a sex educator and school psychologist, next describes her program for integrating social skills training into a sex education curriculum in an inner-city private school. Ernest Collabolletta, drawing from this experience as a teacher and substance abuse counselor, next describes his work integrating social skills and assertiveness training in a group of recovering substance abusers in a suburban high school. In the final chapter, Danya Vardi describes the use of assertiveness training for pregnant and parenting mothers in an inner-city high school. These adolescents, who still live at home and attend high school are struggling with assertiveness issues with their own mothers, learning to handle their babies and toddlers while negotiating the school and welfare bureaucracy.

All the chapters in this section illustrate how clinicians in the school can integrate the educational components of assertiveness and skills training with a therapeutic approach. Whether these programs are presented as communication curriculum for all students, incorporated into rap groups, or targeted for students with special problems, these pilot projects confirm the utility of effective expressiveness and social interactive skills training for adolescents.

REFERENCES

Goldstein, A., Sprafkin, R., Gershaw, J., & Klein, P. (1980). *Skillstreaming the adolescent*. Champaign, IL: Research Press.

Michelson, L., Sugai, D. P., Wood, R., & Kazdin, A. E. (1983). *Social skills assessment and training with children: An empirically based handbook*. New York: Plenum.

12

Communication Training for Adolescent Girls in Junior High School Setting: Learning to Take Risks in Self-Expression

Marilyn Bernstein Shendell

Jennifer is practicing in front of the mirror attempting to look "cool" and "in control." She is sure that everyone else knows just what to say to boys, and only she is filled with fear bordering on terror as the party grows closer.

Allison is fighting with her mother for permission to stay later at the party. They never seem to be able to agree on anything.

Jill is binging on the food in the refrigerator to control her anger and disappointment. She was not invited to a classmate's party.

Samantha sneaks into her room, closes the door, and shakes out an arsenal of pimple cream products onto her bed. She is determined to have clear skin by Saturday night, or she is not going to the party.

ADOLESCENCE AND IMPORTANCE
OF PEER GROUP

The peer group becomes of fundamental importance to the young adolescent as she struggles to establish a separate and independent identity from her family. These relationships provide the bridge away from the "nest of the nuclear family" (Mishne, 1986). Through peer acceptance the adolescent is helped to manage separation issues and to establish her sense of identity. In addition, the peer group provides the adolescent with role models she may choose to emulate.

Peer relationships are affected by the many changes the adolescent undergoes. Physical changes are apparent for everyone to see and may be the occasion for intense self-consciousness, which may manifest itself in problems with social interactions and prompt concerns about body image. Many adolescents ask themselves, "Am I always going to be short? How do I get rid of these pimples?"

In addition, with the increased capacity for social cognitions for example, how people think about other people and themselves, adolescents, more than any other group, become concerned with how others think of them. Their daily life is filled with issues regarding social status—who is going out with whom, what party were they invited to, which one were they left out of, and who is smart, dumb, or popular. These many interactions raise a multitude of questions. Many adolescents ask themselves, "Did I say the right thing? God, did that sound dumb? What did he mean by that? Does that mean he likes me or does he think I'm a nerd?"

IMPORTANCE OF EFFECTIVE SOCIAL AND COMMUNICATION SKILLS

While they are attempting to deal with the physical, social, and emotional changes of this developmental period, young adolescents must also negotiate a more complex social environment that is increasingly broadened to include the school, the community, a work setting, as well as relationships with peers, family, and authority figures. In response to these demands, adolescents are well served if they have the social skills necessary to establish meaningful and satisfying interactions. These interpersonal interactions are dependent on adequate communication skills without which adolescents often falter. We seldom consider whether the average youngster is prepared to know her feelings and then to act on them effectively. Yet, it is apparent that many adolescents do not have these skills. Their communications belie their confusions, uncertainty, and inability to discern their feelings for themselves. Their miscommunications prevent mutually satisfying interactions and instead serve to frustrate adolescents' efforts to negotiate normative developmental tasks.

This chapter describes a small group program developed to address communication and social skills for girls dealing with age-appropriate developmental tasks in a junior high school setting. The goal of this project was to help the adolescent become aware of her feelings, to provide her with the necessary tools to express those feelings, and thereby to achieve more effective and assertive communication skills.

SOCIAL SKILLS PROGRAM

In developing a social skills program within a developmental framework I adapted the approach of Goldstein, Sprafkin, Gershaw, and Klein (1980) called "structured learning." The program of Goldstein et al. incorporates assertiveness training within a hierarchy of stages with skills to be acquired at each level. The program features skill modules that can be used to teach targeted areas of need that lend themselves to focus group work.

Focus of Program

The communication skills program grew out of an ongoing rap group whose focus had been recurrent interpersonal conflicts. As this group evolved, it became clear that the girls had no vocabulary for talking about their feelings. Feelings were confused and often poorly defined. The girls groped to discriminate and define what was going on: What were they feeling and against whom? How could they assert their position? Each girl was uniquely involved in her own struggle for self-worth and social position. Instituting a social skills program at this time was an effort to define more clearly the girls' concerns and difficulties, to help them express and recognize emotions, and to provide them with more adequate methods of coping with problematic situations.

Program of Goldstein et al

Goldstein et al. (1980) proposes that behaviorally disordered youngsters can be categorized in terms of three major types: the aggressive, the withdrawn, and the immature youngster. Each type of child can be viewed in terms of the presence of dysfunctional behaviors as well as the absence of a repertoire of prosocial or developmentally appropriate behaviors. It is the belief of Goldstein et al. that a training program oriented toward the explicit teaching of prosocial skills can remediate what they see as skill deficits. These desirable and functional skills are then added to the youngsters behavioral repertoire. By targeting their skill deficiencies, the "average" adolescent can be given assistance in dealing with the developmental hurdles she faces.

The structured learning approach incorporates the didactic procedures first developed by Bandura (1973). These procedures consist of modeling, role playing, performance feedback, and transfer of training. The program presents 50 target skills that are for the most part concerned with interpersonal behaviors, prosocial alternatives to aggression, and aggression-management behaviors.

Assessment

Goldstein et al.'s (1980) Structured Learning Skill Checklist, which describes numerous social skills and asks the responder to note his or her level of comfort with each skill, was given to each participant as a self-report inventory before and after the program to assess perceived levels of skill deficiency and subsequent changes in self-perceptions. The Mooney Problem Behavior Checklist was administered to help establish the specific target areas most pertinent to the participants. These provided common trouble spots to be addressed, such as peer interactions, family difficulties, and academic concerns. An open-ended individual interview was also conducted at the conclusion of the program to attain additional feedback regarding the program.

Group of participants. Eight seventh-grade girls, ages 12 to 13, who had been in a short-term "rap" group participated in this program. The school guidance counselor co-led the group with the school psychologist (and author). Each of the girls was of at least average intelligence; however, achievement levels varied considerably within the group from just passing to high academic achievement.

The girls attend a small suburban junior high that is located in Westchester (New York). The author is the school psychologist at this junior high school, which is a facility housing 300 seventh- and eighth-grade students.

Procedure

After administering the self-report inventories to highlight deficits, the leader chose appropriate skills to be addressed from Goldstein's 50 skills modules. Most of the girls checked off items that indicated they had difficulty knowing or expressing their feelings. Examples of these questions were: Do you try to recognize which emotions you are feeling? Do you let others know which emotions you are feeling? Therefore, modules were selected that dealt with these skills. In addition, content was based on themes that had emerged during the course of the rap group. Recurring issues centered on peer interactions, communication with parents, and concerns with academic achievement. These themes therefore provided the focus for group discussions. The leaders modified the content questions presented in the skill modules to fit the needs of the group; therefore the steps for learning a particular skill remained the same. Modeling displays were used, however, that were more pertinent to these youngsters' social involvements.

SOCIAL SKILLS DEVELOPMENT

Introductory Sessions

Awareness and Deflection of Feelings

Self-esteem at this developmental level is "risky business" (Kaplan, 1984), and the adolescent functions under a heightened sense of self-awareness. With the emergence of these tender feelings the adolescent often fears they are taking a risk in self-expression in that she is exposing herself. In touch with this risk and afraid to reveal herself, the adolescent tends to avoid and deflect feelings.

Illustration. The girls' inability to label their feelings as well as deny their feelings was quickly seen in beginning sessions. For example, the girls were asked how they might feel if they had done poorly on an exam, and their classroom teacher read their grades out loud. All responded with an air of indifference, stating, "it doesn't matter" or "no big deal." After some probing it appeared that this facade served to protect their more vulnerable feelings, which, after further exploration and questioning, were hesitatingly shared as either embarrassment or stupidity. It did not occur to any of the girls to label the teacher's behavior accurately as inappropriate and therefore as a problem to be solved. The girls' lack of familiarity with their own feelings compounded their need to appear unaffected and indifferent, all contributing to a passive style that limited the development of a sense of self as assertive.

The girls' sense of limited personal power was also seen in relationship to parental authority. The girls were asked: How do you feel when a failure notice comes home?

M: Scared. My mother screams, "I hate that."

M and L stated they would lie and make up some story to try to get out of trouble.

C: My father would be furious at me, I can never get grades that seem to satisfy him. The minute we start talking about anything and he asks me questions I start screaming, then my mother usually comes to me rescue.

As so many of the girls could relate to this situation, we decided to role play an interaction between a father and daughter regarding grades. C volunteered to be the father, and M played the child. M immediately concocted a lie by way of explanation. In ascertaining what M wanted to accomplish, it was evident that escaping punishment was her primary motivation. In contrast to C's description of her own father, she role played a meek and accommodating parent. The girls were asked to role play this situation again, but this time to try and deal directly with what they were feeling without lying. This same situation was played out with several girls; in all instances the interchange became angry and argumentative.

Summary statement. For the girls, expressing angry feelings resulted in heated and defiant confrontations. In this session, it seemed that each of the girls was most comfortable in expressing feelings of anger. They were not concerned with the resolution of the issue nor did they see expression of feelings as a first step toward effective communication. Feeling at times inadequate, superior, frustrated, or misunderstood, there is no understanding that exchanges can be mutually reciprocal; instead, behavior becomes deceptive and antagonistic. What was most apparent was that the girls needed to be able to identify what it was they were feeling. Once the feeling could be labeled accurately they would be in a better position to explore ways of expressing those feelings.

Emerging Skills

Movement from Deflection to Sharing

As the sessions continued the group became more cohesive. Once one of the group members was willing to share her feelings, the rest were able to do the same more easily. The girls were then able to begin to discuss feeling hurt, left out, or betrayed.

Illustration. In the third session the following was presented: "You overhear your friends discussing their plans for the evening, and you have not been included." The girls were asked to consider how they would feel, what might be going on, and what, if anything they would do about it.

The group had a very difficult time with this situation, which was reflected in a great deal of movement about the room, side conversations, and a heightened level of distraction. Role playing consisted of devious manipulations and attacks. Addressing the group's response to this situation, the leader asked the girls to try and focus on what they were feeling before expressing their anger. This was done in an attempt to get the girls to experience their underlying feelings before reacting.

C: That's really lousy. I'd never talk to her again.

M: (a sought after and more confident member of the group): I'd probably go home and cry, that's what happened when J had her party and didn't invite me.

M's open response of feeling hurt stimulated other responses of feeling left out or betrayed.

A: I thought they were my friends and would never leave me out.

S: I'd wonder what I did wrong; maybe they were getting back at me for something.

Summary statement. The situation presented for role playing raised anxiety connected to fears of rejection by the peer group that heightened doubts of self-adequacy and served to impede their ability to respond in a behaviorally appropriate manner. By becoming aware of what they were indeed feeling the girls were learning how to risk expressing those feelings.

Expanding Skills

Process of Learning to Communicate More Clearly

As sessions progressed it was suggested that they were becoming more comfortable with the program, better able to identify situations as problematic, and generally more aware of the difficulties they had in expressing feelings in a way that might lead to effective and satisfying resolutions. C and L brought up situations they wanted to explore. This was the first time the girls were able to use the group as a forum for problem solving.

L wanted help in approaching her mother. L stated that she needed spending money for a planned vacation with her grandparents in Florida. She was certain her mother would say no "just like she always did" and then she would be "screwed."

Two of the girls role played a "battle" between parent and child in which neither party listens, and each grabs at past grievances to hurl at the other. This enactment brought enthusiastic applause of recognition from the girls. This scene was then reenacted by the leaders using prosocial skills that incorporated the past lessons, and stressed "listening" to the other person and "getting" more information before proceeding. In this enactment the leaders, role playing parent and child, negotiated an agreement after first listening to the others concerns. The mother shared financial difficulties, and the daughter was surprised to learn that she was not being indiscriminately punished. The daughter realized that this was not a personal rejection but was based on information she never thought to inquire about. At the conclusion of this modeled behavior, M immediately said, "I can't stay that calm—I get angry instantly." M agreed and said she either cried to get her way or manipulated her parents into agreeing by "forcing" them to chose between two alternatives. A preferred to badger her parents until she "eventually wears them out."

Appraisal. The girls were most familiar and comfortable with either badgering, crying, manipulating, or arguing with their parents, particularly with their mothers, when anticipating that their wishes would not be met. This may be viewed as symptomatic of the conflict surrounding the process of parent–adolescent separation. For these girls, anger and defiance, or subtler manipulations enabled them to feel powerful and in control in the face of parental authority. If the girls could acknowledge and accept their own feelings they would then be in a better position to view themselves as well as their parents more objectively. Without the ability to self-reflect the girls could respond only to their own anxiety, and the parent was then treated as an obstacle. The role of feelings in situations was becoming more clearly differentiated and would then allow for new social perspectives. Strategies could begin to be considered that might include exchanges, negotiations, deal making, compromises, and so forth, all of which would include behaviors designed to protect the interests of the self while considering the concerns of the other more adequately.

Middle Sessions

Evaluation of Progress: Toward a Fuller Understanding of Link between Feelings and Behavior

In this session the examiner sought to assist the youngsters in understanding the link between feelings and behavior. It was clear that as soon as they felt opposed, the girls reacted immediately and almost consistently with anger. The message was, "If you won't give me what I want, I feel furious." It was important therefore to deal with the feelings beneath the anger: sadness, frustration, deprivation, and so on. Although these feelings were evidently quite strong the girls were unable to deal with them. Instead, vulnerable feelings were quickly short-circuited and appeared as anger, an emotion that served to empower and energize. The girls needed help to recognize that their behaviors were motivated by inner feeling states. Without this connection, the social skills training program could not be effective. Prosocial skills could not be learned when they ran straight into the defense. It was unlikely that interpersonal behaviors could be modified before the girls were more in touch with what it was they were feeling.

The leaders shared their perceptions with the group, stating that the girls tended to react with anger and seldom stopped to consider how they were feeling or what they wanted to accomplish. Instead, they merely exploded and were than left with a messy situation. Therefore, in this session they would be encouraged to look for the sources of their behaviors.

Movement Beyond Anger: Exposing the Hurts

Illustration. C volunteered that she and L had just had a "big fight" in the lunchroom and she would like to discuss it with the group. L agreed. C stated that L came up to her and told her the following:

L: Adam's using you just like he used me. Adam likes to go from girl to girl, leads them on, and then dumps them. You should watch out.

C: Why don't you mind your own business?

L defended her position by stating she had been looking out for C's interests and had only wanted to protect her from getting hurt.

C: L was assuming without the facts; she doesn't know about me and Adam.

L was indignant that C had yelled at her and embarrassed her in front of everyone.

L and C were instructed to role play this situation for the group, but this time to concentrate on "how they felt." C was now able to tell L that she felt "offended and hurt" by L's insinuations. L responded that as a new student in the school and new to the "group" she was uncertain of her position with the girls and was always afraid of "being used." She did not know if the girls considered her a friend. She thought if she told C about Adam she would earn a more solid footing with C, whom she perceived as being "very popular." Several girls were surprised by L's admission and hurried to reassure her that she was indeed liked and valued as a friend.

Appraisal. This session was a turning point for the group. Because of the adolescent's vulnerability and need for peer acceptance, she is often reluctant to share her problems and risk being "different" from the other group members. L and C were therefore quite brave in their willingness to broach this topic with the group. The girls were willing to explore both the meaning of their behavior and the emotions that underlie interpersonal transactions. In doing so, they used skills previously discussed in the group, referring to the topics "knowing all the facts" and "stating your feelings." These skills provided them with a framework that gave them the freedom and the safety necessary to expose sensitive feelings.

Efforts to Work on Being More Expressive

The girls' social competence appeared to be compromised by how they envisioned themselves and by what they think others see. As the girls became more unified in their compassion for one another, their sense of understanding and empathy for one another created a strong bond within the group that eased defenses and lead to more open and revealing communication.

Attempts to Talk about What's Wrong

The girls had just received their report cards and were anxious to discuss their feelings, concerns, and reactions to their grades. C stated she had a "lousy grade in math" because the teacher went too fast, and she never knew what was going on. When asked why she did not ask questions in class, she replied that it was more important to "look good" than to ask for help. A supported this feeling and said she hated "feeling dumb" in front of other kids and was afraid they would laugh at her. C felt that some teachers made it worse. Mrs. W made her feel like a "moron" if she gave the wrong answer, and Mr. F was always nice. The group agreed that the teachers' impressions and response to them had a strong effect on how they participated or felt in class.

M: I walk in and expect to be yelled at, but when it happens I still feel like crying.

D, an overweight youngster, stated one of her teachers caught her chewing gum and remarked in front of the whole class, "I don't know why you bother to go to the beauty parlor when you are so ugly in class!"

C: I could have cried for you when that happened.

C liked Mr. K the best because he was impersonal and very structured, he just taught the class and did not get involved with anyone. M, the only girl in the group with learning disabilities surprised the group by cheerfully and adamantly announcing the following:

M: Don't believe what the teachers tell you; I know I'm not stupid. My mother told me not to listen to them.

D: Not my mother; she always tells me how stupid I am.

There was general agreement that their mothers tended to have the same opinion of them as did the more problematic teachers. Only M expressed confidence in her abilities, stating her mother supported and worked with her. She suggested to the group that "you're not what people say you are." L, spurred on by the girls' free expression of their sense of inadequacy stated the following:

L: I never thought you felt like that; everything looks so easy for you.

D: Yea, and I thought only my mother calls me dumb.

Appraisal. It has been suggested (Elkind, 1957) that the extreme self-consciousness of adolescents adds to their belief that everyone is scrutinizing them. This places a terrific emotional strain on youngsters. Sharing these experiences therefore helped to alleviate the girls' sense that they were totally alone and misunderstood. Bravado gave way to expressions of inferiority and the concomitant need to "look good." Only M, who felt encouraged and supported at home, had the ability to shrug off criticism and not have it serve as a ready endorsement of imagined inadequacy, incompetence, or worthlessness. Bolstered by the newfound support of the group along with their discovery of shared fears and vulnerability, the group offered them a first step toward a more consolidated sense of self, independent from the evaluation of others.

The social skills program ended in this session with the completion of the posttest Structured Learning Skill Checklist. Each youngster was interviewed individually in the course of a week to provide further closure and to garner additional feedback information.

Results

A comparison of pretest and posttest scores was made for each girl and for the group as a whole. The lower the cumulative score, the less capable the youngster felt about using a particular skill. Results indicate gains for six of the eight girls, with scores increasing from 2% to 40%, with an average gain of 16%. Only two of the girls' scores decreased an average of 12%, suggesting they felt less comfortable with prosocial skills. Seventy-five percent of the group scores increased, with a net average increase for the group as a whole of 7%.

The individual interviews were most striking in the girls consensus that they would now be able to deal with their mothers more effectively.

M: I'm calmer with my parents now. I used to be really mad; I don't let it get to me now.

L: I used it with my mother the other day. I got my report card, and I sat down and talked to her. In the past I'd be afraid to show it to her. She wasn't really happy, and she still punished me. Guess she thinks that's what she has to do to get me to learn.

C: The acting gave me an idea of what to say to my mother. I got an idea of how the other girls act toward their mothers. It showed me different ways to handle problems—how to confront them.

C: I learned how to deal with my problems in a better way. I've been using it. Like in a fight I had with my mother. I don't go off on her now—I tell my reason and hear hers. Still hard to talk to your mom about personal things though.

M: I learned how to tell people how you feel, how to deal with things. Know how to face my mother with progress reports now.

D: I confront friends more. I ask them if they're talking about me. It didn't change dealing with my family. But I think more about situations now—like getting into fights with my family or friends, I tell them what's wrong.

A: It showed me how to talk about things in my life and how to deal with them. To talk to my parents—before I couldn't do that—mostly to my mom, I would be embarrassed before; I didn't talk to her. It's easier now, I found a different way to talk to her.

C: I was never confident in what I did before; now I think about what I definitely can do instead of what's no good. Still can't talk to my mother. Things happen in school I'm uncomfortable talking to her about—talking to her annoys me; my father too.

Discussion

The results of the present study suggest that the issues of adolescence are responsive to the techniques of social skills training and that social skills training can serve to support developmental growth by expanding the adolescents' skill repertoire. By considering the developmental context of social behaviors, interventions can focus on skill strategies that are developmentally powerful and appropriate.

The literature discusses the seeming contradiction between the need for assertiveness in socialization as contrasted with the expectation of more passive behavior in women. Research in normal female development seems to suggest that women are socialized to rely heavily on external acceptance and feedback to inform their identity. Although men rely on internal standards of judgment, women depend on the responses of others in developing a feeling of worth and competence (Bardwick & Donovan, 1972). Numerous studies (Bardwick, 1971; Douvan & Adekin, 1966; Kagan & Moos, 1962; Simmons & Rosenberg, 1979) suggest that women develop their identity as they experience themselves in relationships to others. As such it may well be easier for men to be assertive as they are socialized to be autonomous and independent, whereas women are taught that compliance, dependency, and interpersonal sensitivity are expected of them (Kagen & Moos, 1962; Weitzman, 1975).

Cultural and ethnic issues also serve to contribute to the girls' orientation. Six of the eight girls shared similar family backgrounds. From second-generation Italian families, they tended to have families in which daughters were more restricted than sons. This study highlighted McGoldrick's (1982) observation that Italian families value the insular family and are more likely then to be at odds with the adolescent social life and peer group involvement whose developmental task is to sustain the adolescent's efforts toward separation and identity formation. It is not surprising therefore that this period of adolescence has been referred to by McGoldrick as extremely stressful for Italian families. It is unlikely, however, that this ethnic group is alone in its struggle with separation issues. Separation issues are generally a charged issue, underscoring the need for added skill development to enhance this process.

Several other factors emerged that may have contributed to the seeming success of this program. As seventh graders, the girls were in the midst of transition from the more protective environment of the elementary school setting to the multiteacher situation of the junior high school. For most of the girls it was the first time that they were provided with a situation that both encouraged and supported them to voice their fears and concerns. The group also served as a forum for them to share their feelings with other peers and thus find that they were not alone in their emerging experiences. In their initial rap group the girls tackled issues of trust and confidentiality that were no longer an issue once the social skills program started. With the exception of A, all the girls had come from the same elementary school, and although they were not in the same social groups in school, they were familiar and comfortable with one another.

CONCLUSION

In summary, by incorporating a developmental and theoretical framework within a social skills program a firmer grasp and understanding of social behaviors is possible. Within this context problematic patterns of reacting can more easily be interpreted and modified toward adaptive and prosocial modes of behavior. The adolescent is not viewed within a deficit orientation, and behavior is not seen as singly determined; instead, the youngster's behavior is understood as an expression of internal and external demands for which she may need help in recognizing and developing more responsive and appropriate behavioral options.

REFERENCES

Bandura, A. (1973). *Aggression: A social learning analysis.* Englewood Cliffs, NJ: Prentice Hall.

Bardwick, I. (1971). *Psychology of women: A study of bio-cultural conflicts.* New York: Harper & Row.

Bardwick, J. M., & Donovan, E. (1972). Ambivalence: The socialization of women. In V. Gornick & B. K. Moran (Eds.), *Women in a sexist society* (pp. 225–241). New York: New American Library.

Chodorow, N. (1978). *The reproduction of mothering.* Los Angeles: University of California Press.

Douvan, E., & Adekin, J. (1966). *The adolescent experience.* New York: Wiley.

Elkind, D. (1957). Egocentrism in adolescence. *Child Development, 4,* 1025–1034.

Erikson, E. H. (1950). *Childhood and society.* New York: Norton.

Goldstein, A. P., Sprafkin, R. P., Gershaw, N. J., & Klein, P. (1980). *Skillstreaming the adolescent.* Champaign, IL: Research Press.

Hin, J. P., & Lynch, M. E. (1983). The intensification of gender-related role expectations during early adolescence. In J. Brooks-Gunn & A. C. Peterson (Eds.), *Girls at puberty* (pp. 201–229). New York: Plenum.

Kagan, I., & Moos, H. A. (1962). *Birth to maturity.* New York: Wiley.

Kaplan, L. J. (1984). *Adolescence: The farewell to childhood.* New York: Simon & Schuster.

McGoldrick, M. (1982). In J. Pearce & J. Giordano (Eds.), *Ethnicity and family therapy.* New York: Guilford.

Mishne, J. (1986). *Clinical work with adolescents.* New York: Free Press.

Simmons, R. G., & Rosenberg, F. (1975). Sex, sex roles and self image. *Journal of Youth and Adolescence, 4,* 229–258.

Weitzman, L. (1975). Sex role socialization. In J. Freeman (Ed.), *Women: A Feminist Perspective.* Palo Alto, CA: Mayfield.

13

Social Skills and Assertiveness Training Integrated into High School Sexuality Education Curriculum

Diane Duggan-Ali

Premature, unprotected sexual activity has caused great problems for adolescents in the United States. Each year 2.5 million adolescents contract a sexually transmitted disease (STD) (U.S. House of Representatives, 1988), adolescent AIDS cases are increasing, and more than 1 million adolescent girls become pregnant (Alan Guttmacher Institute, 1981). In response to these alarming statistics, 23 states have mandated sexuality education programs in the schools, and 23 additional states recommend them (deMauro, 1990). These programs are primarily aimed at reducing unwanted pregnancies and STDs by increasing knowledge, and changing attitudes and behavior. The results of most evaluative studies confirm, however, that although sexuality education courses do generally increase knowledge, they fall short of achieving significant change in the other areas, especially that of behavior change (Kirby, 1984).

One promising approach to this problem is to integrate social skills training into sexuality education programs. The ability to set limits on sexual activity and to negotiate birth control and safer sex depends heavily on good communication skills and the capacity to be assertive. These areas are sometimes addressed in the context of sexual decision making in the more comprehensive sexuality education programs. These longer courses constitute fewer than 10% of all sexuality education programs (Kirby, 1984), however, and even when they are offered, students' skills may be so deficient as to necessitate a more basic social skills training approach. This basic approach can lay the groundwork for more specific application of assertion and communication skills in the context of sexuality later on in the training.

This chapter describes the integration of a basic social skills training component into a sexuality education course. The goals of the social skills training were to increase adolescents' comfort in dealing with sexual topics and to develop communication skills and the ability to be assertive in the face of pressure to engage in premature sexual activity.

The project was run with a group of ninth graders at a small independent high school in a large East Coast city. The school was racially mixed and included students from middle- and working-class backgrounds. Students had received parental consent to participate in a sexuality education class, which was run for the entire ninth grade (20 students). The author is a certified sex educator, and she co-taught the sexuality education class with a school psychologist. The social skills training group was run by the author alone and consisted of three boys and three girls from the sexuality education class.

ASSESSMENT

The project began with an assessment covering three different areas. A pilot self-report scale developed by the author measured students' comfort in dealing with various sexual issues. Their communication skills and ability to be assertive when pressured to engage in sexual activity were evaluated in a role-playing interview, and their apparent level of anxiety in the sexuality education class was assessed through naturalistic observation.

Self-Report Scale

All students in the sexuality education class completed this assessment. It consisted of a forced-choice Likert scale in which students had to rate their comfort in communicating with parents and peers about sexual issues. Topics included talking about sex, deciding and communicating limits, and obtaining and using birth control. The self-report is appended.

Role-Play Interview

In this behavioral assessment, students were interviewed individually in a role-playing format. They were asked to role play a situation in which a boyfriend or girlfriend tries to pressure them into having sex.

They had to respond to eight different "lines," which were adapted from *Postponing Sexual Involvement* (Howard, Mitchell, & Pollard, 1984), a sexual assertiveness training program for teenagers.

The students' verbatim responses and nonverbal behavior were recorded. Both verbal and nonverbal behaviors were analyzed for assertive characteristics, such as adequate volume, and nonassertive characteristics, such as poor eye contact. The results of the nonverbal and verbal analyses were totaled, and a ratio of assertive characteristics to nonassertive characteristics was arrived at.

Naturalistic Observation

Some of the students were also observed in the sexuality education classroom. Their behavior was rated for class participation, eye contact, and nervous behaviors, such as tapping, shaking, or frequent self-touch.

INTERVENTION

Goals

Based on the results of the assessments, the general goals of the project were as follows:

1. Increase comfort in discussing sexual issues in mixed company, as measured by the level of participation in the sexuality education class.
2. Increase comfort in talking directly with members of the other sex about sexual matters, as measured by reported levels of comfort in these interactions.
3. Increase effectiveness in assertively responding to lines pressuring students to engage in sex, as measured by a predominance of assertive versus nonassertive features in verbal and nonverbal behaviors while role playing these interactions.

Social Skills Training

The sexuality education class was one component of the project. It was hoped that the class would provide benefits in two ways: (a) by desensitizing students to the topic of sexuality through exposure in a supportive, nonthreatening environment; and (b) by teaching them to communicate comfortably and effectively about sex through modeling the behavior of the instructors and their more active peers in the class. The instructors, one male and one female, provided a model for students of talking to a person of the other sex about sexuality issues.

The goals of the project were directly addressed in a four-session social skills training group, in which six students participated. Like the class, it provided desensitization to the topic of sexuality and modeling of peers. Its primary purpose was to teach and reinforce techniques of effective communication to help the participants to react assertively when pressured to engage in sexual activity. Concepts such as nonverbal behavior and assertiveness were explained, and students were engaged by eliciting their reactions and examples from their own experience. This was immediately followed by practical application of the concepts, giving students the opportunity to practice and refine their newly developing skills by role playing.

The role playing was done in mixed-gender dyads to give group members practice in using the techniques with other sex peers. Videotaping of the role plays was done during the last session to increase participants' self-awareness by giving them the opportunity actually to see their own behavior. The videotape also documented both the verbal and nonverbal aspects of the final role plays, preserving them for analysis in the postassessment.

The content of the groups was arranged hierarchically in accordance with desensitization principles. A sequence of lessons, starting with nonverbal communication, progressing to general assertiveness, and finally to assertiveness in sexual situations (saying no) was used. Not only did the early skills provide a foundation for later skills, but the lessons were progressively arranged to develop participants' comfort and confidence gradually in increasingly stressful situations.

Session 1: Introduction and Nonverbal Communication

The group began with a discussion of its purpose and formulation of ground rules, which focused on the idea of mutual respect. This was followed by a discussion about what constitutes nonverbal communication, with group members giving examples. The students were then led in warm-up exercises to prepare them for the role playing. The trainer outlined a script and enlisted a student with whom she demonstrated nonverbal behavior as it supports or undermines a verbal message.

After the role play both the student and the trainer gave feedback, focusing on the effect of the nonverbal component of the role play. This was done to illustrate the point and to model the role playing–feedback format that would be followed in subsequent exercises. The group was then broken into dyads to role play a similar situation.

Session 2: Assertive Behavior

The theme of the second group was assertive behavior. After briefly reviewing the ground rules and the previous week's session on nonverbal communication, the trainer talked about passive, aggressive, and assertive behaviors. Students were asked to think of examples from their own experience and then to role play different ways of responding to those situations.

When they gave feedback in the group, one student, Karen, reported with some surprise that being assertive felt "OK, especially when you feel you're right." Another student, Robert, remarked on how difficult and even demeaned he felt being assertive in confronting an aggressive person. He stated that in his opinion it was more face saving to be loud and aggressive back. This drew the group into a discussion about the dangers of escalating aggressive encounters and how to solve disputes constructively by focusing on what you want to get out of the situation.

Session 3: Help for Male Adolescents in Resisting Pressures to Engage in Sexual Activity

At the third meeting the group discussed the pressures on all teens to engage in sexual intercourse. After the students brainstormed specific pressures the trainer emphasized their right to say no and outlined three techniques presented in *Postponing Sexual Intercourse*. Say no and keep repeating it; take the offensive, and state how the person's continued pressuring is making you feel; and if all else fails, refuse to discuss the matter further and walk away from the situation.

The trainer then focused on situations in which an unwilling male adolescent is pressured for intercourse. The group members talked about the specific pressures on male adolescents to always be willing to engage in sex. Robert had a difficult time conceiving a situation in which he would refuse sex if it were offered to him. Group members tried to help him by bringing up negative consequences of sexual activity, but he remained unconvinced.

Sample Role Play: Male Adolescent Resisting Pressure to Engage in Sex. The following scenario explores this issue.

Rationale: To increase adolescent boys' ability to assertively reject unwanted sexual overtures.

Situation: A girl tries to persuade a boy to engage in sexual activity with her, and entreats or belittles him when he will not.

Girl: I care a lot about you, and I want to have sex with you.

Boy: I care a lot about you too, but I don't think we should have sex.

Girl: Why don't you want to? Aren't you a man? (Alternatively: If you don't want to have sex with me that proves you don't care enough about me.)

Boy: (Sample adaptive response) I'm man enough to know when something's not right for me.

The girls were instructed to pressure the boys for sex by questioning their manhood or the boy's feelings for them, as in the previous sample dialogue. The boys had to respond assertively. Two of the boys were rather passive. Bill used humor, stating, "I'm not a man; I'm a mouse." As the role play became more serious in tone he pleaded apologetically, "It's not you, it's me!" as though there were something wrong with him. In the feedback the trainer noted this and reaffirmed his right to say no without apology. Robert continued to have difficulty reconciling the refusal of a sexual invitation with his image of himself as a man. His best defense was, "I'm just not in the mood right now. Maybe later."

Session 4: Help for Female Adolescents in Resisting Pressure to Engage in Sexual Activity

The fourth and final group session was recorded on videotape. It started with a brief discussion about assertive behavior and then went straight to the role plays. Because the previous session had concentrated on assertive behavior by male adolescents, this session started with situations in which girls had to assert themselves.

Karen and Bill worked together and had to start over twice. The first time Karen dissolved into giggles just as she started and could not continue. The second time she stepped out of character to give Bill feedback to show more feeling in his approach to her. This direction from her increased the realism and level of contact in their interaction. As Bill proclaimed his love and urged her to have sex with him, however, Karen ended up passively saying, "I don't know. Let me think about it." The trainer pointed out how effective her direction to Bill had been and how she was wavering in the face of his rather tender entreaties. In a third attempt she was able to be more direct and assertive.

Sample Role Play: Female Adolescent Resisting Pressure to Engage in Sex. The following scenario explores this issue.

Rationale: To increase adolescent girls' ability to reject unwanted sexual overtures assertively.

Situation: A boy tries to persuade a girl to engage in sexual activity with him and entreats or belittles her when she will not.

Bill: I really care for you, but if you won't have sex with me, I just can't see you anymore. It hurts too much!

Karen: Listen. We can have a serious relationship without sex.

Bill: It's not serious enough.

Karen: What we have isn't good enough? We have a strong friend-ship.

Bill: I want more than a strong friendship with you.

Karen: I'm not ready for more.

Bill: Please have sex with me! I care for you so much!

Karen: This is as far as I want it to go.

Bill: But I need it!

Karen: No. If you feel that way then I think we should end it.

In a later role play, Bill showed great improvement from the previous week, remaining serious and firm. Karen, as his aggressor, was persistent and contemptuous, sneeringly demanding, "Aren't you a man?" It was very touching to hear him earnestly proclaim, "I'm 14 years old, and that may not make me an adult, but I'm not a child either!"

After taping we viewed some of the video, critiquing performances in terms of students' ability to be assertive. The students also filled out postassessments. They were all very enthusiastic about the video, and even though the project was completed, they asked to meet again to view the rest of the tape.

POSTASSESSMENT

All group members were evaluated during the final group meeting on their level of comfort in dealing with sexual issues and their effectiveness in assertively rejecting sexual overtures. Students were also evaluated on participation in the sexuality education class on the same day. The instruments used in the postassessment were identical to those used in the initial evaluation.

SAMPLE CASE

Assessment

Karen was a 14-year-old girl from a white, middle-class background who participated in the social skills training group. She was attractive but often wore large sweatshirts and baggy jeans that concealed her body and gave her a childlike appearance. Although informal observations revealed that she got along well with her peers, Karen was shy and noncommunicative in the sexuality education classroom.

Self-Report Scale

Karen's self-report scale indicated that, relative to her peers, she had a great deal of discomfort in communicating about sexual issues. Her self-reported level of discomfort in talking with peers about sex was higher than most other girls in the class.

Role-Playing

Karen was able to assert herself verbally in 50% of her responses. Despite the assertive content of many of her responses, however, her nonverbal behavior undermined her message. Her downcast eyes and low volume detracted from her ability to affirm her own rights in the face of pressure, and her giggling and frequent self-touch suggested embarrassment and vulnerability.

Naturalistic Observation

When observed during the sexuality education class Karen showed limited eye contact with the teacher (less than 10%) and very poor eye contact with peers (less than 5%). She engaged in self-touch gestures such as touching her hair and biting her nails 90% of the time. Although most of her classmates joined in a discussion about talking with parents about sex, Karen did not participate. Informal discussions with some of her teachers revealed that, although she was generally quiet, her participation was better in those classes than in the sexuality education class.

Throughout the three assessments, Karen showed a consistent pattern of discomfort in dealing with sexual issues, especially with members of the other sex present. Although some of this may be attributed to developmental considerations, her peers were clearly more open and relaxed than she. A survey of knowledge about sexuality revealed that, relative to her peers, Karen had adequate knowledge of sexual matters. Thus her discomfort with sexual issues did not seem to be due to a lack of knowledge.

Postassessment

The intervention, although brief, was successful in the areas that were focused on. Karen showed an impressive increase in her ability to communicate assertively in refusing sexual activity. This gain took place largely in her ability to use assertive nonverbal behaviors, such as eye

contact and adequate volume, while communicating a basically assertive verbal message.

Karen also showed a substantial increase in comfort in dealing with
peers of the other sex about sexually related issues, as measured by her
responses on the postassessment self-report rating scale. In the sexuality education class her eye contact with the teacher and other students
increased substantially, and her self-touch gestures, indicators of discomfort, diminished. Karen's participation in the class rose from no
participation to making three separate contributions during the
postassessment observation.

DISCUSSION

Karen's case is a good example of the gains made by all members of the
group. The initial assessment highlighted the need for social skills
training in basic communication, especially nonverbal behavior, for all
group participants. All of the adolescents had difficulty in responding
assertively to lines pressuring them to engage in sexual activity, and all
of them reported some discomfort in discussing sexual topics with other
sex peers. After the intervention all participants showed gains in both
areas. Even Robert, who had trouble accepting the idea of turning down
sex, showed gains in his ability to be assertive and use effective nonverbal communication skills.

Social skills training is effective in working with adolescents for several reasons. One of the main reasons is that its active, direct approach
addresses one of the prominent issues of adolescence, that of learning to
deal with physiological arousal. The role-play situations in social skills
training act as "inoculations" in Meichenbaum's (1985) sense of the
term, in that they expose participants to manageable quantities of
arousal without overwhelming them. The role plays gradually enhance
their ability to cope in arousing situations through acclimation and developing coping skills.

Participants need to be given the opportunity to work up slowly to
sexual issues, which are very stressful for them to deal with in a mixed-
gender group. While the group works on basic communication skills,
they develop familiarity and trust in the process as well as in each
other. This enables them to handle the much more stressful topics of
assertion and sexuality later on in the training.

A mixed-gender group enhances realism and gives participants the
chance to become accustomed to communicating with members of the
other sex. Although all situations are simulations, the presence of

members of the other sex engenders real stress. The participants' ability to handle this stress in the safe, structured environment provided by the social skills trainer develops their ability to deal with such situations in real life. If the initial situations are too stressful the trainer can start with guided imagery or highly structured games.

Impulsivity is another issue that must be addressed in sexuality education programs. Often, engaging in premature, unprotected intercourse is an impulsive act, unplanned and not fully thought through in the heat of the moment. This impulsivity is situational, but often the problem is exacerbated with characterologically impulsive adolescents who are unused to mediating their behavior verbally.

Role playing may be helpful in dealing with this problem. First of all, it is action oriented and therefore appealing to impulsive adolescents. Instead of evoking resistance or apathy, it engages them in the learning process. Within its action format, role playing stresses communication, both verbal and nonverbal. It does this in a structured format that essentially provides the script so that participants do not have to generate their own words. Thus it can help adolescents to begin to use language to delay action, widening the gap between impulse and action with words learned from the role plays.

Involvement is an important consideration in working with adolescents. To derive any benefit, participants must be involved. All of the students in the social skills training group reported that they thoroughly enjoyed the intervention phase of the project. The active, participatory nature of the discussions, and especially the role plays, stimulated them and engaged their attention. The presence of members of the other sex also heightened interest. Adolescents are very interested in interaction with the other sex, even though it often causes some discomfort. The project provided a structured and hence "safe" way of interacting, and the skills they were learning enhanced their feelings of competence. Participants did not have to grope for things to talk about or look for opportunities to interact. These were provided by the social skills training format. Both the content and format of the group engaged the adolescents and helped to develop skills for interaction with peers of the other sex.

To further the involvement of participants, they should play an active role in developing role plays. Situations and dialogue can be brainstormed in the group and written or improvised by group members. This ensures authenticity and relevance to their lives.

It is crucial to be sensitive to the values of the group members, their parents, and the community at large in developing a social skills training program. Involvement of parents is essential. This can be accomplished through preliminary meetings or, at the very least, a note home explaining the nature of the program and inviting their comments. The social skills trainer should be aware of the age when sexual activity typically begins among the peer group and the community's attitudes toward sexual activity, adolescent pregnancy, birth control, STDs, AIDS, explicit language, and the roles of male and female adolescents. These values should be discussed and worked into the social skills training.

The group described previously was composed of 14-year-old ninth graders, none of whom were sexually active, and the focus of the social skills training was on abstinence. Social skills can be used, however, to enhance communication and functioning at other levels of sexual relations as well. Adolescents can learn to negotiate alternative means of sexual expression, other than intercourse, or to question a potential partner about his or her previous sexual history. They can also learn how to obtain birth control and how to negotiate with a partner on its use.

This project focused on male as well as female assertiveness in resisting pressure to engage in sexual activity. Male assertiveness in these circumstances is a relatively neglected area. Many programs focus on female adolescents, as it is the female teenagers who are at most obvious risk for pregnancy. In our society there seems to be an implicit understanding that male adolescents will engage in more sexual activity, and that they can do so with relative impunity. Male adolescents, however, are also hurt by unwanted pregnancy and are also at risk for contracting a STD or AIDS.

Despite this, the idea of male adolescents assertively refusing invitations for sexual activity was very difficult for some teenagers in the group to accept. The role-play scenarios in which boys in the group refused sex seemed to lack authenticity for most of them. They went through the role plays with good will but without conviction. Even the girls, who took on their taunting roles with zest, commented how nicely the boys acted and how they were unlike any of the boys they actually knew.

This may be because turning down sexual advances runs counter to the accepted male stereotype, and young male adolescents, who are in the process of assuming their adult gender roles, tend to subscribe heavily to such stereotypes. These young men need a great deal of support in realizing that they can turn down sexual advances without compromising their masculinity. It is important to foster more realistic appraisals of the situation, which will make it easier for boys to see refusal as a positive, self-affirming behavior. Perhaps the unfortunate example of Magic Johnson, a thoroughly masculine and heroic basketball player who contracted the virus that causes AIDS through unsafe sex, will cause young men to consider the negative consequences of unprotected sexual activity.

More realistic appraisals of the negative consequences of unprotected sexual activity need to be developed among male and female adolescents alike. The cognitive regulation of anger and stress model (Novaco, 1979; Stern & Fodor, 1989) provides a framework for understanding the role of appraisal as a cognitive mediator in stressful experiences, such as responding to sexual pressure. For individuals to react adaptively to a threat, they must have an accurate perception or judgment of its severity. This appears to be problematic for many adolescents. Feelings of invulnerability may distort accurate judgment of the possibility and severity of the consequences of premature, unprotected sex, such as unwanted pregnancy, STDs, or AIDS. Correcting this faulty appraisal is a task that must be addressed in the social skills training. As much as possible the trainer should draw from the group, so that members can educate each other and are not alienated by "preaching" from an adult. Care must be taken not to make the threat seem so overwhelming as to evoke defensive reappraisal. This can result in denial and intellectualization rather than adaptive response to the threat.

Nonverbal behavior has an important place in social skills training within a sexuality education curriculum. Not only does training in nonverbal skills provide a gradual introduction to more stressful topics, but it is an important foundation skill in assertiveness training. Karen is a good example of how nonassertive, nonverbal behavior can undermine verbal content that is basically assertive. Karen and most of the other students showed great gains in increasing the assertiveness of their nonverbal communications.

Videotape greatly facilitates the recording and analysis of nonverbal behavior. Movement behavior is concrete, but it is transitory, and its full expression can easily be lost. When it is recorded it can be viewed repeatedly to extract relevant cues on many different levels. In addition to the obvious advantages it provides the researcher, the video is compelling for the teenaged participants. Although some adolescents may be shy at first, they are virtually all eager to see themselves on screen, as long as they are assured of a supportive, respectful audience.

Future projects of this kind should include a longer intervention phase. At least two sessions on each of the topics (nonverbal communication, assertion, etc.) would be ideal. An additional two-session component on talking with peers of the other sex about neutral topics could be added, before going on to sexually related topics. The extra time spent on each topic would provide an opportunity for the adolescents to gain more practice with the new behaviors and to integrate them into their repertoires.

CONCLUSION

This project demonstrated the usefulness of the social skills training approach in increasing young adolescents' comfort in dealing with sexual issues and in developing assertive verbal and nonverbal behaviors. Social skills training provides adolescents with an opportunity to practice coping with the physiological arousal associated with sexual topics in a safe, structured setting. Scripts provide verbal mediation to aid in delaying impulsive behavior. Adolescents enjoy the active and interactive nature of the role plays, and this increases their level of engagement in the training.

Among the issues that the project raised was the need to focus on male adolescents in developing assertive behavior in refusing sexual activity. Another important issue is the role of nonverbal behavior, and the need to develop adolescents' awareness and skill in this important mode of communication. It is recommended that future projects of this nature include longer intervention phases to provide more practice of target behaviors. It is hoped that this will develop and integrate these skills to help young adolescents to resist pressures to engage in premature sexual activity.

APPENDIX

SELF-REPORT SCALE

Name_____ Date_____

Please rate each statement on a 1 to 5 scale according to how comfortable or uncomfortable you would feel in that type of situation. Even is you have never been in a particular situation, estimate how comfortable or uncomfortable it would make you feel.

Circle   1 if you are (or would be) *very comfortable.*
                 2 if you are (or would be) *moderately comfortable.*
                 3 if you are (or would be) *slightly uncomfortable.*
                 4 if you are (or would be) *moderately uncomfortable.*
                 5 if you are (or would be) *very uncomfortable.*

   1.   Talking with friends of the same sex
        about sexuality issues.   1   2   3   4   5

2. Talking with friends of the other sex
   about sexuality issues.   1 2 3 4 5

3. Talking with your parents about
   sexuality issues.   1 2 3 4 5

4. Talking with friends of the same sex
   about birth control.   1 2 3 4 5

5. Talking with friends of the other sex
   about birth control.   1 2 3 4 5

6. Talking with your parents about
   birth control.   1 2 3 4 5

7. Deciding what level of sexual activity
   (doing nothing, kissing, petting, having
   intercourse, etc.) is right for you.   1 2 3 4 5

8. Setting limits about how far you want
   to go sexually with a boyfriend or girlfriend.   1 2 3 4 5

9. Deciding what kind of birth control is
   right for you.   1 2 3 4 5

10. Buying birth control in a drugstore.   1 2 3 4 5

11. Obtaining birth control from
    a doctor or clinic.   1 2 3 4 5

12. Using birth control.   1 2 3 4 5

REFERENCES

Alan Guttmacher Institute. (1981). *Teenage pregnancy: The problem that has-n't gone away.* New York: Author.

deMauro, D. (1990). A review of state sexuality and AIDS education curricula. *SIECUS Report, 18,* 1–9.

Fisher, W. (1990). All together now: An integrated approach to preventing adolescent pregnancy and STD/HIV infection. *SIECUS Report, 18,* 1–11.

Howard, M., Mitchell, M., & Pollard, B. (1984). *Postponing sexual involvement.* Atlanta, GA: Grady Memorial Hospital.

Kirby, D. (1984). *Sexuality education: Evaluation of programs and their effects.* Santa Cruz, CA: Network Publishing.

Meichenbaum, D. (1985). *Stress inoculation training.* New York: Pergamon.

Michelson, L., Sugai, D., Wood, R., & Kazdin, A. (1983). *Social skill assessment and training with children.* New York: Plenum.

Novaco, R. (1979). Cognitive regulation of anger and stress. In P. Kendall & S.

Hollon (Eds.), *Cognitive-behavioral interventions* (pp. 241–285). New York: Academic Press.

Stern, J., & Fodor, I. (1989). Anger control in children: A review of social skills and cognitive behavioral approaches to dealing with aggressive children. *Child and Family Behavior Therapy, 2,* 1–20.

U.S. House of Representatives. (1988). *A generation in jeopardy: Children and AIDS: A report of the select committee on children, youth and families.* Washington, DC: U.S. Government Printing Office.

14

Social Skills Training for Suburban Substance-Abusing Adolescents: Pilot Recovery Group

Ernest A. Collabolletta

Social skills prevention programs have been used extensively to deter drug abuse (Albee, 1981). The success of social skills resistance programs, such as those implemented and described by McAlister, Perry, and Maccoby (1979) and Pentz (1983), of the coping skills training programs taught in the classroom by Gilchrist and Schinke (1985), of assertiveness skills, anxiety management, and decision making in Botvin's (1983) Life Skills Training, offer proof of social skills effectiveness in primary prevention.

Although such prevention education is necessary, the literature on using social skills training with adolescents in recovery groups merits more exploration. Schools must address the psychosocial needs of returning substance-abusing students because they are returning to the very environment where their substance-abuse problem began or escalated. School psychologists should recognize the potent therapeutic tool that social skills provide for recovering adolescent substance abusers and can teach such skills in recovery groups.

This chapter describes a pilot recovery group that has used social skills training with suburban middle-class adolescents. Although this chapter focuses on recovery, it should be noted that many of the social skill techniques are applicable for adolescents who are experimenting with substances as well as for less severe abusers. In this pilot project no distinction is made between alcohol and drug abuse. Substance abusers are persons whose use of substances have led to a behavior that has negatively affected their lives in such areas as school, the law, family, and interpersonal relationships.

DRUGS IN SUBURBIA

Suburban and affluent communities no longer believe that substance abuse is limited to inner-city populations. They have recognized that good schools, tree-lined streets, and fine-trimmed lawns do not assure a child's psychological safety. Bratter (1989b) offers a profile of what many drug-abusing adolescents are: "These immature individuals have acted out against an environment which they perceive to be hostile, hurtful, or hateful. They have used drugs to medicate themselves which temporarily relieves painful feelings of failure and depression. They are hemorrhaging internally, but conceal wounds from others viewed as enemies who possess the power to inflict more suffering. When these adolescents watch television, they prefer cartoons and situation comedies that provide a relief from the real life acts they perform daily" (p. 4).

Clearly, most suburban families maintain high aspirations for their children. These families value success, especially financial and academic success. For some adolescents, however, the legacy of affluence can be as disabling as poverty. The inordinate amount of pressure put on these adolescents, both by themselves and by their families, often leads to their seeking relief from the pressure through drugs. The awesome goal to compete by achieving the same or perhaps a higher level of success as their parents is disabling. These adolescents are governed by feelings of self-entitlement, anger, and fear of failure. Often they are unable to recognize or understand these feelings so they seek to medicate themselves to reduce a pain they cannot endure.

Approximately 28 to 38 million children and adults live in alcoholic homes (Block, 1981). Because research is lacking on families in which parents are involved in illegal substance abuse, it would appear these numbers are greater. Too often these chemically dependent youths are trapped in a family system in which either the father or mother, or sometimes both, are alcoholic or codependent. When this is the case, too often love, self-respect, and care are lacking. The teens fall prey to neglect, abuse, and learn self-destruction. Deutsch (1982) contends that for many of the children of alcoholics, their parents' use is the primary influence on their psychological development because their emotions, personalities, and behavior are influenced more by this one act than by any other. The substance-abusing adults enable their children to continue their self-destructive behaviors by implicitly encouraging substance abuse. The children view themselves as worthless beings neither capable of giving nor receiving real affection, and this in turn affects their lives and their interpersonal relationships.

Data suggest that susceptibility to alcoholism is neither genetic nor environmental, but an interaction of both. What is certain, however, is for children of alcoholic families, the risk of becoming alcoholics is five or six times greater than for people in the general population (Goodwin, 1971; Winokur, Reich, Rimmer, & Pitts, 1970). Risk factors are probably very similar for those children whose parents involved in drug abuse, but the statistics are not so widely available in the literature.

At-risk adolescents present a challenge to schools. Low self-esteem, impulsiviity, the need to belong, the fear of being different, the fear of rejection by peers, self-indulgence, living in a substance-abusing family, and the inability to delay immediate gratification are some of the characteristics possessed by adolescents who are at risk of abusing drugs and alcohol. There probably is no *one* reason for adolescent drug use. More likely, drug use results from a complex interaction of biological reasons, behavior patterns, and social and psychological determinants (Archambault, 1989). Reviewing research, Beschner and Friedman (1979) offer several reasons for adolescent drug use: First, there is an easy availability of drugs; second, drugs provide a quick, reliable, and easy way to acquire good feelings; third, drugs are one means of acceptance into peer groups, which are important socializing elements in their lives at this time; and fourth, drugs are reliable and effective way to cope with unpleasant feelings and to reduce tension and fear.

In recovery, the substance abusers describe a void, a sense of emptiness in their lives. They recognize how this void was filled by the drugs they had ingested. In recovery, these adolescents are taught how to fill the void without drugs. This is not an easy task because when the substance abuser associates with friends who continue to be drug dependent, the adolescent will feel out of place. Because of past behavior, he will not be accepted by the "good" kids, and yet he can no longer associate with his old friends. Marlatt and Gordon (1985) suggest social skills as an important component of rehabilitation programs. This chapter borrowing from Marlatt and Gordon's suggestion, provides a framework for beginning work in this area.

What are the needs of recovering substance-abusing adolescents on returning to high school? How can the school best assist in their recovery? What role can the school psychologist play in their lives? What are the specific social skills needed to be taught to these youngsters? How do social skills play an important role in recovery?

RECOVERING SUBURBAN SUBSTANCE ABUSER: A PROFILE

Jim is a 16-year-old recovering substance abuser. His mother is a nurse, and his father practices corporate law in New York City. He is reentering his old suburban high school as a junior and is repeating junior year. He has just returned from Minnesota where he had spent 7 weeks at St. Mary's Hospital and 5 months in a halfway house. He is now returning to the high school where his old "using" friends are and his use began. He feels emotionally insecure, academically frightened, and socially incapable of dealing effectively with his last 2 years of high school.

Prior Treatment

Because treatment is paid for by insurance monies, it is obvious why the center of choice of suburban substance-abusing families is the private hospital (Frank, Marel, Schmeidler, & Lipton, 1984). The Herculean task of breaking down defenses begins. The goal has been defined by Maxwell (1986) who describes the defense mechanisms used by addicts: "Chemical dependency represents a severe regression in the defense hierarchy. Unfortunately, not only do chemically dependent persons repeatedly and rigidly use primitive and immature defenses, they also exhibit associated narcissistic or self-centered attitudes and behavior traits that are most commonly seen in young children; such as sustained feelings of unwarranted or deluded superiority, a sense of entitlement, supersensitivity (to oneself, not others), arrogance, and grandiosity" (p. 69).

The now recovering person begins a 12-step program. After about 3 weeks of treatment "family week" begins. Family week consists of 5 days of intensive family therapy, which treats family issues such as "codependency" and "enabling." Not only is the family confronted by their behavior that has further permitted their adolescents' chemical dependency, but for the first time their chemically free adolescents will be confronted on their "using" behavior and the consequences that it has had on the family. After completing 30 days in the hospital, the adolescent usually spends 2 to 12 months in a halfway house. The recovering substance abusers are sent home after the halfway house with a treatment plan. The treatment plan or "program" usually consists of attending at Alcoholics Anonymous or Narcotics Anonymous meetings, getting a sponsor in a 12-step program, participating in a recovery group, attending ongoing individual and family therapy sessions, setting up curfews at home, and understanding expectations in school.

SCHOOL PSYCHOLOGISTS FACING THE RETURNING SUBSTANCE ABUSER

Special Clinical Concerns After Extensive Drug Use

Two primary tasks for adolescents are to develop a positive self-image and to be able to establish interpersonal relationships. These tasks, which are never easy for adolescents, are even more difficult for recovering adolescents.

Adolescent drug abusers have developed relationships with psychoactive substances like nonaddicts have developed with people. Often they have used drugs to solve their personal problems rather than relating to peers. Even the relationships they have had with peers have revolved around drugs—getting high together, "copping" together, and sharing in "drug rituals." If drugs were removed from their relationships, there would be no basis for these relationships. Drugs have become their best friends and lovers, which they depend on not only for pleasure but also relief from pain. When addicts abstain from drugs, they experience a grieving process much the same as a person who mourns another's death. There is denial, anger, and self-pity, depression, and finally acceptance. Psychologists need to recognize this process to help the addicts resolve these issues, which, in many cases, have not been completed in treatment.

Substance abusers have a very negative self-image and low self-esteem. As a result of abusing drugs, these adolescents are consumed by self-hate because they have done things to themselves and others for which they think they will never be forgiven or loved. For many, their abuse has led to scholastic failures, which unless rectified, will bar them entry into the prestigious universities and colleges that they and their families desire.

Returning substance abusers will be facing negative peer pressure once again. These individuals are no longer living in a protective environment peopled by other adolescents who are also trying to stay straight. Refusal skills are crucial to maintaining a drug-free life. They will be facing academic and social pressures of schools compounded by family expectations. Pressures can mount and without the proper tools to deal with them, recovering substance abusers will be doomed to relapse.

It is the goal of the school psychologists, in working in a recovery group, to recognize and remediate their negative self-image, inability to establish relationships, low frustration tolerance, and, by teaching them coping mechanisms, to deal with social pressures, because before they had always turned to drugs for stress management.

SOCIAL SKILLS TRAINING IN RECOVERY GROUP

Special Role of Group Leader

Glasser (1965) provides a good definition of what school psychologists need to be: "The therapist must be a very responsible person—tough, interested, human, and sensitive. He must be able to fulfill his own needs and must be willing to discuss some of his own struggles so that the patient can see that acting responsibility is possible, though sometimes difficult. Neither aloof, superior, nor sacrosanct, he must never imply that what he does, what he stands for, or what he values is unimportant. He must have the strength to become involved, to have his values tested by the patient, and to withstand intense criticism by the person he is trying to help . . . the therapist must, nevertheless, show that a person can act responsibly even if it takes great effort."

The needs of recovering addicts are unique. More confrontation is needed to challenge distortions and denials. Because of the nontrusting nature of the clientelle, school psychologists must be credible leaders, people whom the adolescents can trust and, indeed, emulate in their struggle to remain drug free. School psychologists need to adopt a less traditional role as group leaders. Bratter (1983a) states, "The leader, thus, becomes a responsible role model or ego ideal for adolescents to emulate. As the group matures, stabilizes, and becomes self-actualizing, the leader subtly decreases his/her charisma, activity, and domination by assuming a more therapeutic posture" (p. 167).

School psychologists need to be clear not only about their personal feelings concerning psychoactive substances but about their personal use of such chemicals including alcohol. Overtly or covertly, their own feelings will be communicated to adolescents. These adolescents will mistrust adults, especially those who assume authority roles with contradicting messages. Teaching appropriate behavior by means of example (modeling) is a key element in the therapeutic alliance.

In working with these adolescents, school psychologists should recognize that time will be spent in consultation with teachers in the school. Although recovering adolescents are attempting to be honest, they have spent years being deceitful, manipulating systems, and trying to get the most for themselves with the least amount of effort. When recovering adolescents realize that the group leader communicates with teachers, it will lessen the chances of deliberate denial and distortion.

Confrontation and Assertiveness: Therapeutic Tools for School Psychologists as Group Leaders

Being active and direct while confronting the substance abusers' self-defeating attitudes and behaviors require school psychologists to modify and renegotiate many traditional roles of psychotherapy. Most training programs prefer nondirective, empathetic, and reflective roles. This being the case, school psychologists who choose to work with these youngsters need to be clear about their own values regarding directness and assertiveness. School psychologists need to confront at-risk youngsters during crisis and point out self-destructive behaviors. This often extends the parameters of traditional psychotherapy. In most cases psychologists may need additional training in this area. How comfortable do psychologists feel forcing change on an individual, or questioning honesty or truthfulness? Let us consider the following vignette and see how assertive the leader must be in confronting group members.

Jim, a new member of the group, was forced by his parents to attend a group session for his drug and alcohol use to be evaluated. Brian, who has been recovering for some 18 months, is confronted by the group leader regarding his risk taking in relationships.

Leader: Brian, Jim told you that he was going to drink last night?
Brian: Yeah.
Leader: Jim, did Brian try to talk you out of it?
Jim: No, he said it was my decision and my life.
Leader: (sarcastically): What a caring thing to say, Brian! Do you think Jim has a problem with drugs?
Brian: Yes, I do.
Leader: Do you think that he has the potential to really abuse alcohol?
Brian: Yes.
Leader: Then why wouldn't you try to do something about it?

Brian (to leader):	It's his life. He has the right to do what he wants.
Leader:	Even if it's potentially dangerous to him?
Brian:	Yeah.
Leader:	Does anyone have any feelings about this?
John:	Yeah, I do. Brian, if this guy is a friend of yours, don't you owe it to him to say something to him?
Leader:	That's my opinion too, Brian. That's selfish, egotistical "using" behavior. You did the same when your best friend, Keith, was using. You backed off, you didn't even try to stop him.
Brian:	It wouldn't have helped if he really wanted to drink that night.
Leader:	Really? Well, let's ask Jim. Jim, what would have happened if Brian had tried to talk you out of it?
Jim:	I really don't know.
Leader:	Let me put it another way. What would you have thought or felt if Brian had done that?
Jim (pause):	That he cared.
Leader:	And would the fact that you felt he cared have affected you in any way?
Jim:	Well, it might have stopped me from drinking that night if I could have hung out with him.
Leader:	Brian, do you care about Jim?
Brian:	Yeah.
Leader:	Well, your actions that night did not tell him that you cared. (To another group member) John, did you get the message that I called you yesterday?
John:	Yeah.
Leader:	What did it say?
John:	That I had better be at the meeting today.
Leader:	What was my message to you?
John:	You cared about my being here.
Leader:	Brian, I called you, too, and left a message. What was yours?
Brian:	To get my ass here at 3 p.m. sharp.

Leader:	Brian, we haven't even been getting along that well and I know that you could have blown me off and interpreted it as my getting on your case. But did you?
Brian:	No.
Leader:	How come?
Brian:	Because I know that you give a shit.
Leader:	And guess, what? Both you guys are here tonight!
Leader:	So what's the real story with you, Brian?
Brian:	It's more that I'm afraid to risk. You know how sensitive I am and I'm tired of being hurt.
Leader:	So if you left Jim know you care, you're afraid that you might be hurt. Well, you might be hurt and you surely will be vulnerable. I know I put myself in a vulnerable position when I called you guys. I could have been rejected by you. Brian, this week I want you to take one risk in relationships and share it with the group next week. Have you ever done that before?
Brian:	Yeah.
Leader:	How did you feel after you did it?
Brian:	I felt good.

Besides confrontation and assertiveness, the school psychologist modeled risk-taking behavior for his group.

Group Sessions

Group sessions are the most powerful and effective therapeutic intervention to use with recovering adolescent drug abusers. The power of the group can influence individuals to change values, attitudes, and behaviors that cannot be done in individual therapy. Smith (1985) suggests that "Abusers are alienated from institutions that might socialize them not to use drugs." A recovery group provides a positive social system which becomes a refuge from alienation. Bratter (1983a) identifies these four crucial and curative functions of groups: "First, the group can serve as a rational restraining force for those adolescents who have elected to engage in potentially dangerous and self-destructive drug-related behavior. Second, the group collectively learns how to help everyone begin to identify negative attitudes in social contacts, how to avoid placing oneself in a 'no win' situation, and how to unlearn being dependent on mind altering substances. Third, the group becomes a corrective emotional experience. Fourth, the group becomes a caring community."

The group leader must mobilize the group to value abstinence so that each member exerts pressure on the others to achieve their mutual goal. Simply stated, a minicaring community is established in which the group assumes responsibility for each member. Healthy behavior is fostered, whereas self-defeating, self-destructive behavior is condemned and challenged. By the group leader's demonstrating responsible concern, group members begin to internalize positive values and gain greater self-respect, a sense of obligation to others, and begin to act more responsible.

Although drugs are an integral part of the adolescent culture today, the school psychologist, as group leader, seeks to create a positive counterculture in the recovery group. The culture of the group not only promotes the idea of being drug free, but elevates it to a desirable and highly achievable goal. When these expectations become group norms the social skills that will be taught can be more readily internalized by the adolescent.

The Contract

If group members have been to a rehabilitation center or participated in a 12-step program, these adolescents are sophisticated in terms of group process and dynamics. During the first session, the contract is explained to all participants.

1. The goal is to promote abstinence and responsible and productive behavior.
2. Confidentiality is extended to all in the group. Confidentiality is violated if there exists imminent danger to self or others.
3. All data gathered about an individual becomes a concern of the group.
4. If a group member uses a drug it becomes the individual's responsibility to notify the group. If others find out about a member's use, it is also their responsibility to disclose such behavior. For persons who have slipped, there will be 1 week to report the slip to a significant other or else it becomes the responsibility of a group member or the leader to do so.
5. There will be no physical manifestation of violence in the group, no weapons, no threats, and no intimidations toward group members.
6. Each individual has the right to speak without interruptions.

INCORPORATING OF SOCIAL SKILLS AND ASSERTIVENESS TRAINING INTO ONGOING RECOVERY GROUPS

Coping Strategies to Relieve Stress

Adolescence is a stressful period of one's life. For recovering adolescents, the stress and anxiety is magnified because their chemical response to stress no longer is an option for them. New strategies must be taught by the leader and implemented by the group members. The two principal coping strategies to relieve stress and anxiety for these adolescents involve both covert cognitive coping skills and overt relaxation techniques.

The following is a typical occurrence of an adolescent who has returned from a halfway house and is trying to cope with life without chemicals.

Mark: I'm feeling real scared. I've been getting a lots of urges lately. I have 12 months of sobriety, and I'm still feeling bad, nervous, really stressed out.

Tony: You know that used to happen to me a lot too. It's gotten better, but it never all goes away. What has worked for me is the self-hypnosis we learned in group. I liked it because it made me feel like I was in control, I was controlling something—my nervousness.

An example of what group members had practiced is the following (adapted from Davis, Eshelman, & McKay, 1980; Jacobson, 1974):

Sit in a comfortable position with your eyes closed. Now begin to picture a peaceful scene, perhaps a beautiful beach, where the sand is white and the water is clear, and the sun is shining. You are lying on the sand. Begin to relax all your muscles. Start with your forearms and biceps. Tighten them first, then relax them. Notice the difference between the tension and the relaxation. Tighten and relax your face, your neck, and your shoulders. Take deep breaths as you relax your chest. Tighten and relax your stomach, your buttocks, your thighs, your calves, and your toes. Now, suggest to yourself that you are going deeper and deeper; imagine riding an elevator that is descending and descending from the tenth floor to the basement. Go down deeper and deeper. When you wish to come back to full consciousness, count backwards from three. You will awaken and feel relaxed and refreshed.

Chemically dependent adolescents often think that living without the drugs and alcohol will produce intolerable anxiety for them. Their perceptions need to challenged, and cognitions need to be changed.

Peter: Staying away from the pot is impossible for me. I get so damned nervous.

Leader: It sounds like it's difficult, but is it impossible?

Peter: Well, I feel so nervous and anxious.

Leader: So you feel nervous and anxious, but is it impossible to live with these feelings?

Peter: I don't want to feel these feelings.

Leader: And you control the universe?

Peter: Well, I guess I can live with these feelings and maybe learn to control them better.

Leader: I really believe you can. Now say, "It's not possible to live a drug free day, only difficult."

Refusal Skills

Although instructed to avoid "persons, places, and things" that might influence them to use again, most recovering adolescents will find themselves in situations in which drugs and alcohol are being used. For them to say "no", group members are taught self-statements to maximize the probability to refrain from using psychoactive substances. Consider the following interaction between a group member and the group leader:

Eric: I know I can hang out with my old buddies because they respect what I have been through and I know they would stop me from doing anything I would regret.

Leader: "Bull! How can they stop you from doing anything when they can't even stop themselves? Misery loves company! Andy that's what you have to keep telling yourself!

These kinds of comments need to be rehearsed and meditated on so they become part of the adolescents' repertoire when they find themselves in situations or with people that threaten their abstinence.

"How many addicts do I know who can smoke one joint (or drink one drink)? None! I won't do it."

"What harm will it do me if I start using (drinking) once in a while? A great deal of harm. There's the potential to lose my family, my new friends, and, most important, my self-respect. No way."

"Do I wish to throw away_____days of sobriety for that one drink (coke)? No, it isn't worth it! What I have now is worth more than what I ever had when I was using. I don't want to."

How to Go to Bat for Yourself

Often recovering adolescents find themselves treated as second-class
citizens not only among their peers, but with school personnel as well.
Some erroneously view these students as academic cripples. Although
their scholastic accomplishments may have been affected adversely
while they were abusing drugs, there is reason to believe they are capable to achieve academic excellence. Adolescents themselves will forget
this and be unable to stand up for their rights. Consider how Chris, a
junior, lacked the ability to stand up for his rights in the following scene
with a college advisor:

Chris: Well, I really thought that I would like to go to New York
            University.

Advisor: Chris, you missed a whole year of school while you were
            "away." Your grades in freshman year were not too good.
            Don't you think that Westchester Community College
            would be more appropriate for you? At least for 1 year?

Chris: Yeah, but I kind of had my heart set on N.Y.U., and being
            in the city at a big university. You know?

Advisor: There's more pressure at a big university and being in the
            city and all. Couldn't that be dangerous, you know, more
            of a temptation for you?

Chris: Well, I guess you're right.

Advisor: Good, Well, let's see. You need to take the S.A.T.'s in
            May. . . .

When Chris came to group after this meeting and recounted his
story, he was very upset that he had been convinced to do something
against his will. He was upset that no one had faith in him, and he could
not convince the counselor. The real issue, however, was simply stated
by another group member when he said to Chris, "Hey, man, you really
need to go to bat for yourself."

The remainder of the group that day was spent teaching Chris assertive statements such as the following:

"In freshman year I was using drugs, now I'm not. I'm a different per-
son who is capable of doing well in school"
"Drugs are very much a part of this school, and I have not relapsed.
What makes you think I will in New York City?"
"Pressure can get bad here too. It bothers me that you do not recog-
nize I am responsible and abstinent."
"I deserve to try to enter a college of my choice, not one picked for me. I

deserve the best. I went through a lot to get where I am today. I can apply to N.Y.U."

After rehearsing these, a group members practiced a role play with Chris. Shortly after, Chris made another appointment with his advisor and wrote to N.Y.U. for an application.

CONCLUSION

Social skills training has proved to be a useful modality to promote self-actualizing abstinent behavior. Primary prevention programs have become part of school curricula. Peer pressure resistance, anxiety management, and assertiveness training are all a part of schools' attempts to combat drug abuse.

When more adolescents return from treatment programs, schools must implement other programs that will address the social–psychoeducational needs of those students who have not been helped by prevention programs.The adolescent recovery group offers support. The school psychologist, as the leader of a recovery group, should realize that a necessary component of the group is social skills training.

Although this chapter has been a pilot study for such a group, further research needs to be conducted using preassessment and postassessment in recovery groups. It is this author's conviction that the more therapeutic tools that are available to the group leader, the more success one can expect from recovering adolescents. Therapists must not rely on one treatment modality but rather an eclectic approach to repress the disease. Although no statistical evidence is available to support clear success of social skills in this pilot recovery group, and clearly the many variables such as group leader, treatment centers, individual personalities, and time spent in treatment need to be considered, the students have faired well, remained drug and alcohol free, and successfully integrated themselves back into school life.

REFERENCES

Albee, G. (1981). Preventing prevention in the community mental health centers. In H. Reshik, C. Aston, & C. Palley (Eds.), *The health care system and drug abuse prevention: toward cooperation and health promotion.* Washington, DC: National Institute on Drug Abuse.

Archambault, D. (1989). Adolescence: A physiological, cultural and psychological no man's land. In G. Lawson & A. Lawson (Eds.), *Alcohol and substance abuse in specific populations* (pp. 223–245). Rockville, MD: Aspen.

Beschner, G. M., & Friedman, A. S. (Eds.). (1979). *Youth drug abuse: Problems, issues, and treatment.* Lexington, MA: D. C. Heath.

Block, C. (1981). It will never happen to me. Denver, CO: M.A.C. Printing and Publishing Division.

Botvin, G. J. (1983). Lifeskills training: Teacher's manual. New York: Smithfield.

Bratter, T. E. (1989a). Group psychotherapy with alcoholic and addicted adolescents: Special clinical concerns and challenges. In F. J. Azima & L. Richmond (Eds.), Adolescent group psychotherapy. Madison, WI: International Universities Press. New York: International Universities.

Bratter, T. E. (1989b). Mentoring: Extending the psychotherapeutic and pedagogical relationship with adolescents. *Journal of Reality Therapy, 8,* 2.

Davis, M., Eshelman, E. R., & McKay, M. (1980). *The relaxation and stress reduction workbook.* Richmond, CA: New Harbinger Publications.

Deutsch, C. (1982). *Broken bottle, broken dreams: Understanding and helping children of alcoholics.* New York: Teachers College Press.

Frank, B., Marel, R., Schmeidler, J., & Lipton, D. (1984). An overview of substance use among New York State's upper income households. *Advances in Alcohol and Substance Abuse, 4,* 11–26.

Gilchrist, L. D., & Schinke, S. P. (1985). Preventing substance abuse with children and adolescents. *Journal of Consulting and Clinical Psychology, 53,* 121–135.

Glasser, W. (1965). *Reality therapy: a new approach to psychiatry.* New York: Harper & Row.

Goodwin, D. W. (1971). Is alcoholism hereditary? A review and critique. *Archives of General Psychiatry, 25,* 545–549.

Jacobson, E. (1974). *Progressive relaxation.* Chicago: University of Chicago Press (Midway Reprint).

Marlatt, G. & Gordon, J (1985). *Relapse prevention.* New York: Guilford.

Maxwell, R. (1986). *Beyond the booze battle.* New York: Ballantine.

McAlister, A., Perry, C., & Maccoby, N. (1979). Adolescent smoking: Onset and prevention. *Pediatrics, 63,* 650–658.

Pentz, M. A. (1983). Prevention of adolescent substance abuse through social skills. In T. J. Glynn, C. G. Leukefeld, & J. P. Ludford (Eds.), *Preventing adolescent drug abuse: Interventions and strategies* (National Institute on Drug Abuse Research, Monograph 47, DHHS Publication No. [ADM] 83–1280, pp. 195–232). Washington, DC: U. S. Government Printing Office.

Smith, T. E. (1985). Groupwork with adolescent drug abusers. *Social Work in Groups 8,* 55–63.

Winokur, G., Reich, T., Remmer, J., & Pitts, F. N. (1970). Alcoholism: II. Diagnosis and familial psychiatric illness in 259 alcoholic probands. *Archives of General Psychiatry, 23,* 104–111.

15

Assertiveness Training for Pregnant and Parenting High School Teenagers

Danya Vardi

This chapter originated from the author's work with a group of pregnant and parenting female adolescents who attended a public high school in the Bronx. During the course of several months, it became clear that these young women had enormous difficulty asserting themselves with their mothers, children, boyfriends, community agencies, and school personnel. A program was designed to address these needs. The goal of the project was to increase the adolescent mothers' interpersonal problem-solving skills so that they would be more able to assert themselves in a variety of social situations. In addition, the work focused on increasing the repertoire of assertiveness skills with the hope of preventing repeat pregnancies.

POPULATION DESCRIPTION

The high school in which the program occurred is located in one of the poorest neighborhoods in the Bronx, New York. Acculturation, poverty, inadequate health care, violence, and crime are problems that the young women who participated in the program face on a daily basis. They also experience a lot of difficulty negotiating the school environment and community agencies. The result is that they rarely obtain what they want, often get discouraged, and drop out of school.

In addition to assertiveness difficulties with school personnel and community agencies, the adolescent mothers in the group had significant difficulty asserting themselves at home with their mother and their boyfriends. A clear pattern of passivity, always putting other's needs before their own and not viewing themselves as capable human beings who voiced their opinions freely emerged. Deficits in interpersonal problem-solving skills that cut across many domains were evidenced. Their specific assertiveness difficulties in each domain are delineated as follows:

Acculturation Issues

Seventy-five percent of the young women in the group have recently immigrated to the United States from places such as Puerto Rico and the Dominican Republic. They are forced to adjust to a foreign culture as well as cope with poverty, discrimination, violence, and childrearing responsibilities. The school places them in the lowest level classes in the bilingual program (many of them are no more literate in their native language than they are in English), which makes them feel inadequate and makes the idea of obtaining a high school diploma untenable. They are given little support and do not see much promise for themselves in school. In addition, they are unable to ask the school to better serve their needs. The remaining 25% of the group are natives to their environment, although many of their parents were immigrants to the United States. Thus, in many ways they too must learn to adjust to two cultures simultaneously.

Problems with Public Assistance Agencies

Poverty is perhaps the central problem from which many of the other problems mentioned stem. These young women all are supported by public assistance and are placed at the bottom of the socioeconomic ladder. Inadequate housing and insufficient amounts of food are daily problems for them. Often there are more than six people living in a one-bedroom apartment that has lead paint peeling from the walls and is poorly heated. The food stamp and Women and Infant Care (WIC) office is always extremely crowded, and lines are several hours long. The adolescent mothers reported that they frequently have difficulty obtaining what they need from these offices. They stated that they usually leave the offices feeling upset and worried.

Health Care Problems

Adequate health care and early treatment of pregnancy is often not a reality for these young women. The community in which they live has the highest number of reported AIDS and lead-poisoning cases in the city, as well as one of the five highest pregnancy rates in New York City. These problems are further complicated by a scarcity of clinic and child care facilities, low birth weights, as well as infant mortality rates that exceed city, state, and national averages.

The few clinics that are available are overcrowded, have inadequate facilities, and an overworked, poorly paid staff. The young women describe going to the clinics as a "nightmare" in that you have to wait most of the day to see a doctor, and often the clinic then sends you elsewhere to obtain services they cannot provide. In addition, the school requires a note from the clinic if an absence is to be excused and the clinic staff refuse to write notes for students, stating that "they are too busy." The adolescent mothers then get in trouble at school, as teachers do not let them make up work unless their absence is officially excused.

Violence and Crime in the Community

Violence both in and out of the high school makes these young women fearful for their safety. Across the street from the high school is a crack house that is in operation most hours of the day. The park in back of the high school is full of hypodermic needles and, despite attempts to "clean up" the park, it remains a center for the sale of drugs. As is often the case, the interior of the high school mirrors what is happening in the community. A leading newspaper has recently rated the high school as having the most violent incidents of all high schools in New York City. Many students come to school armed with knives and guns. Fights in the cafeteria occur at least once a week. Pregnant adolescents often do not attend school for most of their pregnancy, for fear of harming their unborn child. The security system in and surrounding the school is lacking and thus they prefer to stay home. When the young women asked if they could be escorted in the building, the administration said that could not be done. The young women were too afraid to pursue this issue further.

Problems With Teachers and Counselors

Many of the teachers and counselors in the school are self-proclaimed "burnouts." They feel isolated, unsupported and often undermined by the administration. Many of them state that the administration has no idea how much remediation many of the children in the school need, and expect them to work miracles. One teacher claimed that she cried when she found out she had been placed at the high school. Another teacher stated that he is so afraid of getting hurt that he walks right by students fighting in the halls and does not even look back.

Most teachers are sympathetic to the special needs of adolescent mothers and the problems they face attending school on a daily basis. Given that they have 40 students in each class and only one period of preparation time in a day, however, it is difficult for them to take the time out to help the adolescent mothers, although they would like to. Frequently they do not have the time to go over in detail the class work the adolescent mothers miss as a result of their absences from school. The adolescent mothers often remain silent in these circumstances, do not ask the school for after-school tutoring services open to them, and the unfortunate result is failure to complete the course.

Problems With High School Administration

The high school administration is extremely insensitive to the needs of pregnant and parenting adolescents. Their policy toward teenage pregnancy is to ignore the statistics that state that 20% of all young women in the school are either pregnant or are parents, and that historically teenaged parents have a 50% higher risk of dropping out of school (Jones et al., 1985). They view adolescent mothers as having no academic potential and try to place them in trade schools and schools where they can obtain a high school equivalency diploma. Even the brightest adolescent who attends school regularly receives no support from the administration. In fact, the administration recently rejected an idea in which there would be an all school awards assembly in which those adolescent mothers who were attending school and doing well would be recognized.

Problems with Mothers

The mother–daughter relationship is complex, unique, and emotionally charged, with adolescence being the most difficult period for this dyad (LaSorsa & Fodor, 1989). The relationship is further complicated when the adolescent mother has a child of her own. As adolescent mothers are struggling to achieve self-definition and separation, they are put into a position in which they very much need to be close to their mothers, and have their mothers give them support and guidance (Kendall & Williams, 1986).

Unlike most other relationships, problems with one's mother can be life long and, if not worked out, some of these problems may linger long after the parent's death (Fodor & Wolfe, 1987). The adolescent mothers in the program complained more about their difficulty in asserting themselves with their mothers than any other assertiveness difficulty. Many of the adolescent mothers' parents were watching their children at home while they attended school. Many of these grandmothers are still raising children of their own in the home. Thus, many generations reside in those homes. In addition, many of the grandmothers were the disciplinarians with their daughter's children and gave their daughters orders on what to do with their children. The adolescent mothers stated that they were scared to assert themselves, as they were completely dependent on their mothers and grandmothers. They stated that they needed them very badly for guidance and support. At a school party for the adolescent mothers, one adolescent mother was observed threatening her child "if you don't stop that I'm going to tell grandma!"

Although reduction of anger, guilt, and anxiety is important in teaching adolescent mothers to assert themselves with their mothers, cognitive restructuring is often more important than specific skills training (Fodor & Wolfe, 1987). The adolescent mothers needed to be shown how to communicate their needs and feelings openly so that they could begin to relate to their mothers as two adults who enjoy a special bond of closeness and sharing (Fodor & Wolfe, 1987).

Problems with Boyfriends

Next to assertiveness difficulties with their mothers, the adolescent mothers reported assertiveness difficulties with their boyfriends. For many of the adolescent mothers, the teenaged fathers of their children were their first sexual partners, and the first men that they had "fallen in love with." Thus, they are forced to learn how to get along in a relationship (e.g., communicate positively, make their needs known, take into account another person's needs) and learn how to be a parent at the same time. It is thus not surprising that many of the adolescent mothers stated that their boyfriends almost always "got their way" and that their needs in the relationship were secondary. They did not view themselves as equal partners in their relationships and felt that it was their job to please their boyfriends rather than themselves. All but one of them stated that they could not bring themselves to ask their boyfriends to wear a condom. Many of them stated that they were afraid that if they disagreed with their boyfriends, their boyfriends would not give them any financial support and they would leave them. In addition, given that more than 50% of the students at the high school come from single-parent homes, most of the adolescent mothers and their boyfriends come from female-dominated households. In these homes, males are rarely present, and any male in the home is given special status. There is no consequence for the male when he gets a female pregnant, it is her responsibility to care for the child.

ASSESSMENT PROCEDURE

The assessment procedure occurred over several weeks, during which group members became comfortable speaking with the group leader and with each other. The group leader was a school psychologist with several years experience working with adolescents. She was young enough that the group was able to trust her and relate to her in a more informal way than they do with individuals who are of their parents generation. One group member described her as "a big sister to the group."

Like many other social skills assessment and intervention projects, this study used multiple informants and baselines to gain a more realistic assessment of the adolescents' social skills (Baum, Clark, McCarthy, Sandler, & Carpenter 1986; Franco, Christoff, Crimmins, & Kelly, 1983; Jackson & Bruder, 1984; Serna, Shumaker, Hazel, & Sheldon, 1986; Wolf & Edwards, 1988). Adolescent mothers were asked to provide data on how they perceived themselves and their peers, guidance counselors, and teachers were asked to provide data on how they perceived each group participant and the group leader provided data on how she viewed each group member.

The instruments used in the assessment process were a slightly modified version of the Children's Assertive Behavior Scale (CABS) developed by Michaelson and Wood (1982) that included the first sixteen questions of the questionnaire. This questionnaire was filled out independently by group members. A sociometric questionnaire to facilitate identifying the most shy group members was independently filled out by group members and all adult observers. The Attitudes Toward Contraception Scale developed by Gough, and the Contraceptive Embarrassment Scale developed by Herold were completed by group members. The final assessment task was a group exercise in which the group was asked to generate responses verbally to a series of pressure lines to have sex, assuming they did not want to have sex.

The Actual Assessment Process

The group complained about CABS. They stated it was too "boring" and that the situations "did not seem real." The measure was chosen because it was geared for a fourth- to sixth-grade reading level, which is the level that most of the adolescents in the group were reading at, and because with slight modifications the questions could be appropriate for adolescents. The group members stated that they were uncomfortable with the forced-choice format of the questionnaire, as often they would not have responded in accordance with any of the available choices. In addition, they stated that the format of the instrument was completely unlike the way that they think and go about making decisions. This result is consistent with the results of prior researchers, who found that a decision–theoretical model may reflect a cognitive strategy that only some adolescent mothers employ, and that for others it appears that neither reflection or benefit, weighting alternatives, or deliberate decision making takes place at all (Flaherty, Maracek, Olsen, & Wilcove 1983).

The group seemed to enjoy filling out the sociometric questionnaire where they rated each other as passive, assertive, or aggressive much more than filling out the CABS; however, many of the group members were anxious about the task. They needed additional assurance that the results would be anonymous. There was a lot of giggling during this task. One of the more assertive group members pointed to another assertive group member and stated "you know what I'm going to rate you as!"

In contrast to the giggling and cheerfulness during the sociometric questionnaire, the group was extremely quiet when asked to fill out the contraceptive inventories. Only one of the more assertive group members spoke at all during the process. She stated "I'm trying hard to be honest, but when I'm here I'm not embarrassed, I can think clearly and I know what I should do . . . . When I'm with my boyfriend things are different." The group seemed to empathize with her, and many stated that they had the same problem.

After this discussion the group proceeded to finish the forms. By the time they were asked to generate the responses to pressure to have sex they were very vocal. By allowing the group to ask Karen questions, have discussions with each other, and vent their anxieties they appeared to become more comfortable in discussing this difficult topic. They seemed to enjoy this task most of all, and many of the shyer group members became involved in the brainstorming process. A copy of the groups' responses to the pressure lines is included in Appendix 1.

Results of Assessment

The results of the CABS indicated that group members tended to have a higher percentage of correct responses to positive statements, negative statements, requests, conversations, and feeling statements when they were speaking with an adult than when they were speaking with a peer. In addition, they had the lowest average percentage of correct responses to negative statements said to them by adults or peers. Unfortunately, there were no norms to compare this profile with. The only norms Michaelson and Wood obtained dealt with internal consistency and test–retest reliability. Results of the sociometric questionnaire indicate that group members perceived each other as more assertive than they perceived themselves.

The results of informant ratings indicated that the teachers, guidance counselors, and the group leader tended to rate group members more passively than they rated each other and more passively than group members rated themselves. An exact breakdown of informant sociometric questionnaire results is included in Appendix 2.

The results of the contraceptive inventories indicate that, despite being well aware of the threat of AIDS and the disease prevention advantage of the condom, the only birth control method the group rated as acceptable was the birth control pill. Many group members stated that the other methods were "messy." One group member stated "I could never touch myself *there.*" The group also did not find a vasectomy or tubal ligation acceptable unless you "were old and already had your kids." The only place group members stated that they would not be embarrassed to obtain a prescription for birth control pills was from a clinic doctor in a different neighborhood where they did not know anyone. An exact breakdown of the contraceptive questionnaire results is included in Appendix 3.

Conclusions from Assessment

Results of the assessment indicated that these young women had difficulties asserting themselves in a multitude of situations and with a multitude of people, such as their mothers, boyfriends, school personnel, community agency personnel, and health clinic personnel. The intervention was designed to address problems in asserting oneself with each of the previously mentioned groups of people.

Across all rating scales a consistent assertiveness hierarchy emerged. Five members of the group were consistently rated as behaving most assertively, and two members of the group were consistently rated as behaving most passively. The group members tended to rate themselves as more assertive than the informants rated them, but less assertive than their peers rated them.

As a group, the adolescent mothers feel totally responsible for providing contraception. They also perceive their boyfriends needs to be more important than their own. They are unable to ask their boyfriends to wear a condom and are extremely uncomfortable touching their own bodies.

INTERVENTION PLAN

The goals of the intervention plan were to teach some general knowledge of social skills, to enable the group participants to assert themselves with clinic personnel, their mothers, welfare workers, and school personnel, and to increase the group members' level of comfort in discussing sexual issues such as telling a boyfriend to wear a condom, asking a physician questions about sex, and requesting contraception at a pharmacy.

A focus on interpersonal problem solving skills, using behavioral–assertiveness training techniques, was chosen based on prior research. Several researchers have found that by only focusing on increasing adolescent access to contraceptive services and educating adolescents about contraception the pregnancy rate still remains high (Cvetkovich et al., 1975; Kane et al., 1974). With more family planning services, easier access to contraception and more prevention programs than ever before, the rate of teenage pregnancy in the United States is at an all time high of 18.6% per 1,000 teens age 15 and under in 1987 (*New York Times*, 1991). In addition, in at least three studies, teenage child-bearers receiving intensive family planning education postnatally had roughly a 50% rate of repeat pregnancies within 2 to 3 years after giving birth (Flaherty et al., 1983). Manion et al., 1988, found that significant improvement in parenting risk and child behavior problems were evident only for mothers who received behavioral/assertiveness training coupled with parent education.

The program intervention was four sessions long. The group leader spoke at the beginning of every session and then the group participated in a series of role plays of situations they had experienced where they had difficulty asserting themselves. The first intervention session focused on assertiveness difficulties with community agencies and clinic personnel, the second intervention session focused on assertiveness difficulties with school personnel, the third intervention session focused on assertiveness difficulties with mothers, and the final intervention session focused on assertiveness difficulties with boyfriends. The order of the topics was chosen that the more sensitive material would be brought up at the end of the intervention, when group members were less anxious.

Intervention Session 1: Assertiveness Difficulties with Community Agencies and Clinics

The first session began with a review of what the group members had defined as assertiveness and reviewing the verbal and nonverbal aspects of assertiveness. The group seemed to have no trouble remembering what they had previously stated. After that, the group leader explained that the next four group meetings would be spent talking about what it was like dealing with clinic workers, school personnel, mothers, and boyfriends.

When asked how they would feel about role playing some situations a few of the more assertive group members stated that they would be willing to volunteer. Although the shy members of the group stated they would not volunteer to role play a situation, they stated that they would participate in the discussions and help give feedback to role play participants. The first two group members to participate in the role play were Tammy and Ebbonie. They chose to role play a situation in which Tammy had difficulty asking for what she wanted from a clinic worker. Ebbonie played the clinic worker. The transcript is as follows:

Tammy:	I need a note to my school stating that I was here so my absence can be excused.
Ebbonie:	No! (says in a very loud and forceful tone).
Tammy:	Please, I will not be allowed to make up the work if my absence is not excused (pleads).
Ebbonie:	Can't you see I'm busy, go away (barely conceals a smile)!
Tammy:	(Looks at the group leader.)
Group leader:	(Addresses the whole group and asks what Tammy should do.)
Linda:	Ask to see a supervisor if she still refuses.
Angie:	Try to be nicer to her, tell her you know she is busy but it's important.
Tammy:	(takes a deep breath): I know you are really busy, but I need the note. If you can't give it to me I want to see a supervisor.
Ebbonie:	(giggles): Here (hands Angie a piece of paper).

The group stated that they liked the way that Tammy had been sensitive to the woman being busy, yet assertive in her request. They also stated that Ebbonie played her role convincingly but giggled too much.

Intervention Session 2:
Assertiveness Difficulties with High School
and Institutional Bureaucracies

The second intervention session began with a brief discussion about the difficulties group members encountered in working with high school personnel. One group member stated she had to drop her baby off at day care at 8:30 a.m., and thus always missed her first-period English class.

She stated that her guidance counselor told her that if she dropped that English course she would have to enroll in an average-level English class and withdraw from the College Bound Program. Several other students jumped in with scheduling problems they were having. They stated that the guidance counselors never remember them and do not consider the fact that they are mothers when making up their schedules.

Marisol then began to discuss the fact that teachers do not let her make up work when she misses school for her child. She recounted a situation in which a teacher refused to give her the work. Other group members agreed with her and stated they were having similar problems. When asked if she would role play the situation she agreed. Angie volunteered to play the part of the teacher.

Marisol:	I wasn't here yesterday and need the work I missed (says in a loud demanding tone). Wait ... I just heard myself ... can I start over?
Group leader:	What did you just do?
Marisol:	I was very nasty and acted like he was going to give me trouble before he even spoke.
Group leader:	Why don't you go ahead now and redo the role play keeping those things in mind.
Marisol:	Hi, are you busy? I need to talk to you for a minute.
Angie:	Sure, what's up (class giggles and tells Angie to "talk like a teacher")?
Angie:	(smiling) What can I do for you?
Marisol:	I need the work I missed in class yesterday.
Angie:	Come by my office at 3 p.m., and I'll give it to you.
Marisol:	Thank you.

The group stated that Marisol had done a much better job the second time and that Angie, like Ebbonie, should not have smiled a giggled so much. They stated that Marisol was polite and respectful of the teacher.

Intervention Session 3:
Assertiveness Difficulties with Mothers

By the third intervention session, the group was relaxed and many more group members were vocal. All but two group members conceded that they frequently fought with their mothers over child rearing issues. Battles over discipline and who was in charge were the main problems group members stated they needed help with. Because of the interest this topic generated, the group decided to do three separate role plays. Marisol and Angie volunteered for the first role play, which they named, "mom is always right."

Marisol:	Mom, come help me hang these curtains up in Tariana's room.
Angie:	Sure.
Marisol:	I think that they should go here (pretends to place curtains).
Angie:	Oh no, they need to be over here, come on—let's move them (pretends to move them).
(Group starts to laugh).	
Marisol:	This is my house and I'll put them where I want!
Angie:	If you're going to act like that good-bye (said in a loud and forceful tone of voice)!

At this point the group leader interrupted and asked both of them to state what went on. Marisol stated that she resented Angie telling her what to do and Angie stated that Marisol was "being a bitch and she didn't want to be yelled at like that." When asked what happened in the real-life situation Marisol stated that her mother did exactly what Angie did, and she went over later in the day to apologize. When asked what they would do differently, Marisol stated that she should have been more understanding and controlled her temper. Angie stated that she should have told Marisol nicely that she did not want to be treated that way. When asked to do the role play again both seemed slightly uncomfortable but agreed. The second role play went as follows:

Angie:	I think the curtains should go here . . . why don't we move them over here?
Marisol:	Mom, I really think they should go over here and that is where I am going to put them, thanks for your help and suggestions though.
Angie:	Well . . . OK, we'll put them there if that's really where you want them.

The tone of voice used throughout the role play was much softer. When asked to comment on the second role play the group nodded in agreement that it seemed much better. Karen said "you both were considerate of each other's feelings and that was nice."

The group entitled the next role play session "whose baby is it anyway." Linda volunteered to role play a situation in which her mother had wanted to take her daughter down South for Easter because her relatives never met her. Linda stated that she wanted her daughter to be with her during Easter since she would be all alone and off from school. She stated that she spent Easter all alone feeling terrible and missing her daughter. Karen stated that she would role play Linda's mother in the role play.

Karen:	I'm leaving on Saturday to go down South and I want my relatives to see Makeeba. We'll be back on Tuesday.
Linda:	Mom (says softly and looks as if she is about to cry . . . she becomes silent) . . .
Group leader:	What's happening now?
Linda:	I can't do it . . . I feel too guilty . . . she watches Makeeba all day while I'm in school and even on weekends when I want to go out. She doesn't make me help around the house . . . how can I say no to her?
Group leader:	It's fortunate that she helps you as much as she does, however, it's important that you realize that you are an adult and that Makeeba is your daughter. You can explain to your mother how much you appreciate what she does for you but also express your own needs.
Ebbonie:	You could have told her that you would plan a trip to see the relatives another time, but that Easter was not a good time for you.
Group leader:	That was a good suggestion . . . do you want to continue the role play? (Linda nods yes.)
Karen:	I'm going down South to visit the family, and I'm taking Makeeba with me. We'll be back on Tuesday.
Linda:	Mom, I know you want to have everyone meet her, but I really want to have her with me on Easter. It's her first Easter, and I want to be with her. Maybe this summer we can go down South together and they can meet her. (Her voice became much softer toward the end of the sentence.)
Karen:	I may not be able to have time off this summer, and I really want to take her with me.
Linda:	Mom . . . please (pleads and looks as if she is about to cry).

Group leader:	You started off fine . . . what is happening?
Linda:	I'm letting her get her way as usual.
Group leader:	What could you do differently?
Linda:	I could stop crying and whining when I talk to her. Even when I say what I want it also comes out like I am afraid to say it.

The group entitled the third role play "disciplining your child." Sadie volunteered for the role play. She described a fight she had recently had with her mother in which her 13-month-old son hit her, and her mother told her to hit him back or he would never respect her. Sadie was torn between not wanting to hit him, wanting him to stop misbehaving and wanting to please her mother. She stated she hated being hit as a child and did not want to do that to her son. Aurania stated she felt the same way and recently had a fight with her mother who hit her 2-year-old son for dropping a plastic cup full of juice on the carpet. Many of the other group members expressed similar feelings of hating being hit as a child and being in conflict with their mothers over how to discipline their children. Aurania then stated she would play Sadie's mother in the role play.

Aurania:	(Pretends to hit child.)
Sadie (in a loud and forceful tone):	Mom! please don't hit him. Only his father and I are responsible for disciplining him and we don't believe in hitting. If you don't like what he is doing, and he won't listen to you then tell me, and I'll handle it.
Aurania:	(Taken by surprise) . . . uh . . . okay . . .
Sadie:	That was great.

The class applauded Linda and stated that she was direct, forceful, and stated her opinion clearly and confidently. They stated that she maintained constant eye contact, was stern but not abusive and held her head high. The group agreed that was what assertive behavior should be.

Intervention Session 4:
Assertiveness Difficulties with
Boyfriends/Husbands.

The final intervention session focused on sexual assertiveness. This session was the most difficult for the group. The group leader began the session by writing on the blackboard. She made a column entitled "His Needs" and another column entitled "Your Needs." Items the group put under "his needs" were feeling good, getting over, and feeling powerful and manly. Items the group put under "your needs" were preventing repeat pregnancies, not getting AIDS (many of their boyfriends are intravenous drug users and refuse to wear condoms). For the first time nobody in the group volunteered to role play a situation in which they had to ask their boyfriend to wear a condom. The room was silent and most group members were looking at the floor or wall. Finally, Angie stood up and said "You're all wimps . . . I'll role play the situation." The role play went as follows:

Group leader:	Lets go . . . I can't wait all day.
Angie:	Uh . . . I'm looking for a condom . . . I think you should wear one (looks at the floor and speaks very softly).

(The group starts giggling and Karen states that she never saw Angie so shy in all the years she has known her.)

Group leader:	What is happening now?
Angie:	I can't do this . . . even though I know I have to and that I could get AIDS . . .
Group leader:	Can anyone in the room help Angie out? (Everyone is silent.)
Angie (takes a deep breath):	I want to try and finish this . . . (Looks at group leader and continues . . .) I care about you and like being with you, but if you don't put a condom on I won't sleep with you.
Group leader:	Don't you trust me?
Angie:	No (says in a loud and assertive tone). (Group starts laughing and applauding.)
Group leader:	That was much better—who can tell me what was good about the way Angie spoke to me?
Karen:	She let him know she cared about him but also let him know that she meant what she said.
Aurania:	She was blunt and put her foot down.
Marisol:	She let him know she wasn't going to budge.

CONCLUSION

The group then spent the remaining part of the session filling out evaluation forms of the program and saying their good-byes to the group leader. Many of them became friends over the course of the few months that the project lasted and continued to socialize after the group finished. During the course of the rest of the school year many of the teachers, guidance counselors and adolescent mothers came back and stated that they had really found the program helpful. Even the shyest members of the group stated that, although they did not participate as much as some of the more assertive group members, they were able to benefit from listening and watching others model assertive behavior.

Several projects also resulted from the program. Five of the group members went to the principal and lobbied for a shorter school day for mothers in which they could come in later, not eat lunch, and only take basic requirements, which he granted them. Ten of the group members became involved in lobbying for a day care center on school grounds, which will be completed next year. The final thing that came out of the program is a clinic pass, which is prepared by the school, that the doctor initials.

The program described earlier departs from the assumption that information and education alone is enough to influence adolescent's behavior. This program used assertiveness training to teach the group members how to apply information to interpersonal problems and how to assert themselves in a variety of situations. Both students and faculty involved in the program agree that it was a successful pilot program, and are now making it part of the school's curriculum for pregnant and parenting adolescents. It is hoped that the school will ultimately realize that all students in the school can benefit from these techniques.

There are a few modifications that are currently being made. Sessions need to be longer than 45 minutes a day thus; the principal of the school is now allowing the session to run into lunchtime. This will extend sessions by 20 minutes. Booster sessions are an essential component of such a program and are currently being implemented. Group members who meet twice a month are getting together for a party lunch or class.

APPENDIX 1. Group Responses to Pressure Lines to Have Sex

Pressure line	Group response
Everybody's doing it	That's everybody's business. I'm not doing it. Everyone but me.
If you love me, you'll have sex with me	Well I don't love you. Ain't that much love in the world.
If you won't have sex with me, I won't see you anymore.	Bye There's more fish in the sea.
I know you want to do it, your just afraid of what people will say.	I don't care what others say. I'll do what I want to do.
Come on and grow up, you can't be a kid forever.	That's not growing up. You are the kid.
Let's do it. You know I want to marry you someday.	When we get married, we'll talk about it.
We had sex once before, what's the problem now?	I changed my mind. I didn't like it.
Don't you want people to think you're a real woman?	Sex has nothing to do with being a real woman.
Don't you want to try it?	No!!!!!!
But I have to have it!	Get it somewhere else.
If you want to be popular you'll do it.	I don't need to be popular
If you get pregnant, I'll marry you.	I'm not getting pregnant cause I'm not doing it.
You want it as much as I do.	If I wanted it, I'd do it.
If you love me you'll do it.	I don't love you.
Come on, try me, I'll be the best you ever had.	Get lost.
Come on, take a drink, it will get you in the mood.	I don't drink.
If you don't someone else will.	Let them go ahead.
A lot of your friends do it.	That's their business. I'm different.

From the *Life Skills Program*, 1985.

APPENDIX 2.   Results of *The Contraceptive Embarrassment Scale*

Please answer the questions below to the best of your ability. Do not put any identifying information on this sheet. Your responses will be kept confidential.

Read each statement below. If you find you are embarrassed or would be embarrassed by the statement, check the second column "embarrassed by statement." If you think you are not embarrassed or would not be embarrassed by the statement then check the third column "not embarrassed by statement."

Statement	Embarrassed by statement (mean group rating n=12)	Not embarrassed by statement (mean group rating n=12)
Obtaining condoms from a pharmacy close to where my parents live.	10	2
Obtaining contraceptive foam from a pharmacy close to where my parents where my parents live.	10	2
Obtaining birth control pills from a pharmacy close to where my parents live	9	3
Obtaining a prescription for the birth control pill from my family doctor.	11	1
Obtaining condoms from a pharmacy distant from where my family lives.	10	2
Obtaining contraceptive foam from a pharmacy distant from where my family lives.	10	2
Obtaining birth control pills from a pharmacy distant from where my family lives.	4	8
Obtaining a prescription for the birth control pill from a clinic doctor.	4	8

Courtesy of Edward S. Herold, University of Guelph.

APPENDIX 3. Results of *The Attitudes Toward Contraceptive Methods Scale*

Instructions: Ten contraceptive methods are listed below. Please rate each one for its acceptability to you, using this scale.

5=very acceptable
4=somewhat acceptable
3=not sure, uncertain
2=not acceptable
1=very unacceptable

Contraceptive Method:	Mean Group rating: (1–5) (n=12)
Condom	3.1
Diaphragm	1.3
Foam or jelly	1.6
Vasectomy	1.4
Tubal ligation	1.6
Abstention	2.2
Rhythm method	1.0
Withdrawal	1.0
Intrauterine device	1.0
Birth control pills	4.2

Courtesy of Harrison Gough, University of California at Berkeley.

REFERENCES

Barth, R. P., Schinke, S. P., & Maxwell, J. S. (1985). Coping skills training for school-age mothers. *Journal of Social Service Research, 8,* 75–94.

Baum, J. G., Clark, H. B., McCarthy, W., Sandler, J., & Carpenter, R. (1986). An analysis of the acquisition and generalization of social skills in troubled youths: Combining social skills training, cognitive self-talk, and relaxation procedures. *Child and Family Behavior Therapy, 8,* 1–27.

Flaherty, E. W., Marecek, J., Olsen, K., & Wilcove, G. (1983). Preventing adolescent pregnancy: An interpersonal problem-solving approach. *Prevention in Human Services, 2,* 49–64.

Fodor, I. G., & Wolfe, J. L. (1987). Assertiveness training for mothers and daughters. In R. E. Alberti (Ed.), *Assertiveness: Innovations, applications, issues.* San Luis Obispo, CA: Impact.

Franco, D. P., Christoff, K. A., Crimmins, D. B., & Kelly, J. A. (1983). Social skills training for an extremely shy young adolescent: An empirical case study. *Behavior Therapy, 14,* 568–575.

Jackson, H. J., & Bruder, J. N. (1984). Social validation of nonverbal behaviors in social skills training programs for adolescents: I. *Journal of Clinical Child Psychology, 13,* 141–146.

Jones, E. F., Forrest, J. D., Goldman, N., Henshaw, S. K., Lincoln, R., Rosoff, J. I., Westoff, C. F., & Wolf, D. (1985). Teenage pregnancy in developed countries: Determinants and policy implications. *Family Planning Perspectives, 17,* 53–63.

Kendall, P. C., & Williams, C. L. (1986). Therapy with adolescents: treating the "marginal man." *Behavior Therapy, 17,* 522–537.

La Sorsa, V. A., & Fodor, I. G. (1989). *The adolescent daughter/midlife mother dyad: A new look at separation and self-definition.* Manuscript submitted for publication.

Michelson, L., Sugai, D. P., Wood, R. P., & Kazdin, A. E. (1982). *Social skills assessment and training with children.* New York: Plenum.

Serna, L. A., Schumaker, J. B., Hazel, S. J., & Sheldon, J. B. (1986). Teaching reciprocal social skills to parents and their delinquent adolescents. *Journal of Clinical Child Psychology, 15,* 64–77.

Stake, J. E., DeVille, C. J., & Pennell, C. L. (1983). The effects of assertive training on the performance self-esteem of adolescent girls. *Journal of Youth and Adolescence, 12,* 435–442.

Werry, J. S., & Wollersheim, J. P. (198). Behavior therapy with children and adolescents: a twenty-year overview. *Journal of the American Academy of Child and Adolescent Psychiatry, 28,* 1–18.

Wolfe, D. A., Edwards, B., Manion, I., & Koverola, C. (1988). Early intervention for parents at risk of child abuse and neglect: A preliminary investigation. *Journal of Consulting and Clinical Psychology, 56,* 40–47.

Young teen-agers have more babies. (1991, August 31). *The New York Times,* p. 10.

Conclusion

Iris G. Fodor

Assertiveness training in its beginning phase had an advocacy component. Alberti and Emmons (1970) popular book, *Your Perfect Right* encouraged people to learn to be assertive to take charge of their lives. In
the 1970s, this charge was taken up by groups using assertiveness techniques as vehicles for social change. One of the most widespread move-
ments was that of assertiveness training for women. This author,
among others, was an early advocate of women learning to be assertive
to overcome prior sex role socialization. Women were taught to be active, not passive, assertive not self-denying or compliant (Jackubowski-
Spector 1973; Osborn&Harris, 1975; Phelps&Austin, 1975; Wolfe &
Fodor, 1975). Although society did not fully change, many women did.
Societal receptivity to women's assertiveness is still questionable; for
example, assertive women are often considered too aggressive (Fodor &
Epstein, 1983). There is no question, however, that these techniques
enabled women to fight job discrimination, sexual harassment, and
abuse, and to help foster equality in relationships (Fodor, 1988).

With the shift in the 1980s toward deemphasizing assertiveness and
stressing skills training, there was a shift toward society (teachers, parents, and the schools), defining what was socially appropriate for children and adolescents. Social skills techniques were used to change
behaviors, considered more problematic by the agents of society, than
they were for the students. Even the concept of social competency is
value laden. We must ask, socially competent for what role in society
(i.e., to fit into a discriminatory, racist society) (Cheek, 1974).

As I review the chapters in this book that address adolescent assertiveness and social skills training, some trends are apparent. Most social skills assessment and intervention programs have been developed by psychologists for mainstream populations. Many of the adolescents described by this book's authors are disadvantaged, living in poor neighborhoods with limited resources. They represent diverse cultures. The chapters on ethics and high-risk black adolescents, Asian Americans, and Latin Americans aptly demonstrate the problems in adapting concepts and programs developed in Euro-American culture for culturally diverse groups. As the chapter authors described the development of programs for such adolescents, the standardized assessments and treatments had to be modified. Several chapter authors argued for the development of specific measures to address the special needs of adolescents from other backgrounds or with specific handicapping conditions.

The most innovative work described in this book, adheres to the original goals of assertiveness training. That is, to enable adolescents to define their own goals, work out their own responses to the problematic situations in their life, and use these techniques to fight for change. For example, Vardi's chapter on parenting and pregnant teenagers in a disadvantaged school district is a good model of the use of assertiveness training as a tool for advocacy. She demonstrated that with a limited amount of exposure to assertiveness training, these young mothers were able to make some changes in the way the school responded to their needs. It is hoped that these adolescents also learned about empowerment.

In assimilating the work described in the book, what I am arguing for is to work from the bottom up. That is, when possible, clinicians, school psychologists, and counselors should begin working in schools with classes of students to form rap groups to discuss their own assertiveness concerns. Following a psychoeducation model, with the trainers in a facilitative role, such discussion groups would enable the students to assess their own social interactive problems and together work on the behaviors they wish to change. By including all students in such programs, the students with the "maladaptive" behaviors would not be singled out. Ideally, such programs should begin in the early school years and be part of the regular curriculum. Because most adolescents do want to achieve, have effective peer relations, get along better with their parents, and find their place in society, these programs should foster society's goals as well. It is important, however, not to neglect the advocacy role as well. Training adolescent members in a democracy to assert themselves, speak out, and work together to fight injustice and discrimination is the best hope we have to train further leaders and work for change.

REFERENCES

Alberti, R. E., & Emmons, M. L. (1979). *Your perfect right.* San Luis Obispo, CA: Impact.

Fodor, I. (1988). Assertiveness training in the 80's: Moving beyond the personal. In L. Walker & L. Rosewater (Eds.), *Handbook of feminist therapy.* New York: Springer.

Fodor, I., & Epstein, R. (1983). Assertiveness training for women: Where are we failing. In P. Emmelkamp & E. Foa (Eds.) *Failures in behavior therapy.* New York: Wiley.

Cheek, D. (1974). *Assertive black/puzzled white.* San Luis Obispo, CA: Impact.

Dodge, K. A. & Murphy, R. R. (1984). The assessment of social competence in adolescents. In P. Karoly and J. Steffen (eds.). Adolescent behavior disorders: Foundations and contemporary concerns. Lexington, Mass. D. C. Heath.

Jakubowski-Spector, P. (1973). Facilitating the growth of women through assertive training., *The Counseling Psychologist, 4,* 76–86.

Osborn, S. M., & Harris, G. G. (1975). *Assertive training for women.* Springfield, IL: Thomas.

Phelps, S. & Austin, N. (1975). *The assertive woman.* San Luis Obispo, CA; Impact.

Wolfe, J., & Fodor, I. (1975). A cognitive/behavioral approach to assertiveness training in women: Special issues on assertiveness. *The Counseling Psychologist. 5,* 45–59.

Index

Stress inoculation approach,
   158–160
Structured learning approach, 23–24
Structured Learning Skill Checklist,
   208, 215
Student Health Psychiatric Clinic,
   UCLA, 105
Suburban substance-abusing adoles-
   cents, social skills training for,
   234–247
Sullivan, H. S., 35–36

Talking about what's wrong,
   214–215
Teacher Rating Scale of Social
   Skills, 46
Teachers, problems of pregnant
   teenagers with, 251–252
Teenagers, pregnant, *see* Pregnant
   and parenting teenagers
Therapeutic encounter, with black
   adolescents, 91–92
Therapeutic tools for school psychologists, 240–242; *see also*
   Treatment *entries*
Thought implications, capacity for,
   32
Training
   anger control, 23, 160–161
   anxiety management, 23
   assertiveness, *see* Assertiveness
      training
   communication, for adolescent
      girls, 205–218
   interpersonal cognitive problem-
      solving, 154–155

social skills, *see* Social skills training
Treatment, *see also* Therapeutic *entries*
   appraisal of, 44–45
   in anger control, 152–153
   evaluation of outcome of, 45
   substance abuse, 237–238
Treatment package, for assertive
   and social skills, 22–23
Treatment programs, behavioral, for
   angry adolescents, 154,
   158–161
Triggers, of anger, 152–153

Unassertive scripts, self-talk and, 15
United States, major Latino groups
   in, 115–118
U.S. Bureau of the Census, 83, 114
U.S. House of Representatives, 219
University of California at Los An-
   geles, 105
Upward Bound Students, 183, 185,
   187

Vignettes, 54–56
Violence, in community, 251

Waksman Social Skills Rating Scale
   (WSSRS), 48
Walker Social Skills Curriculum, 46
Women, new Asian-American, 106;
   see also Female adolescents
Women and Infant Care (WIC), 250

Your Perfect Right, 3, 9, 269